Requirements Management

Colin Hood · Simon Wiedemann · Stefan Fichtinger
Urte Pautz

Requirements Management

The Interface Between
Requirements Development and
All Other Systems Engineering Processes

 Springer

Colin Hood
Simon Wiedemann
Stefan Fichtinger
Urte Pautz

Keltenring 7
82041 Oberhaching
Germany

Colin.Hood@Hood-Group.com
Simon.Wiedemann@Hood-Group.com
Stefan.Fichtinger@Hood-Group.com
Urte.Pautz@Hood-Group.com

ISBN 978-3-642-08002-9   e-ISBN 978-3-540-68476-3

DOI 10.1007/978-3-540-68476-3

Cover Design: KünkelLopka, Heidelberg

Printed on acid-free paper

9 8 7 6 5 4 3 2 1

springer.com

The authors

Colin Hood is founder and Chairman of the HOOD Group. He has been responsible for the development of control systems from relay based systems to modern electronic and software controlled systems. Colin holds an BSc(Hons) in Electrical Engineerig and Electronics, a Diploma in Management Studies (DMS), and an MBA. Colin is also a founding member of the International Requirements Engineering Board (IREB).

Simon Wiedemann has been a Senior Consultant with the HOOD Group for a couple of years and is now focussing on his responsibilities as a member of the HOOD Group's technical board, approving publications and training consultants. His PhD is on mathematical methods for numerical simulations of flexible multibody systems. Simon is a professor for mechanical engineering at the Munich University of Applied Sciences.

Stefan Fichtinger is a Senior Consultant with the HOOD Group. Since the beginning of his professional career, Stefan has been involved in the requirements definition of software products such as product data management (PDM) and logistics systems. As a software product manager, Stefan was responsible for market analyses and successful roll-outs.. He also has experience as process manager. Stefan holds a Dipl.-Ing. degree.

Urte Pautz is a Senior Consultant with the HOOD Group, supporting customers in introducing and establishing requirements mangement and engineering processes. To this end she uses assessments, seminars, workshops and coaching. Urte has many years of experience in configuration and change management, and also has a strong background in information technology and software development. Urte holds a Dipl.-Inf. degree.

To contact the authors of this book, please use the following email address:

Technical-Board@HOOD-Group.com

You are also welcome to visit the HOOD Group's homepage using:

www.HOOD-Group.com

Preface and Dedications

We wrote this book to help people that have been trained in one discipline at the expense of achieving a balanced view of complete systems. We are systems engineers that are experts in requirements. We are systems engineers first and foremost, because without an appreciation of all of the disciplines of systems engineering we would not be able to appreciate the finer points of our speciality. Without an appreciation of all of the disciplines of systems engineering we could not be experts in our field.

We gratefully acknowledge the support we received from a team of people from the HOOD Group in the writing of this book. Amongst them, we specially want to say thank you to

Gabi Leibmann: she kept a lot of administrative work away from us

Stefan Fichtinger: for doing much more than has been agreed

Michael Jastram: for all his incredible support

Munich, October 2007
Colin Hood

Table of Contents

1 Introduction

1.1 Aim of Book

The aims of this book are to motivate successful improvements to requirements management, to promote understanding of requirements management as one of an interrelated set of systems engineering disciplines, and to understand these systems engineering disciplines and their interfaces to requirements processes.

1.2 Benefit to be gained from book

By understanding and following the guidance in this book you will be able to reap benefits of synergy between team members and across departmental boundaries by coordinating efforts in requirements management as part of your systems engineering activities.

We have seen organisations that as they have grown have developed to become a collection of independent departments. Too often these departments concentrate increasingly on achieving their departmental aims, eventually to the extent that their departmental aims become more important than the aims of the overall organisation. What we need is coordinated teamwork where each part of the team pulls in the same direction.

This book helps a team to understand the central role played by requirements in systems engineering projects. It shows that no one systems engineering discipline is more important that any other. It shows that all the systems engineering disciplines are interrelated and interdependent.

This book will establish the need for, and legitimise the use of requirements management and engineering.

Managing requirements consists of managing changes to requirements, managing various versions of requirements, managing multiple configurations of requirements, managing deliveries of requirements on time, in budget and to the correct quality without taking undue risks. And all the time ensuring that all those who need to know, know who is responsible for what. All of this requires communication and commitment.

Product and services produced to meet requirements must be checked against requirements to ensure that the specified and agreed requirements have been achieved

A perfectly optimized system is a set of suboptimal subsystems. If teams try to optimise each subsystem there will be conflict. Following the advice in this book teams will be inspired to see the big picture and be able to concentrate on getting the system built as required.

To introduce terms such as RM&E (requirements management and engineering) and relate to other nomenclature so that CMMI (Capability Maturity Model Integration) terms may be used throughout the book

1.3   Definition of terms

CMMI: Capability Maturity Model Integration. A framework for scoring an organisation's ability to work with systems engineering processes. CMMI comes from the Software Engineering Institute (SEI) of Carnegie Melon University in Pittsburgh U.S.A. Various trademarks and service marks of the SEI relating to CMMI are acknowledged.

HCM: HOOD capability model. A model for judging the quality of the implementation of a process mainly by considering the quality of its work products. Often used to support motivation of change programmes by measuring and publishing progress.

Process: (see also Software Process). A sequence of steps performed for a given purpose; for example, the software development process.

Requirement: A statement identifying a capability, physical characteristic, or quality factor that bounds a product or process need for which a solution will be pursued.

Requirements Definition: The process of producing documented and agreed requirements by means of elicitation, specification, analysis (quality check: judgment of requirements against quality criteria), and review (leading to acceptance, rejection, or return for rework) of requirements.

Requirements Development: The purpose of requirements development is to produce and analyze customer, product, and product-component requirements.

Requirements Engineering: See Requirements Development.

Requirements Management: The set of procedures that support the development of requirements including planning, traceability, impact analysis, change management and so on.

Requirements Management: The sum of the interfaces between requirements development and all other systems engineering disciplines such as configuration management and project management. The purpose of requirements management is to manage the requirements of the project's products and product components and to identify inconsistencies between those requirements and the project's plans and work products.

RM&E: Requirements management and engineering. The overall term used to include all requirements related processes.

Note to RM&E: In the 1990's the overall term used was requirements management. Then towards the end of the 1990's and early in the new millennium a trend gathered momentum to split the management of requirements from the development of requirements. Some organizations made the distinction along the lines that developing or defining requirements was requirements engineering. Others disagree. Some organisations use both terms requirements management and requirements engineering and consider that their understanding is the one and only true definition. Other organisations use definitions that completely contradict the understanding of others, and also consider that their understanding is the one and only true definition. Some use the CMMI definitions of requirements management and requirements development and combine these by using requirements engineering to encompass everything. So we use the term requirements management and engineering in an attempt to include all people, while acknowledging that there are a variety of definitions. At work we use whatever terminology our customers wish. There are more important battles to fight than who has the best words. People who get hung up on whose definition is correct, (or more normally the fight is who is incorrect!) should read A. A .Milne and learn from Winnie the Pooh; "We can use words to mean whatever we wish them to mean". As long as we understand each other we can work together. We advise the use of standards wherever possible. Where there is no single standard we must agree amongst ourselves.

Software Process: (see also Process). A set of activities, methods, practices, and transformations that people use to develop and maintain software and the associated products.

Stakeholder: A "stakeholder" is a group or individual that is affected by or in some way accountable for the outcome of an undertaking. Stakeholders may include project members, suppliers, customers, end users, and others.

Alternative definition: People who will be affected by the project or can influence it but who are not directly involved with doing the project work. Examples are managers affected by the project, process owners, people who work with the process under study, internal departments that support the process, customers, suppliers, and financial department.

Alternative definition: People who are (or might be) affected by any action taken by an organization. Examples are: customers, owners, employees, associates, partners, contractors, suppliers, related people or located near by.

Alternative definition: Any group or individual who can affect or who is affected by achievement of a firm's objectives

Test: (See Validation and Verification). The activity of checking correctness.

Verification: Although "verification" and "validation" at first seem quite similar in CMMI models, on closer inspection you can see that each addresses different issues. Verification confirms that work products properly reflect the requirements specified for them. In other words, verification ensures that "you built it right."

Validation: Validation confirms that the product, as provided, will fulfill its intended use. In other words, validation ensures that "you built the right thing."

1.4   Structure of the Book

This book is divided into three parts. Part one is Requirements Management and Engineering: requirements management is greater than the sum of its parts. In this first part the aim is to introduce the book and to establish a common understanding of terminology with the reader.

Part two is Getting Down and Dirty: the low-down on systems engineering disciplines and their interfaces to requirements processes. In this part the aim is to discuss in detail the systems engineering disciplines, and specifically to define the interface between each systems engineering discipline and requirements development.

Part three is A Practical guide: helping to motivate and support successful implementation of requirements driven improvements with HOOD capability models (HCM).

Part one starts with Chapter 1 Introduction. This is the introduction to the book and describes the aims of the book and the benefits to be gained from reading the book. Some terms are defined that aid the understanding of the following chapters. Some terms are defined more than once quoting from various sources to show that the terms, although used often, are not standardized. If these definitions are contradictory it is made clear which definition is to be used in this book. The structure of the book is explained and a guide is given how to read this book to get the best advantage.

Chapter 2 Why Requirements Management and Engineering? In this chapter the need for and benefits of requirements management and engineering (RM&E) are explained. Terms such as RM&E and other nomenclature are explained so that CMMI terms may be used throughout the book. Definitions and detailed introduction of interfaces between systems engineering disciplines is not done here, but are investigated later in chapter 5.

Chapter 3 is Processes and Methods in Requirements Management and Engineering. The aim is to introduce the other systems engineering disciplines and process including those described by CMMI which will be explained in detail to form the structure of Part 2, the main part of this book.

Chapter 4 is Introduction to Requirements Engineering. The chapter introduces and defines requirements engineering, requirements development, and the HOOD requirements definition process.

Chapter 5 is Introduction to Requirements Management. Requirements management is firstly defined in terms of its activities and also in terms of its results. This is the introduction to a discussion that is the main part of this book. After the main discussion involving all the other disciplines, requirements management according to HOOD will be redefined in the more advanced, inclusive, and sophisticated way.

Part 2 starts with Chapter 6 Project Management. Project management is introduced, and its relationship to requirements development is investigated. The overlapping responsibilities between a project manager and a requirements manager are discussed, and the information common to both disciplines is exposed. The similarity and differences between tasks on a project plan and the requirements in a specification are explored.

Chapter 7 is Configuration Management. Configuration management is introduced and its relationship to requirements development is investigated. The overlapping responsibilities between the roles of configuration management and a requirements manager are discussed, and the information common to both disciplines is exposed. The idea of requirements and related information as configuration items and a set of requirements as a specification are explored.

Chapter 8 is Measurement and Analysis. Measurement and analysis is introduced, and its relationship to requirements development is investigated. The role of measurement and analysis is discussed, and the information common to measurement and analysis and requirements development is exposed. The similarity and differences between measurements of requirements and the requirements in a specification are explored. Particularly the need for measuring to support an aim rather than measuring just because a measurement is possible is emphasised.

Chapter 9 is Risk Management. Risk management is introduced, and its relationship to requirements development is investigated. The overlapping responsibilities between a risk manager and a requirements manager are discussed. The information common to both disciplines is exposed. The different types of risks and risk mitigation and their influence on the requirements in a specification are explored, as is the influence of requirements as a source of risk.

Chapter 10 is Test Management (Verification and Validation). Test management is introduced, and its relationship to requirements development is investigated. The overlapping responsibilities between a test manager and a requirements manager are discussed, and the information common to both disciplines is exposed. The similarity and differences between test cases in a test plan and the requirements in a specification are explored. The difficulties encountered when using a test plan as a requirements specification are recounted.

Chapter 11 is Change Management. Change management is introduced, and its relationship to requirements development is investigated. The overlapping responsibilities between a change manager and a requirements manager are discussed, and the information common to both disciplines is exposed. The similarity and differences between change requests and the requirements in a specification are explored.

Chapter 12 is Advanced Requirements Management: the complete specification. This chapter is the summary of all previous chapters in Part 2, showing requirements management as a complete specification of the interfaces between requirements engineering and other systems engineering disciplines.

Part 3 is a practical guide, helping to motivate successful implementation of requirements driven improvements with HCM. Part 3 starts with Chapter 13 The HOOD capability models. This chapter provides motivation for supporting change. Psychological reasons why we need to measure and publish progress or lack of progress is described. Chapter 13 The HOOD capability models is an introduction to Chapters 14 and 15 which describe the HOOD capability models in detail.

Chapter 14 is HCM for Requirements Definition. The aim of this chapter is to introduce and define HCM for requirements definition. Help is offered for introducing improvements in practical terms. A stepwise introduction is recommended and supported, rather than present a theoretical treatise.

Chapter 15 is HCM for Requirements Management. The aim of this chapter is to introduce and define HCM for requirements management. Help is offered for introducing improvements in practical terms. A stepwise introduction is recommended and supported. This chapter pulls together the threads of all previous chapters and weaves the themes together to create a tapestry of all the ideas presented thus far. Each thread remains distinct but still takes its place in the overall picture.

1.5   How to read this book

There are many ways to use this book. Consider it a resource from which we may take as we please. The book may be read from beginning to end or it may be used as a reference book and dipped into time and again with random access as a project progresses.

The book is divided into three parts. Part 1 is an introduction and sets the scene for the rest of the book. Part 2 deals with systems engineering disciplines and their relevance to requirements management. This is the main part of the book that you will use as a reference for technical information within your project. Part 3 deals with the challenge of introducing the ideas of Part 2 into your organisation. Part 3 is the part of this book that you will use as a reference for management information to support your team during the introduction of improvements.

Reading from beginning to end is particularly useful not only for those beginning to grapple with the complexities of requirements management. Also, those with many years experience might enjoy seeing things explained that previously had been taken for granted. You may agree with some or all of the various opinions presented. We hope that if you at first disagree with some of the opinions that this will help you to respect the fact that there are many dearly held opinions, and that our industry is still in its infancy and there is much still to be standardised. We have tried to represent various views while being sure to tell you what we have found to work in practice. In cases where there is disagreement we fall back on the author's years of experience in engineering since 1977 and use our common sense. Remember that this subject is no longer a technical challenge; we are dealing with peoples' understanding and people's failure to understand. We are dealing with peoples' weaknesses and insecurities. So please be kind to those with a different opinion to yourself. As my Father said, "You can learn something from any idiot". Your challenge at work is to include others and to strengthen the team. We hope this book helps you better to construct and explain your arguments in order that you can convince. We hope this book helps you better to understand the opinions of others that you can benefit from a broader view.

Using the same principal as is used in good training courses, information will be introduced in context to be defined later in detail. This organisation of information enables and supports the reading of the book from beginning to end. Learning is supported and encouraged by introducing topics in a broad way. By using a technique similar to active listening, the reader is encouraged to ask questions. By asking questions the answers to the questions become much more relevant than if the information is presented in a series of unrelated and surprising facts. By removing the element of surprise as another piece of information is presented learning is supported. In this book when information is dealt with in detail there is no surprise as we have prompted the questions by the manner of the introduction.

Consider your brain to be a series of cupboards, drawers, and shelves. The stuff you store on shelves is easily visible and can be found without much structuring. You just have to scan the shelves for what you want, and when you see what you are looking for your search is over. But your shelf space is limited, and anyway, even if you could replace all of your drawers and cupboards with shelves the search would take too long. Only having shelves for storing information would be like the advice given in the comic Viz, "If you have trouble finding things, just thread all of your possessions onto a piece of string. If you lose anything, just follow the string from one end to the other and you will be sure to find what you are looking for." Now, that is a technical challenge!

So we need more than just shelving. We need more structure. If we have lots of things put away we need to file things in some order so that we can find them again. We need cupboards so that we can store different things in different places. The cupboards may contain shelves but these are only visible when we have opened the cupboard door. If we do not later shut the door properly the contents may fall out.

The early chapters can be considered to be an explanation of which cupboards we have. By explaining the aims of each chapter and each part of each chapter we open the cupboard doors so that you may file the information away in your brain. By summarising each chapter we help you to close the cupboard door to prevent the contents falling out. The aims at the beginning and the summary at the end of each chapter support learning.

The modular form of this book supports the reading of the book as a reference book so that detail is easy to find just when your project needs it.

2 Why Requirements Management and Engineering

2.1 General

To ask why requirements management and engineering should be used is rather simplistic. A better question would be: "Why and when is it recommended and important to use RM&E methods and processes in projects?" This, however, is an excessively long title.

In recent years, management started to give RM&E more and more importance. For instance, management may require the introduction of requirements management in an organization by a specific deadline .

This approach implies that until that point there was no requirements management in the organization at all, but this is never true:

Every organization offering a product or a service practices requirements management. If this were not be true, the organization would have perished a long time ago. All organizations have a relationship between customer and contractor. And customers have aims that they are trying to achieve by using the contractor's products and services.

If there is the aim to fulfil the customer's wishes with products and services, requirements management takes place – at least implicitly.

Why is this topic more important for some organizations than for others? Why did the implementation of RM&E methods and processes gain so much importance during the last decades?

If we investigate small companies that develop a relatively simple product, requirements management is typically not a big deal. In such organizations, the development department usually communicates directly with the customer. They know the customer and their needs as well as the product or service to be developed.

Under these circumstances, it's just a small step from customer need to product or service, as only a small number of people is involved. The team members can communicate verbally and have little difficulty coordinating. The complexity of the product or service isn't high enough to require division of labour. Under these circumstances, acceptable and even good results can be achieved.

But if an organization grows rapidly, if the complexity of the products increases and if separation of labour becomes more common, the importance of using structured methods and processes in requirements management increases as well. Modern RM&E methods originate, not surprisingly, in the air and space flight industries. After all, these industries have always been pioneers in designing highly complex system that are highly coupled. On top of that, development is highly distributed which means that small coordination problems can produce fatal and expensive consequences.

In the last decades, the importance of electronics in vehicles increased significantly. The functionalities in electronics are a major distinguishing factor between car manufacturers. The method described earlier – to keep the requirements solely in the heads of the people – worked fairly well initially. But there is a limit, at which even the "local heroes" of an organization loose sight. This is even more fatal, as this process happens silently. But at some point, the number of errors becomes overwhelming and the costs explode.

To sum it up: The methods and processes of RM&E are indispensable for organisations that develop complex products or services using separation of labour.

There is one issue, however, that makes it very difficult to introduce RM&E methods into projects: A neglect of RM&E in the starting phase of a project materializes only during the final phase of a project.

In his book Software Engineering Economics, Prentice-Hall, published in 1981, Böhm states that the cost for fixing errors raise drastically, the later in the development process they are discovered. Today this is considered common knowledge.

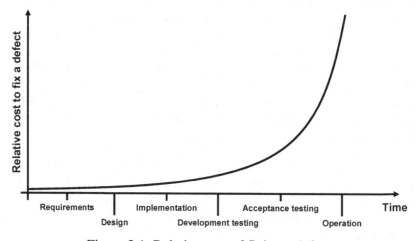

Figure 2.1: Relative cost of fixing a defect

This finding is even more significant, if we look at the areas where errors are found.

F. Sheldon analyzed a US-Air Force project, where 40% - 60% of all errors were found in the requirements. Only a third of the errors were found in design and code.

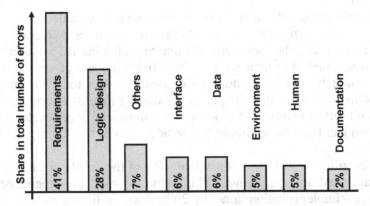

Figure 2.2: The share of errors in requirements in total number of errors

In other words: The highest savings can be achieved by focussing on finding errors – or avoiding them in the first place – during the early stage of a project by consequently using requirements management.

The advantages of RM&E methods and processes are even more visible if we investigate the connection to other disciplines, like project management, version management, configuration management, design, architecture, solution finding process, purchase, supplier management, customer service, distribution, marketing, as well as test management.

2.2   Advantages of RM&E in project management

2.2.1   Advantages of project planning

The aim of project management is to produce in the required quality with a calculated time and money budget. Typically, the estimate is documented in a contract.

A serious estimate can only be produced, if contractor and customer agree on the requirements of the system to be developed, at least roughly. Supposedly there are project managers or sales people who are capable of creating a time frame and cost estimate contractually, without even formulating the requirements of the system under development. But this approach reduces the chances of success for the project from the very beginning.

Highest priority goal should be to develop as soon as possible a mutual understanding of the system under development between customer and contractor. This will serve as the foundation for a serious estimate of cost and time.

We should wonder why, in spite of this insight, countless offers contain cost and time estimates, but only a vague notion of the deliverable. It may have to do with the fact that collecting and eliciting the requirements for the first round of estimates takes a significant amount of work that neither the contractor nor the customer allocated a budget for. The start of the implementation is often the perceived starting time of a project. But this doesn't reflect reality: The moment when the decision of developing a new system had been made should be considered to be the starting point of the project.

According to RM&E best practice, 40% of the development time should be allocated for specifying. This value is based on experience. This reduces implementation time to 20%, leaving the remaining 40% for testing.

What does this mean for the creation of offers? The customer should allocate a budget of time and money before the bidding even starts, in order to produce a good requirements specification that will serve as a basis for the call for bids. Likewise, the contractors must have enough time to analyse the requirements specification and to write a target specification.

Both sides benefit from this approach, as a common understanding in regard to the system under development is being established. This will improve the quality of the project plan (time and budget), and ultimately for the implementation phase, which tends to be more expensive. The result is a more precise calculation of the system architectures, optimal resource planning, and avoidance of aberrations (based on misunderstandings). All this results in a reduction of costs

2.2.2 Advantages during the implementation phase

There is a high risk that changes in requirements won't be documented in the implementation phase. There are many reasons for this which are detailed in chapter 11 of this book.

In a proper realization of RM&E best practices, a process should be defined that regulates the handling of changes during all stages of the project.

Advantages for project management are manifold. For instance, contractor and customer both have an up to date project plan that they agree upon. All relevant stakeholders always have an up to date project status. Conflicts that are based on different understanding of the services to be rendered are thus avoided in the first place. Coordination of tasks is simplified, as changes are being discussed and decided upon in the open. All project tasks refer to a consolidated specification and can be traced to the implementation of the solution. Due to prioritizing of requirements, unforeseen influences can be dealt with quickly by adjusting the project plan. In other words, the methods of RM&E support the project manager's responsibilities.

2.2.3 Advantages during the acceptance phase

The final acceptance, also called buy-off, typically marks the end of a project. But acceptance can only happen if the acceptance criteria are fulfilled. The criteria, in return, should have been formulated together with the requirements.

If the specification has not been updated during the course of the project, it is difficult to define acceptance test, or to perform a final acceptance in the first place.

An up to date specification is the basis for test planning. Test cases can and should be developed based on the requirements. Feedback in the form of test results allows the project manager to estimate the actual quality of the product under development, and whether the project is on schedule.

A defect list based on tests is the foundation for making the decision of finishing a project.

There are real projects that continued on for years, because contractor and customer couldn't reach agreement on the final acceptance, caused by an outdated specification.

2.2.4 Advantages in regard to version and configuration management

Version and configuration management is a complex field in itself. Every business that continuously develops products consisting of components must deal with this topic.

Typically, there is a concept that regulates the versioning and configuration of products. There is the definition of a product structure, a component structure and an organization structure.

RM&E must develop an information infrastructure for specifying requirements based on these concepts, corresponding to the structures of organization, product and development.

Definitions for criteria must be defined that associate requirements with product versions, product variants, module versions and module variants.

The advantages are obvious:

- Product management is aware of dependencies of requirements and knows at every time which requirement is implemented in which product version or variant
- Product management can estimate the implications of changes on product versions or variants
- Key requirements are specified only once; changes are mapped automatically on the relevant development projects
- Problems with the respect to implementation or realization can be traced to specific product versions and variants
- Specific requirements can be reused for multiple product versions and variants

2.3   Advantages for finding solutions in design and architecture

2.3.1   Advantages design and architecture

Agile methods are a hot topic in software development. Here, a system with minimal basic functionality is developed at the beginning of the project. Subsequently, the system is extended in small steps in close collaboration with the customer. This stands in stark contrast to the waterfall model in software development, where the system is specified completely before implementation starts.

As so often, reality is in between these two approaches. For instance the fundamental general conditions and aims of the project shouldn't change. To exaggerate, a system shouldn't start as a bookkeeping system to become a CAD System during the course of the project.

On the other hand, changes must be allowed during the implementation phase.

Everybody who ever built a house knows what is meant by this. The fundamental architecture must stand before implementation starts (e.g. number of floors, location, type of heating, etc.). Nevertheless, some adjustments during the construction phase must be possible (e.g. the type of doors and windows, partitioning of rooms, etc.).

In other words, the basic requirements must be clearly defined and consolidated and be sufficient to build a stable architecture and design. Without this, an expensive redesign of the architecture may be necessary later on in the project. RM&E methods help through elicitation, modelling, analysis and review to create a foundation of these fundamental requirements. This will give the system a stable and sustainable architecture.

During development, RM&E helps to accommodate changes that will come without doubt. This is supported by structured processes. Working based on different states of the specification is a common problem especially in big teams. This discrepancy often shows up only during integration. RM&E methods help to execute change management in a structured fashion, which helps avoid erroneous development in its early stages.

2.3.2 Advantages in finding solutions

The key here is the capability to innovate. Especially companies and developers who used a specific technology for a long time for solving customer problems have the tendency to keep improving the technology in use, rather than to consider new avenues.

Examples help to explain this in detail. A central user requirement may be: "The user must be able to see the picture the most 5 minutes after taking it." This user requirement could be realized thanks to the development of the Polaroid camera in the late 40s. It is based on the technology of special films that develop and fixate the photograph. The technology was improved over the decades, until digital cameras entered the market. Digital photography was a disruptive technology that solved the actual user requirements better and much cheaper than the technology based on photographic film. Bottom line: The Polaroid camera was almost completely replaced by digital cameras and is only left in a few niche markets.

There are numerous examples like this.

RM&E support the ability to innovate by providing elicitation methods for requirements on all levels and their traceability. To realize this, user requirements are specified in a way that they don't contain any unnecessary limitations or solutions, due to technology or otherwise.

2.4   Advantages in purchase and supplier management

Typically, the purchasing department insists on a clear description of the scope of work for the system to be developed. This simplifies comparing offers from suppliers based on the work description, or user requirements specification. Ideally, the specifcation is sent to various suppliers, who in return create offers. The purchasing department can then pick the cheapest offer.

What are the advantages for the purchasing department? It can focus on the commercial aspects, like selecting the offer with the most favourable conditions and the cheapest price.

RM&E can only support the purchasing department with some aspects. For instance, it can support the creation of the user requirements specification, which is then sent to all potential suppliers.

But in addition, it is expected that the suppliers create a target specification, where they elaborate on how they intend to solve the problem. The department that commissioned the project should support the purchasing department in the evaluation of the target specification. Thus, the ultimate decision is made by the purchasing and commissioning departments together, and price is just one aspect in the decision making process.

The advantage of this approach is that the decision has a solid foundation, simplifying significantly the purchasing negotiations and supplier assessments.

2.5   Advantages in customer service, sales and marketing

Customer service can be an indicator of the service quality of an organization. Customer service typically has great interest in the high quality of the product delivered. If this is not the case, the effort of customer service will be unproportionally high compared to other departments.

Why is this? If problems are recognized by customers after delivery, customer service must take care of them. The most expensive problems are those where customer service must do this on site for a large number of users. But customer service has to deal with more than just product defects: They also deal with complains regarding lack of functionality or bad usability.

This makes customer service a universal communication channel that allows the company to gather feedback regarding the quality of the product. Unfortunately, often this channel is underutilized for product improvements.

If customer service is used as the source for product requirements, the effort and cost of customer service could be lowered.

Customer service can also be used as a source of requirements for performing system diagnoses, which is another advantage of RM&E methods. Upon a customer service request, a potential system error must be identified quickly, so that it can be fixed without delay.

This, too, reduces effort and thereby costs for customer service.

Other beneficiaries of implemented RM&E methods are sales and marketing. Those are the groups that are typically the departments in an organization that are the closest to the customer. This makes it particularly important that requirements from the customers are not only captured precisely and accurately, but also that they get clearly communicated to the development department.

Communication is the most common problem in this area. Sales and marketing on one side and development on the other side need to have a solid foundation for talking to each other. It is often difficult to establish a common understanding regarding the system under development. But this is a crucial precondition for the development of a successful system. RM&E methods support the selection of appropriate modelling techniques and specification languages, which for the foundation for communication and avoid ill developments.

2.6   Advantages in test and verification management

The department for testing and verification management benefits the most from the active use of RM&E methods. The main task of this group is not only to asses the quality of already developed products and systems, but to accompany the whole development process and to verify intermediate results like specifications.

In order to execute this task, a reference between the current and desired state must be established. Thus, the definition of the desired state for the system under development is a prerequisite. Typically, this is captured with a specification. But far too often specifications are neglected and have a low quality. They tend to have gaps, are out of date or missing completely. RM&E not only accounts for verification of the system under development, but of the specifications as well, thereby creating a foundation for the creation of test cases.

Has this been missed, only few options are left: to develop new test cases through drawn-out interviews with the stakeholders or development department, or simply to use "common sense" and hope for the best.

This results in different understandings of the system under development. Not only different understandings between supplier and customer, but also between departments and individuals. In such a situation, every statement regarding the quality of the system must be put into perspective, as there is not even agreement on the end product.

Using the methods of RM&E, an up to date specification can be guaranteed at any time. This results in a fairly accurate agreement on the end product between the stakeholders. This in turn is a solid foundation for the creation of test cases. The implications of changes during the course of the project can be traced and test cases adapted to the changes, if necessary. Unnecessary test efforts are avoided and the information value in regard to the quality of the system is improved.

3 Processes and Methods in Requirements Management and Engineering

The previous chapters have given an introduction to the subject requirements management and engineering and have shown its meaning and why it could be desirable to take requirements management and engineering activities into account in product development projects.

This chapter gives information on the history and background of requirements management and engineering, thus laying the foundation for the detailed discussions in the following chapters.

Common methods and processes associated with requirements management and engineering are presented, the details of which will be explained later. This overview also serves as a more detailed introduction to the subject, giving information to understand the current status of the development of requirements management and engineering as a project discipline in its own right.

3.1 The roots of Requirements Management and Engineering

The roots of requirements management and engineering go very far back in history, depending on what point of view one takes. If in a very simple approach we define requirements engineering as trying to understand what a customer wants, then it goes back to the first craftsmen that have created anything for anyone else but themselves.

However, the idea of requirements management and engineering as we know it today has its roots in more recent days. It has been born together with the computer, or more precisely with the birth of what we call software, and has fully grown during the time of what is nowadays called the software crisis. The software crisis is usually thought to have taken place sometime around 1970, but events such as the Ariane explosion or products such as the common operating systems for personal computers may lead an observer to think that this crisis is far from being over. In fact, the more complex things become (and they always become more and more complex), the higher the probability that something goes wrong somewhere.

Figure 3.1: Persian craftsman artwork (source: wikipedia)

It will be interesting to see whether the industry will ever learn that decent products do not necessarily have to be complex in order to work properly. Do you know of any industrial product that became simpler throughout the years?

3.1.1 The progress in computer engineering

The dawn of computer systems marks a milestone in the development of modern industries (for the interested reader we take the liberty of pointing out to the fact that the first freely programmable computer system was actually the ZUSE, and not the ENIAC as some people would rather have you believe).

Although very complex systems were known before the first computer, such systems were always physical, which means that the product was fully defined by what is today called the hardware only. There was not more inside than you could see from the outside. In other words, before the computer there was no such thing as software. But why is this such an important difference?

The difference between hardware engineering and software engineering is that hardware engineering is usually inevitably constrained by physical laws. For example, if you want to build a sports car that shall be able to accelerate from zero to 100 kilometres per hour within 4 seconds, you have to relate the car's total mass to the necessary power of the engine. Doing this you will quickly find out that there is only a very narrow range of possible or realistic combinations of combustion engine power and car mass that allows for the basic requirement to be met.

Figure 3.2: First freely programmable computer, Zuse Z1 (source: wikipedia)

By contrast, software engineering is usually only constrained by the physical properties of the computer hardware used. For example, it is pointless to programme a graphical user interface with a resolution of 100 dots per inch if the screen you are using only has a maximum resolution of 50 dots per inch. But if the screen allows for such a resolution, then you can build your user interface in an infinite number of ways. You can use buttons that must be mouse-clicked, or you can use command line input, or you can use speech recognition and so on. If you use click buttons, you can line them up at the bottom, or at the top, or just spread them all over the screen, and so on. If you line them up at the top, you can create them to have all the same size, or to have different sizes depending on their labels, or to have random sizes and so on. If you decide to make them have all the same size, you can distribute them along the width of the screen or just place them next to each other, independent of how much space this consumes. And so on and so forth.

It will be seen from this simple example that the freedom of implementation is usually incomparably larger in software engineering than it is in hardware engineering. It is exactly this general freedom that has caused so many problems throughout the last 4 decades.

Although mechanical or hardware systems have also become very complex recently, owing for example to the findings of material science such as smart materials with memory or materials that change their aggregate state due to electric current, many people and organisations still believe that requirements management and engineering is the province of software engineering only.

It will be shown in this book that requirements management and engineering covers so many aspects of development projects that there is little doubt about the benefit for both software and hardware engineering projects.

3.1.2 Programmers – from artists to facilitators

The first computer systems were exclusively managed and programmed by specialised engineers that often were owned by the inventors of the system. While at the very beginning the principle feasibility of such systems had been one of the main aims to be proven, computers were soon used for special purposes like doing numerical maths.

Figure 3.3: Punched cards controlling a mechanical loom (source: wikipedia)

The main challenge with these early systems was to actually make them work the way the inventors intended them to work. The programmers had a complete plan in their heads, and this plan was usually so simple that there was no questioning that. For example, many of the early systems simply had to add or subtract any two numbers that were entered with punched cards. Some of the early systems were even designed to only perform one task such as adding two numbers, so that the arrangement of the hardware itself represented an invariable programme.

In these days, a programmer was very much an engineer and an artist in a new field of science. Apart from academia and warfare, people in general had little interest for computer systems and all applications were specially designed and very individual.

Thus the development of computer systems dragged itself along, its impacts unrecognised by most of the world. Due to the electric parts that then were state of the art and their physical constraints, this development had rather been slow and not every spectacular to the common people.

Figure 3.4: Front panel of the IBM 650 (source: wikipedia)

Another huge leap was taken during the advent of astronautics. The physics of space travel make it necessary to build everything as light as possible. It was soon found that it is impossible for example to build a satellite with 10 kilogramme of equipment when this equipment needs 100 kilogramme of computer hardware to operate. Thus the quest for new computer hardware led to the invention of semi conductors amongst others, and this in turn quickly led to the invention of integrated circuits.

With integrated circuits it was first possible to build small and powerful multi purpose computer systems that could be programmed more or less arbitrarily.

In those days, programming changed from an art to a special skill that was mainly the domain of technicians in the new field of information technology. The average programmer was used to customers who did not know very much about the subject and its implications and who fully had to trust his or her knowledge and experience.

The customers roughly defined what they needed, and the programmers did all the work and made all the necessary decisions based upon personal experience, skill and inspiration. The motivation of the early programmers to document anything was often low. This way the computer remained some sort of black box that could be made to do anything, but not by everyone.

A few years later the idea of the personal computer for everyone forever changed the way of working of most of the people. Small multi purpose computer systems were soon produced in masses and could be found in almost every office. They were meant to support in every day activities such as writing letters, doing calculations and so on.

Figure 3.5: The Commodore C64 personal computer (source: imageafter.com)

The personal computer first made it necessary to produce computer programmes for thousands of users and more, because solely buying individual solutions would have been impossible for most of the users.

Programming then became the skill of guessing people's needs. Programmers did what they could, but still mainly programmed and often failed to realise what their customers really wanted. Many programmes were created that were hardly or never used, for they would have changed so much the way people used to work that the programmes were unacceptable.

It was then realised that what was necessary was to find out the problems and visions of the future users of the system. The art of programming then changed to devising and applying the most effective and promising ways of doing that sort of research and of delivering what is wanted on time and within budget. Some organisations were very good at this, and some went on completely ignoring their customers' needs.

So all in all, the success of a typical software project still depended largely on the skills of the programmers. Therefore, methods and processes were soon introduced to make the results less dependent of the programmers, more reproducable and more stable in terms of quality. Concepts such as structured programming were invented, and programmers were told to use flow charts and the like to explain to their customers what they plan to implement in a language that he or she might understand.

These various methods and ideas finally culminated in the modern concept of requirements management and engineering. The roots however are still the same and may be summarised in one sentence: trying to find out what the customer really wants and building it. Thus the modern programmer has finally become a facilitator whose skill is not programming, but making it possible that the customer and the technicians can understand each other. So much for the theory.

3.1.3 Requirements Management and Engineering today

In reality, many ideas in requirements management and engineering remained almost unchanged throughout the decades, although people would not stop giving them new labels.

It appears to be fashionable these days to have many processes, methods and maturity models at hand, but the impression remains that this is blurring rather than clearing the picture. Many organisations and people talk a lot about CMMI, RUP, SPICE, V model and others. We will go into more detail with a selection of these maturity models in later chapters.

Only very few have understood that if things are properly done like they should be done, most of the requirements of the common maturity or capability models would automatically be met. This is not amazing, for the better models only reflect the activities that should normally be carried through in every larger project, nothing more nor less.

But instead of taking their time to realise this, organisations try to reach a certain maturity level according to some capability model that is currently "in". They strictly follow the letters but have little understanding of what they actually mean. It must be said, a few organisations are good in following the letters, but many are not. The reason is that without the deeper understanding and experience, the word will remain meaningless. This is the main reason for organisations failing to introduce requirements management and engineering processes and methods. They believe that if they proceed as advised in some book on the subject, they will have a functioning requirements management system within a couple of days. This regularly turns out to be an illusion.

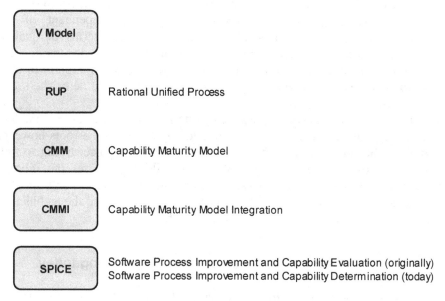

Figure 3.6: Overview of currently fashionable maturitycapability models

This said, it is clear that we suggest the definition of the ends towards which to work to be centre of interest, rather than formalities, however smart they may be or appear. Never lose sight of why we are doing what we do, and do not blindly follw a model.

3.2   Common concepts in Requirements Management and Engineering

From the previous section on the history of requirements management and engineering it is clear that throughout the years a certain set of concepts has formed that is usually common to all requirements management and engineering approaches. As has been mentioned, the names of these concepts may change, owing to current fashions, but the ideas behind stay the same.

We will examine some of these basic concepts now and use this in later chapters as the basic foundation from which we start our discussions on the subject.

3.2.1   The systems engineering concept

The first of the most important concepts in connection with requirements management and engineering is the separation of the various process subjects or, as they are usually called, process areas into different disciplines that although being closely related to each other can be distinguished nonetheless. The following figure shows one common separation.

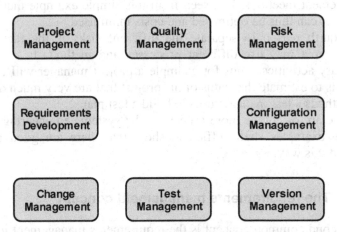

Figure 3.7: Separation of project activities into different process areas

This separation or distinction is commonly called systems engineering. It was soon found out that the more complex projects are best mastered when the various necessary activities are grouped with respect to the main subject they are associated with. This has a number of advantages.

One obvious advantage is that the whole lot of the project is cut into more manageable pieces. This alone would be worth while, for the more one goes into detail with each set of activities, the more reliable estimates and plans will be.

A second reason for separating all the project activities into different areas is that the project members can specialise in their respective fields of expertise. Thus in larger projects there will usually always be a project management staffed with people with experience in managing projects, a risk management staffed with people with a background in risk detection and management, a test management with experienced testers and so on. There are very few larger projects today where in principle all staff are able to carry out all activities at the necessary level of quality so that there is no need to distinguish between certain activities.

Another reason to categorise the various project activities is the possibility to examine the relationships between each of the different categories of activities. This allows for a most effective planning and an optimum performance. For example, once the activities are grouped as depicted in figure 3.7, it may be realised that in a certain project the quality management is not very closely related to the version management, but it is very closely related to the test management. In this situation it may be decided that it is not necessary for the quality manager to take part in version management meetings, but that it is mandatory to take part in test management meetings. It is seen from this simple example that the use of resources can thus be optimised and costs minimised.

A fourth reason to separate the different tasks is the fact that each process area may use different processes and methods to carry out the necessary activities. Thus for example a project manager will usually use methods to estimate the status of his project that are very much different to the methods a test manager uses to build a test plan.

There are of course more aspects to the systems engineering approach, but the examples shall suffice to show that there are good reasons to proceed this way.

3.2.2 The requirements management concept

The second common concept is the requirements management idea. All of the capability models currently used in the industry take requirements management and engineering into account as being one of the most important process areas. This is usually reflected in the fact that even to reach the lowest level of maturity or capability in the state-of-the-art models, there must be at least some kind of requirements management and engineering.

This is not surprising, for requirements engineering is the term that summarises all efforts to find out what shall actually be built, and requirements management is the term that summarises all efforts to make sure that the data created with requirements engineering remains valuable and usable throughout a project. And it is of course clear that every sensible project should not ignore the customer's or end user's needs and wants, and that this should be so for all the project.

But the following chapters will show that there is much more to requirements management than just a simple administration of a handful of text pieces called requirements. Requirements management integrates all the available project data with the available requirements data, thus creating a flow of information for all of the different project members to benefit. From this point of view, requirements management may be seen as the heart of project information administration.

3.2.3 The process quality concept

A third central concept of systems engineering in general and requirements management and engineering in particular is the idea of the process quality.

The maturity models currently used try to measure how far advanced an organisation is with respect to a certain systems engineering disciplines. In order to do this, these models try to estimate the maturity and quality of the processes that are applied for carrying out the necessary activities.

The underlying idea of such an approach is the belief that a high quality of processes governing the development of a system will be reflected in the quality of the system or product itself. Many examples exist that support this point of view, relating repeatability of product quality to process quality and vice versa.

3.3   Processes and methods in Requirements Management and Engineering

Now that we have an overview of what requirements management and engineering are and how they fit into the process landscape of a normal project we will have a closer look at the various processes and methods commonly applied.

The examinations starting here will continue in the following chapters, where still more details and aspects will be introduced and explained. This section is meant to give a rough introduction and overview of what requirements management and engineering actually means in daily business.

3.3.1 Requirements engineering

There are many definitions in the literature of what requirements engineering is. We use the term requirements engineering to indicate that within this process area, requirements are created or engineered. Thus a totally equivalent term would be requirements development.

In requirements development or engineering the main process that takes place, according to the HOOD Group's point of view, is the requirements definition process.

This process contains all activities that are necessary in order to develop requirements and is separated into two sub processes:

- Definition of scope
- Definition of requirements

The first of these two sub processes, the definition of the scope, can be further separated into three main activities:

- Identifying interfaces
- Defining interfaces
- Defining stakeholders and roles

The second sub process as listed above can also be separated into a small number of key activities:

- Elicitation
- Specification
- Analysis
- Review

All the activities introduced here together with their meaning will be explained in detail in the following chapters. In the meantime it may suffice to note that all these activities can take place at the same time. It is one of the secrets of an efficient requirements management and engineering philosophy that most of the work can be carried out in parallel, although many process models implicitly or explicitly suggest that there be a certain order of the single activities.

Some of the methods commonly applied for identifying and defining interfaces, stakeholder and roles and for elicitation are:

- Modelling
- Document analysis

- Checklists
- Brainstorming
- Mind maps
- Interviews
- Observation
- Use cases
- Scenarios and stories

These methods can be used for example to identify and define interfaces, stakeholders and roles as well as to elicit requirements. As maybe not all readers are familiar with the above terms, one or two sentences shall be spend in order to give brief explanations.

Modelling: basically, a model is a copy of a certain finite fraction of reality. As such, a model may contain less detail or information than the original, but never more. In more practical terms, a model may be anything describing a certain aspect of reality from plain text to a picture. In this sense modelling is not really a method in its own right, but many methods are modelling techniques.

Document analysis: as the overwhelming majority of development projects nowadays have some kind of predecessor projects, large pieces of the necessary information are usually gained by the analysis of existing documentation, for example old requirements specifications, old stakeholder lists and so on.

Checklists: this term is rather self-explaining. Checklists are used to make sure that none of the most important activities or pieces of information has been accidentally left out. Checklists are a simple and effective way of embedding knowledge in an organisation.

Brainstorming: the idea of a brainstorming session is to produce a lot of ideas, associations and the like in a very short amount of time, thus building a first basis for a development project to lift off from. This is made possible by the strict rule that during the brainstorming, no criticism is allowed. Only after the phase of free association, the various concepts and ideas developed are analysed for feasibility and so on.

Mind maps: a mind map is a graphical representation of associations with a certain subject. Usually, the main subject is centred in the middle of a piece of paper, and the main ideas and thoughts in connection with that subject are ordered around the centre. Every such main idea builds another centre around which sub ideas and more detailed associations can be grouped.

Interviews: an interview is simply asking someone directly for his opinion on a certain subject. Experience shows that although this idea is quite obvious, it is usually one of the least effective methods. It may be necessary but it is not sufficient.

Observation: many data and important pieces of information can be gathered by simply observing people doing something. As observation usually has a touch of secrecy, this method may appear unethical to some.

Use cases: use cases are a combination of graphical and textual representations of one or more ways in which to use a system to be developed. As such, they are a typical case of modelling. Use cases became a fashion some two or so decades ago when it was found that the customers of complex systems usually understand a picture much easier than for example a piece of source code.

Scenarios and stories: scenarios and stories are similar to use cases in that they may use graphics and text to describe possible ways of using a system to be developed. Some people use scenarios to cover many more ways of using the system than use cases.

For the specification of requirements, typical methods that may be used are:

- Templates
- Quality criteria
- Weak word analysis

Templates: there may exist templates for tables of content, which will support in structuring the requirements during specification. There may also be templates for example for the syntax of single sentences.

Quality criteria: requirements are usually specified according to some quality standards that are defined through quality criteria. Typical criteria for requirements are identifiability, traceability, atomicity and lack of redundancy. It is important to note that these quality criteria must be agreed on before the requirements are specified.

Weak word analysis (Quality Check): we call a word a weak word if it transports little information blurs what should be expressed. Typically, adjectives and adverbs are weak words, for example "really fast", "not too slow" and so on. Instead, depending on why the requirements are being written it is sometimes be better to say "faster than 100 kp/h", "no quicker than 10 pieces per second". However, if the aim of writing and publishing requirements is to trigger innovation, then it might be better to say "really fast" in a customer requirements specification to see what the various suppliers can supply. This type of requirement that at first sight appears weak is in fact really useful for guiding a choice between various offers. Rather than specifying a maximum cost for a project, it can be beneficial to specify that low cost is important to see from a selection of potential suppliers what is possible.

For the analysis and review of requirements there are various special methods. Many people have their own favourite. The trick is to do what is best suited to the current situation rather than blindly following a recipe without understanding it. The basic activity during analysis is evaluating a certain subset or all of the requirements with respect to the quality criteria agreed on before the specification, and this simply means studying all relevant requirements. During the review the only task that has to be carried out is making the decision whether a requirement or a set of requirements can be accepted as is, or has to be rejected, or must be revised before being analysed and reviewed again.

3.3.2 Requirements management

As has been briefly mentioned above, we define requirements management to be the set of activities which ensure that the requirements information is always up to date and can be accessed by all project staff that may benefit from it. In other words, requirements management integrates all relevant pieces of information from all the other systems engineering disciplines. A more complete and detailed definition will be given in the following chapters.

It is seen from figure 3.7 that the main process areas associated with requirements management are:

- Project management
- Quality management
- Risk management
- Configuration management
- Version management
- Test management
- Change management
- Requirements engineering

As requirements management integrates requirements engineering with all the other systems engineering disciplines as listed above it is hard to define a requirements management as a single process.

Rather, the requirements management process is a collection of processes that all interface with requirements engineering. Thus for example, whenever there are changes in a project, the requirements documentation must be changed accordingly. To give a second example, the requirements must be filterable or selectable with respect to the various product versions.

A selection of some of the most common concepts or methods of requirements management is given as follows:

- Identifiability
- Filterability

- Traceability
- Linking
- Additional information
- User rights

Identifiability: Requirements management has to make sure that each single requirement is identifiable. Although this may seem superfluous for very small projects, people usually soon find out that if they always have to talk about "the third sentence of the second paragraph on page number five", misunderstandings and errors are almost inevitably. In a simple approach identifiability can be reached by giving each requirement a unique number. It is important to note that even when requirements are deleted, their identifier should not be assigned a second time, for this may cause misunderstandings and ambiguities. Problems with this very common approach can arise when more than one requirements document or specification has to be managed. In such a situation it is very likely that one number has been assigned more than one time in different specifications. Adding a unique prefix to the number for each individual specification resolves this problem, and finally all requirements are really uniquely identifiable.

Filterability: It will be seen in the following chapters that a functioning requirements management focuses on information rather than documents. For example, keeping all requirements in one place allows for a central administration of this important information, and all relevant project staff may access all existing information. There are many advantages to keeping the information together and only extracting what is needed at the moment, instead of having distributed and fragmentary pieces of information all over the place. One such advantage is the possibility to maintain all existing information and keep it consolidated, which would otherwise be probably impossible. This approach is also motivated by the fact that usually data bases are used to administer the requirements and associated information. If people share a common data pot it is necessary that they can all extract the pieces of information that are currently necessary. For example, a test manager will need other information than the project manager. Thus filterability of the information is a mandatory precondition for shared information. But even with regard to only one person, say the requirements manager, it is necessary to filter the information, for example to create requirements specifications for different versions of the product.

Traceability: How far traceability can go will be shown in the following chapters. For the moment we note that in principle traceability covers at least two important aspects: the first aspect is traceability between various pieces of information at one point in time, for example traceability between customer requirements and system requirements. The second aspect is traceability of one single piece of information throughout time, for example how one requirement changed during the course of a project. As the second aspect is usually closely related to what is commonly called change management or change history, we will limit the concept of traceability to the first aspect from here on. As a consequence, traceability and linking (see next paragraph) are two terms that are more or less interchangeable.

Linking: This term is commonly used in the requirements management and engineering literature for the documentation of relationships between different pieces of relevant information associated with requirements. For example, linking the requirements information to the test information means documenting somehow which requirements will be tested by which test cases and which test cases cover which requirements. If unique identifiers as described before are used, linking can be a simple text entry. In our example, the identifiers of the requirements covered by one test case can be entered so that they can be identified as belonging to this test case, and the identifier of the test case can be entered in each requirement. This would represent a bidirectional traceability between tests and requirements. Commercial requirements management tools usually offer the possibility to create such linking in a more or less comfortable way.

Additional information: Another important method in requirements management is the separation of the requirements information from additional information. Note that this separation is not always obvious and may be carried out in more than one way. The additional information is commonly stored in attributes that are defined at the beginning of a project. Once an attribute is defined it means that every requirement will possess this attribute, and this usually means that this attribute must be filled in and maintained for each single requirement. Typical examples of such additional information that belongs to a requirement but should not be part of the requirements information itself are the identifier, the author, the date of creation, the owner, comments, priority and so on. The link information described in the previous paragraph can easily be stored in one attribute.

User rights: One very important aspect that must be taken into account in requirements management is the question of user rights. Since all project members share one common pot of information as has been described above, there have to be rules regarding the administration of this information. For example, the test manager must usually be able to see the requirements information, but there may be no need at all for him or her to be able to change this information. Therefore an information access policy must be defined and implemented to make sure that data is only seen and edited by a certain number of people and according to certain rules.

3.4   Summary

This chapter continues the brief introduction given in the previous chapters on requirements management and engineering.

To this end its history is briefly repeated, from which it is seen that the modern idea of a requirements management and engineering approach for development projects has been born together with the first commercially available computer systems. It is shown how the main job of a programmer has changed from writing code to finding out the needs and visions of the customer.

The most common concepts in requirements management and engineering are presented, amongst them the systems engineering concept and the process quality concept. The systems engineering concept divides all project activities into different process areas, and the process quality concept is the believe that a high process quality will be reflected in the quality of the products created by these processes.

An overview is given of the most important processes and methods in requirements engineering and requirements management. In requirements engineering, the two main processes according to the HOOD model are the definition of the scope and the definition of the requirements.

The definition of the scope can be separated into three main activities, the identification of the interfaces, the definition of the interfaces and the definition of the stakeholders and their roles. The definition of the requirements can be divided into the elicitation, the specification, the analysis and the review. Typical methods applied during the identification and definition of interfaces, stakeholders and roles and during the elicitation are modelling, document analysis, checklists, brainstorming, mind maps, interviews, observation, use cases, scenarios and stories. Typical methods that may be used for the specification of requirements are templates, quality criteria and weak word analyses.

In requirements management it is not easy to define a process as such, for requirements management integrates requirements engineering with all other systems engineering disciplines and thus is rather a collection of all the processes that interface with requirements engineering. The systems engineering disciplines whose interfaces to requirements engineering are analysed in this book are the most prominent. They are project management, quality management, risk management, configuration management, version management, test management and change management.

Some of the most important concepts of a functioning requirements management are presented and explained briefly. These are identifiability, filterability, traceability, linking, additional information and user rights.

4 Introduction to Requirements Engineering

This chapter introduces and defines requirements engineering, requirements development, and the HOOD requirements definition process.

4.1 History of Requirements Engineering

In the 1970's the need for creating, understanding, and agreeing requirements specifications was not questioned. It did not have a fancy name it was just engineering. Engineers were trained to produce specifications in whatever method of presentation was necessary. This was sometimes text, sometimes tables of data, and very often drawings were used.

All of these specifications and methods of documentation produced models of the system. We did not talk about modeling, we spoke of requirements specifications. And these specifications were used as the basis for tests when product was created.

In the 1970's customer needs were documented in a customer requirements specification.

In the 1980's it was thought that the word customer was too restrictive. The word customer could unfortunately be understood to represent only the requirements of the person paying for the system. To combat this the word user was used. Customer requirements specifications became user requirements specifications.

In the 1990's it was considered that the use of the word "user" was too restrictive, and could give the impression that only the end-user was considered, possibly ignoring all requirements for such things as Test, Maintenance, Sales, and Transport. So in the 1990's the word stakeholder came into fashion. User requirements specifications became stakeholder requirements specifications.

During this time the processes used for ensuring that requirements specifications were of the correct quality (correct, up-to-date, complete etc.) became known no longer as just plain old Engineering, but now it was to be known as requirements management.

Around the turn of the millennium some people started to refer to requirements management as requirements engineering. Quite soon these terms, originally identical, started to get different meanings. All of these meanings were of course correct. We use words to mean whatever we want them to mean. It was just such a huge shame that changing the meaning of words introduced such a lot of misunderstanding and strife.

Humpty Dumpty took the book and looked at it carefully. 'That seems to be done right --' he began.

'You're holding it upside down!' Alice interrupted.

'To be sure I was!' Humpty Dumpty said gaily as she turned it round for him. 'I thought it looked a little queer. As I was saying, that seems to be done right -- though I haven't time to look it over thoroughly just now -- and that shows that there are three hundred and sixty-four days when you might get un-birthday presents --'

'Certainly,' said Alice.

'And only one for birthday presents, you know. There's glory for you!'

'I don't know what you mean by "glory",' Alice said.

Humpty Dumpty smiled contemptuously. 'Of course you don't -- till I tell you. I meant "there's a nice knock-down argument for you!"'

'But "glory" doesn't mean "a nice knock-down argument",' Alice objected.

'When I use a word,' Humpty Dumpty said, in rather a scornful tone, 'it means just what I choose it to mean -- neither more nor less.'

'The question is,' said Alice, 'whether you can make words mean so many different things.'

'The question is,' said Humpty Dumpty, 'which is to be master -- that's all.'

Alice was too much puzzled to say anything; so after a minute Humpty Dumpty began again. 'They've a temper, some of them -- particularly verbs: they're the proudest -- adjectives you can do anything with, but not verbs -- however, I can manage the whole lot of them! Impenetrability! That's what I say!'

'Would you tell me please,' said Alice, 'what that means?'

'Now you talk like a reasonable child,' said Humpty Dumpty, looking very much pleased. 'I meant by "impenetrability" that we've had enough of that subject, and it would be just as well if you'd mention what you mean to do next, as I suppose you don't mean to stop here all the rest of your life.'

'That's a great deal to make one word mean,' Alice said in a thoughtful tone.

'When I make a word do a lot of work like that,' said Humpty Dumpty, 'I always pay it extra.'

'Oh!' said Alice. She was too much puzzled to make any other remark. 'When I use a word,' Humpty Dumpty said, in rather a scornful tone, 'it means just what I choose it to mean -- neither more nor less. '
Words   from   Through   the   Looking   Glass   by   Lewis   Carol
http://www.sabian.org/alice.htm

Some people use requirements management with its original meaning, some use requirements management to include requirements engineering, some use requirements engineering to include requirements management. The HOOD Group use the term "requirements management and engineering" to mean the sum of requirements management and requirements engineering. Requirements management is the sum of the interfaces between requirements development and all other systems engineering disciplines such as configuration management and project management. HOOD use the terms requirements engineering and requirements development interchangeably. Requirements development is defined by SEI in the CMMI specification to be "…to produce and analyze customer, product, and product-component requirements." My advice to you is to use whichever words your customer uses and ensure that all people involved share a common understanding. It is no accident that words used in this book are defined in Chapter 1. We hope that you encounter the words and learn their definition before you need to understand and use them.

In the 2000's the strict interpretation of stakeholder led some people to think that a stakeholder requirements specification should include requirements from all stakeholders, even those stakeholders further down the chain of requirements specifications from suppliers. This unfortunately led to what should basically be a documentation of customer requirements becoming a documentation of not only the customer requirements, but also the solution being supplied, and many other requirements from stakeholders that had no connection with the customer. Some customers even edited their documentation so it appeared that their requirements were identical to the systems requirements as written by the suppliers. This is not the intention of a specification supplied by a customer. The intention of a requirements specification has remained the same during the 30 years that I have been associated with the industry. That is, a requirements specification supplied by a customer is intended to define what is to be achieved by whatever the customer is buying, and also to define the constraints which have to be conformed to when supplying a solution. Constraints are requirements that restrict the choice of solution, for instance underground trains supplied for Munich in Germany have to be the blue colour of the Bavarian (Southern German) flag. I would include a picture of the Bavarian flag but this book is due to be printed in black and white only. Oh why not, you can imagine the colours.

Figure 4.1: Bavarian flag (white and blue)

So in the 2000's the requirements specification supplied by a customer is once again known as a customer requirements specification. If you do not like this I am sure that you need only wait a while. It has taken 30 years for changes to arrive back to where we started.

The more things change the more they stay the same.

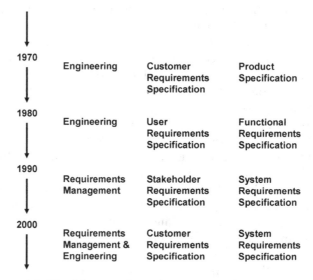

Figure 4.2: The history of requirements engineering at a glance

4.2   HOOD Requirements Definition Process

4.2.1   Aim of this part

In this part, first a general definition of a process is worked out, followed by the specific case of the HOOD requirements definition process. This allows the differences and similarities between requirements definition and requirements development to be defined and understood. Requirements development is a term used and defined by the Carnegie Mellon University as part of the CMMI specification. We use the terms requirements engineering and requirements development to be interchangeable. We acknowledge that there are many varied and contradictory definitions currently used.

This chapter Introduction to Requirements Engineering is included because requirements management is defined as the interface between requirements engineering and all the other systems engineering activities and processes. To understand better this interface we need to understand both sides of the interface.

4.2.2 What is a Process?

According to the IEEE, a process is "a sequence of steps performed for a given purpose". This simple definition is too restricted, and in practice leads some people to think that a process is like a straightjacket and is designed to prevent movement.

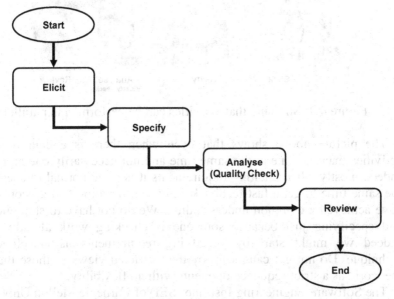

Figure 4.3: Requirements definition process shown as a flowchart with unnecessarily strict sequence restrictions.

Many people define a process by specifying a flowchart with a straight flow, which is a set sequence of activities to be performed. This may be correct but is often not what is intended nor required. Consider the above simple process for requirements definition. In this simple example only activities and the sequence for performing the activities are shown.

But what does the flowchart mean? Does it mean that no specification may be done before the elicitation is finished? Does everything have to be complete before the first review can take place?

This is what is suggested by a strict interpretation of the flowchart. And indeed it is unfortunately how many people choose to interpret some process specifications.

In fact the four activities described thus far do not have to be sequential. Years of using flowcharts and dealing with sequential computers based on von Neumann architecture have led some of us to believe that activities can only be performed sequentially. What about using a team to perform the activities?

Elicit   Specify   Analyse   Review
                          (Quality Check)

Figure 4.4: Showing that activities can be performed in parallel

The picture above shows that even when there is a data flow the activities may be done at the same time and not necessarily one at a time. Indeed mostly when eliciting requirements it is quite normal to specify at the same time to get a fast feedback and a confirmation that all concerned have achieved a common understanding. We do not have to stop eliciting and specifying just because someone is checking work already done. Indeed we might start by specifying requirements as an elicitation technique. Do not get caught up by the restricted views of those that see the world as a strict sequence of events with no flexibility.

The Software Engineering Institute (SEI) of Carnegie Mellon University expands upon process to define a software process as „a set of activities, methods, practices, and transformations that people use to develop and maintain software and the associated products". This is an improvement on two counts; it removes the idea of a process necessarily having a set sequence; and it introduces the idea that process is used by people. I wanted to write that the second point is particularly important, but then again so is the first! So many process improvement attempts fail because of a feeling of users of the process being unnecessarily restricted, often due to a misguided definition or interpretation of a process specification. So it is important to consider people as part of the process, and therefore to consider flexibility where possible and where necessary.

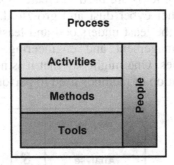

Figure 4.5: A process specification consists of more than just activities

The activities of the HOOD requirements definition process are described in the following section.

4.2.3 The activities of the HOOD Requirements Definition Process

The activities of the HOOD requirements definition process consist of more than the four basic activities we have discussed so far, that is; Elicit, Specify, Analyse (Quality Check), and Review (Approve). These four activities do form the heart of the process, and they are necessary but not sufficient.

This section includes descriptions of the aims of the four basic activities and develops an argument to support the need for further activities.

4.2.4 Modelling

We have seen in the previous section that a process consists of a set of activities, which will be executed using methods, which may be supported by tools. To execute the four basic activities listed above we could use various methods. Many people consider the act of modeling to be a requirements definition activity. But when asked why this activity is done they may not have an answer. If you are feeling mischievous ask your tool vendor why they use graphical modeling techniques. The answer should be to support whichever of the other activities you are performing! Modeling is not an end in itself; it is a means to an end. Some people think that modeling is just something that one does for its own beauty. These are the sort of people who talk a little louder when explaining the points on which their reasoning is not fully thought out. This may be why some of the really good modelling tools are used to create models that are never used. The models just gather cyber dust and grow old. But modeling is great! Modelling is one of the least understood and least exploited things we do in requirements management and engineering. Modelling is done to support other activities. One might say that it is not really an activity, but more like a classification of methods used to perform activities.

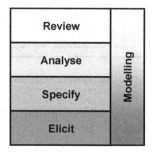

Figure 4.6: Modelling is performed to support other activities

Please do not misunderstand our views on modeling. At HOOD we are firm supporters of and experts in the use of models and also work closely with partner companies that do little else other than support customers improve their modelling expertise.

4.2.4.1 Scope

As an input to the above activities we need to consider the context within which the system being defined will operate. We need to consider what is inside the system and what is outside the system. Without a clear and shared view of what is the system and what is outside of the system any development consisting of more than one person is almost bound to fail or take an inordinate amount of time. Wasting time is also a failure. So the scope of a system under consideration needs to be defined, communicated, and understood.

When considering scope most people think immediately of system boundaries and physical interfaces. This is good as far as it goes. But it does not go far enough. Later we will discuss the role of people and systems interfacing to the system under development.

A physical interface to a system has at least two aspects; the static interface, and the dynamic interface.

A static interface consists of such things as port numbers for computers, pin allocation for electronic hardware, and size of fitting for mechanical constructions.

A dynamic interface consists of such things as data and the meaning of data (information) which may vary with time through a computer port, voltages and the meaning of certain voltages which may vary with time for electronic systems, and movement for mechanical systems.

Considering an alternative view of systems, lets move away from the purely physical view of the interfaces as seen from within a system, and consider the systems within the enclosing environment including people with interfaces to the system under development. It is necessary to ensure the elicitation of the requirements of people who are to use the system, and those affected by the system either by its use or abuse. We call these people stakeholders. It is sometimes advantageous to also consider as stakeholders the systems with interfaces to the system under development.

I have had many discussions with colleagues from previous employment about the definition of the term stakeholders, so please excuse me distilling my experience to you here.

For the purpose of defining requirements it is necessary to collate requirements from all roles which may affect, and are affected by, a system. During this collection it is necessary to know what role a stakeholder has, the better to understand their requirements.

Requirements may be defined which influence the system under development during various phases including; inception, development, commissioning, use, maintenance, upgrading, retirement, and disposal or recycling.

The reason why I have switched to talking about defining requirements for roles rather than stakeholders is that it is often impossible, or not preferred, to spend the time (time is money) speaking to every possible user of a system. It is normally sufficient to capture requirements from a suitable selection of users, at least covering all roles. The trick here is defining and understanding "suitable". The reason we attempt to capture requirements from all roles is to be effective in an attempt to get a full set of requirements. The reason we might not capture requirements from every stakeholder is to be efficient in our use of resources.

Let us consider a one-off system made for a specific customer involving few stakeholders. It is highly likely that we might try to capture requirements from all stakeholders. But if you were producing cars for the mass market would you attempt to capture requirements from everyone that purchased your cars? Perhaps not. But I am told that Nissan Cars do, and that Nissan have the top customer satisfaction rating of all mass car manufacturers! Why could that be?

Our customers are like our eyes toward the future: they show us where to go. Knowing what concerns our customers, what they are not satisfied with—listening carefully to the voices of our customers is the very starting point for our business.

For example, there are certain things that may be hard to elicit from a survey or questionnaire: the comfort of a driver's seat or changes to car parts over the years. With this in mind, employees who work on the cutting edge of new car development and production personally conduct In-Car Interviews to get important feedback from our customers.

Technical engineers all over the world, as part of their routine work, have the opportunity to ride along with customers in their cars and receive their frank opinions. The feedback gained during these one-on-one sessions provides important input for our new product development.

Our Customer Support Center also helps us get important feedback. Our Japan Support Center, for example, gets over 180,000 calls per year with questions, complaints, and praise. This outlet helps clue us into a wide array of opinions, which we then collect and analyze. The information gets posted on our company-wide intranet system and is used in many areas to make quality and service improvements. We have seen many real examples of how customer feedback has led to opportunities for improvement. Our major global operations also actively utilize input from our customers.

Nissan Sustainability Report 2004 (http://www.nissan-global.com)

Just to be sure that we have the same understanding of stakeholders and roles, here is a short example.

We take the example of a requirements management and engineering training course with 10 participants in a training room. What activities are to be done? The course needs to be designed and written, course material may have to be printed, the date for the course has to be agreed and published. The room has to be booked. Is over-night accommodation necessary for the trainer or any participants? The course has to be delivered to the participants. Feedback will be collated at the end of the course. Requests for payment for the cost of the course must be sent. Payment for the course must be received. People must be able to know that the courses are available so probably some promotion will be done. Hopefully the course will make a profit.

The people available to perform the tasks are Bob, Claudia, Charles, Gabi, Mascha, and Urte, plus of course the participants in the training.

When defining requirements with whom do we need to get requirements from? Let us see how the two scenarios could work in practice. The following table links task to roles to stakeholders.

Tasks / Roles / Stakeholders		
Task	**Role**	**Stakeholder**
Design training. Write course.	Author	Charles Urte
Advertise training.	Marketing	Gabi
Print training material. Send request for payment. Receive payment. Book training room. Book accomodation.	Administration	Claudia Mascha
Give training. Collect feedback.	Trainer	Bob Charles Gabi Urte
Make profit.	Employees	Bob Claudia Charles C...
Take part in training.	Participant	

Figure 4.7: Table showing relationship between roles and stakeholders

We can see from the above table that roles may be performed by one or more stakeholders, and stakeholders may perform one or more roles.

So back to our question; who do we get requirements from? We could try to elicit requirements from every stakeholder, or we could try to elicit requirements from representatives from every role. Consider the case before the course is written, the participants might not be known so someone will have to represent their views. This is often seen as a part of the role of marketing, to be a surrogate for customers.

It is very important when eliciting requirements that a stakeholder understands on behalf of which role they are providing information. We have seen above that a stakeholder may perform more than one role, and it is possible that they give their major role precedence and neglect any secondary role.

If we tried to get requirements from everyone we would have to deal with sixteen people, that is six employees and ten participants. If we were more efficient we could choose three people for example: Charles, Claudia, and Gabi. This is possible because this is one of the combinations of people which cover all roles, with Gabi representing the concerns of the participants. To be more effective, after the course was given we would collate requirements from feedback of participants and others, and use this information to improve the course iteratively.

As an input to the aforementioned activities of requirements development we need to provide information pertaining to the scope. As discussed above we can consider this to be physical interfaces and also a list of stakeholders and their roles. The four activities of the HOOD requirements definition process are supplemented by the activities of identify interfaces, define interfaces, and define stakeholders and their roles.

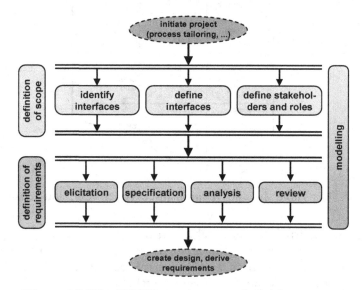

Figure 4.8: The HOOD requirements definition process

The above diagramme shows that there are 2 major parts to the HOOD requirements definition process. Definition of scope and definition of requirements. Strictly the scope is also a requirement, but we separate it here to show its importance. In practice it is also easier to think of these parts as separate but related. Normally the scope is defined before the work on defining requirements begins in earnest. For instance a systems integrator such as a car manufacturer will have performed some systems engineering work to define their system in terms of subsystems and their interfaces. We could also say they have defined their product in terms of components and their interfaces. It is also normal that the definition of the scope is changed during the requirements definition activities as more information becomes known. Many people complain that the requirements change during a project, but this is better than not correcting incomplete or incorrect requirements. The definition of the sub-systems may be passed onto the next stage, often an external supplier, with the definition of interfaces in the form of constraint requirements, and requirements and use-cases defining the expected use of the sub-system.

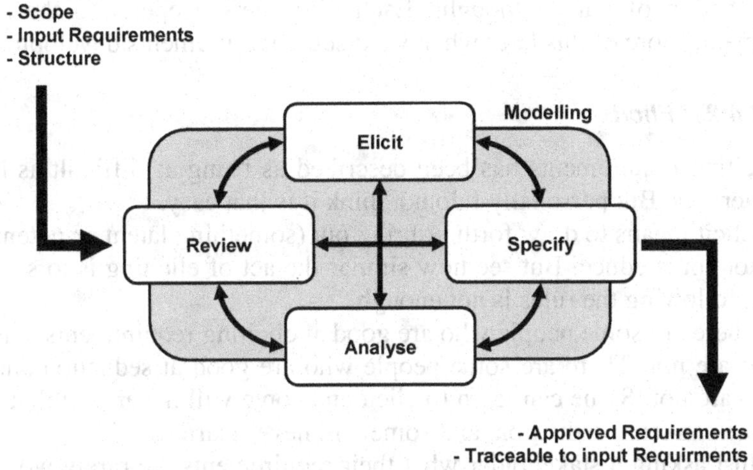

- Scope
- Input Requirements
- Structure

Modelling

Elicit

Review

Specify

Analyse

- Approved Requirements
- Traceable to input Requirments

Figure 4.9: Requirements definition with scope being an input

The above diagramme shows the process as a machine or a rotating drum which churns away deriving approved output requirements from the input requirements. The diagramme deliberately does not place any restrictions on the sequence of the activities nor the number of iterations it takes to produce approved requirements. Structure is shown as an input as often there it is required to produce information in a particular structure, for instance certain documents may have to be produced. If structure is not given as an input to the process the process itself must create some structure to enable requirements to be read in context and to facilitate requirements to be found when searched for. It is very important that a group work together using a common information model. This facilitates sharing information and re-use of information such as requirements and tests.

The input not shown on the diagramme is the energy that powers the machine which is engineering innovation. The diagramme shows that approved requirements are produced or derived based upon input requirements and other information. There might be a slight problem with considering the requirements to be derived, as if there is no choice involved in the production of requirements. The use of the word "derive" is not meant in a mathematical sense, but merely that the output requirements are based upon the input requirements. Normally each stage of the overall requirements development process that uses requirements definition brings us closer to the implementation. That is, each stage of requirements definition normally introduces more constraints on how the system is to be implemented. This cannot be automated; we still need the innovation of human thought. Each stage gets deeper into the solution domain. More of this later when we discuss requirements development.

4.2.4.2 *Elicit*

Eliciting requirements has been described as being as difficult as herding butterflies. But personally I do not think it is that easy.

Elicit means to draw forth or bring out (something latent or potential). A synonym is educe. But see how similar the act of eliciting is to seduction. Just following the rules is not enough.

There are some people who are good at eliciting requirements, and some who are not. There are some people who are good at seduction and some who are not. Some can learn to elicit and some will never be able to learn. Some can learn seduction, and some will never learn.

Just asking a stakeholder what their requirements are rarely works. It is said that the customer is always right. Well that may be. In fact the customer is always busy and normally has far more urgent things to do rather than speak to someone in a suit about requirements for a system that is not even due to be delivered within 2 years.

The first thing to be sure of when eliciting requirements is that we have to get the stakeholder into a state in which they want to talk to us. To return to our comparison with seduction, you had better be sure that the house is tidy and the baby is not crying.

4.2.4.3 *Specify*

We specify to convey to others the requirements that we have elicited. The most important person to communicate this information to is the person from whom the information has been elicited. If the stakeholders do not recognise and agree with their own requirements then we have no basis on which to build.

There are many methods for specifying requirements. A choice must be made so that the people or machines that need to understand can actually understand.

Around 1985 I introduced to an organisation a method of specifying requirements supported by a graphical language. We had tremendous success within the organisation and the quality of work increased dramatically, and timescales reduced dramatically.

There was one problem. The customers did not fully understand the diagrammes we were using. We see the same mistakes being made today with UML. Some suppliers assume that their customers will understand UML and make people feel stupid if they do not understand. This is no basis for seduction and does not work for requirements elicitation. Not everyone is strong enough to admit when they have not understood, and we have seen long drawn out expensive discussions about everything other than the real problem.

When specifying requirements we must ensure that all parties understand what is being documented. We have to speak the language of our customer.

What do we do if requirements from various stakeholders conflict? To start with we have to document the requirements otherwise they may be overlooked. Specifying requirements does not consist of just writing down what we understood was said. We need to document requirements and then sort out the conflicts. In order to create a consistent set of requirements we need to consolidate the set of requirements. Consolidate can have many meanings such as merge or combine. More than just merging the set of requirements, what we mean by consolidation is to remove inconsistencies to produce a consistent set.

Theoretically one might prioritise requirements and take the requirements with the highest priority. There are problems with this; i)This might result in an inconsistent set of requirements ii)giving requirements priorities is difficult and full of internal political challenges such as organisations that only allow high priority requirements, and iii) it is often not the requirements that are actually prioritised but the stakeholders that own the requirements. To put it simply the boss normally gets his way.

Setting priorities is a great idea but some (most) organisations are not mature enough to do this successfully. Setting priorities helps us to understand the results of tests that show that not all requirements have been fulfilled. So what? Is the system usable and is it worth delaying acceptance for a few requirements? If we have not properly prioritised requirements in advance of the tests we are forced to start negotiations when we are under pressure to commission the system.

Despite the problems outlined above, I implore you to document how important requirements are, and how urgent requirements are.

4.2.4.4 Analyse (Quality Check)

Analysis of requirements has been used to mean many things. Tom de Marco used the term Structured Analysis to mean a process used to understand requirements and to facilitate achieving a common understanding between parties. Analyse is also used in general terms to mean; study, examine, investigate, scrutinise etc. We use the term here to mean a quality check. Requirements are assessed with respect to quality criteria. The result of the analysis is used as an input to the review activity. The result of the analysis is a measure of quality. A measure of how well the quality criteria have been fulfilled.

Some organisations refer to the activity of analysing the quality of requirements as "Inspection". We believe that this is more likely the name of a method used to perform the analysis. It is very easy to mix up the methods with the activities but this can cause confusion. Keep clear the activity that is being performed as this defines the aim of what we are doing. If we concentrate on methods and do not consider for which activity the methods are being used we might loose sight of what we are doing. Some methods may quite legitimately be used for a variety of activities, so keep the activity in mind. Do not blindly always use the same methods. Consider the activity and choose the methods that best fit the situation each time.

4.2.4.5 Review

Once again the nomenclature used in our industry is poorly defined so for clarity we state here what we mean.

Review	
Activity	Description
Analyse (Quality Check)	Requirements are assessed with respect to predetermined quality criteria
Review Meeting (Approval)	Decide if requirements or a document are acceptable or if improvement is required before approval may be granted
Improvement	To improve a document or requirements following a review, and in preparation for the next review; this will normally involve another iteration of elicitation and specification

Figure 4.10: Analysis and Review

An input to the review activity is the result of the analysis (quality check) activity. It may be decided on the balance of needs that a requirement or set of requirements might be accepted and therefore approved even though not all quality criteria are fulfilled. For instance requirements might be incomplete or not exactly unambiguous but the risk associated with this might be acceptable compared to the delay that would be needed to rework the requirement or document.

This is why the activities of Analyse and Review are separate. Just because a quality requirement is not fulfilled does not mean that the requirement or document is unacceptable. The people performing each activity need different skills. The person performing the analysis needs to be able to deal with large amounts of detailed information. The person performing the review needs to see the big picture and be prepared to accept a compromise, to understand and take a risk, and be prepared to take the consequences.

A mistake that some beginners make is to assume that all requirements need to fulfill all quality criteria all the time. Having read a book is not enough. Having a list of quality criteria is not enough. You need experience and you need to be big enough to balance needs.

Who should be invited to review requirements?

The easy answer is to invite all stakeholders. But this will normally not work. The cost will be enormous and the likelihood of everyone being available is slim. Similar to selecting stakeholders for eliciting requirements, a sub-set of stakeholders is more efficient.

Consider roles of those who need to use the requirement or document. Do not forget those responsible for testing; they know what a good requirement is, or at least they know a bad requirement when they see one. Think of designers that need to design a solution to fulfill requirements. Think of implementers. Think of customers in order to check that they understand what they are going to get delivered. Do not wait until a system is complete before ensuring that the customer and supplier share a common understanding. Think of the authors. Will they recognise what they have written after a few people have "improved" their work?

4.3 Requirements Development and Requirements Engineering

Requirements engineering and requirements development are used interchangeably. According to CMMI the purpose of requirements development is to "produce and analyze customer, product, and product-component requirements".

We have already discussed that the word Analyse (or Analyze) and have stated that it can have many meanings. CMMI use this term to mean more than just checking the quality of requirements. In this case CMMI use Analyse also to mean "understand".

CMMI requirements development consists of the following activities: Elicitation, analysis, validation, and communication of customer needs, expectations, and constraints to obtain customer requirements that constitute an understanding of what will satisfy stakeholders; Collection and coordination of stakeholder needs, development of the life-cycle requirements of the product, establishment of the customer requirements, and establishment of initial product and product-component requirements consistent with customer requirements.

When using a CMMI model, you will encounter goals and practices that include the phrase "establish and maintain." This phrase connotes a meaning beyond the component terms; it includes documentation and usage. For example, "Establish and maintain an organizational policy for planning and performing the organizational process focus process" means that not only must a policy be formulated, but it also must be documented and it must be used throughout the organization. It is not enough to define a process, you have to live it!

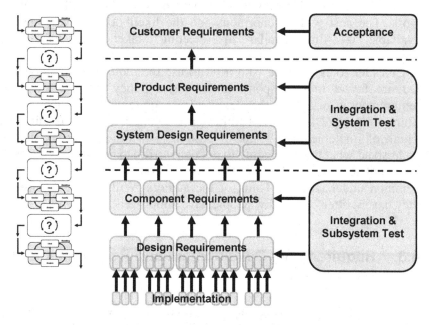

⌐☐⌐ Requirements Development = Requirements Definition

⌐ (?) ⌐ Understanding Requirements

Figure 4.11: Requirements development within information model

So requirements development consists of requirements definition, from customer requirements through product requirements to product component requirements. Whereas we have said that the requirements definition process is used at all levels of the information model for all types of requirements, requirements development is specifically pulling all levels together and making connections between them.

The word product is used to be synonymous with system. The word component is used to be synonymous with sub-system.

Requirements development and requirements definition are very similar. The difference is that requirements development emphasises the holistic view of the use of requirements. Requirements Definition also has this view but does not emphasize it. When we teach the definition of requirements it is unfortunately very easy for people to concentrate on the current requirement or the current document at the expense of seeing the big picture. Of course everything that is written about requirements definition, such as lists of quality criteria, is to be considered as part of something bigger. Requirements do not exist in isolation. Showing requirements development to be the totality of defining requirements from customer requirements through to implementation helps to emphasize the systems view necessary.

4.4   Summary

This chapter gives an introduction to requirements engineering. At first we show how the terms commonly used in this area have changed throughout the decades.

Thus it is important to note for example that what has been called customer requirements in the 1970's has later been called user requirements, still later stakeholder requirements and today again customer requirements. In the following we use these different terms interchangeably, indicating that it does not so much matter which word you use as long as you have a common understanding.

The later sections of this chapter give an overview of the HOOD view upon the requirements engineering process. We believe that it can be divided int o two main steps and their corresponding activities:

Definition of scope:

- Identifying interfaces
- Defining interfaces
- Defining stakeholders and roles

Definition of requirements:

- Elicitation
- Specification

- Analysis
- Review

It is also explained how modelling is the one activity that supports all other activities, and as such does not belong to one or some activities exclusively.

The last sections of this chapter explain why the requirements engineering process is iterative, and how the individual activities fit into a corresponding requirements information model. It can be seen that the activities are carried out again and again, thus shaping the requirements with respect to quality on each level of the information model and with respect to greater detail from one level of the information model to the next.

5 Introduction to Requirements Management

The previous chapter has given an introduction to requirements engineering or, in other words, requirements development. The meaning of requirements development has been shown briefly, and the benefits of structured requirements development processes have been explained in detail.

The present chapter will go into more detail regarding the lifecycle of a requirement and the interfaces of requirements development to adjacent systems engineering disciplines. It will be shown that this lifecycle analysis quickly gives rise to a number of questions.

The following chapters will answer all these questions in detail, analysing each interface separately and explaining the information that should ideally flow through each interface.

5.1 What is Requirements Management

Requirements management is the sum of all activities in connection with requirements that take place after the requirements have been developed or engineered.

For example, if changes of requirements are desired, these changes must somehow be coped with. This usually implies an analysis of what the change means to the project in terms of effort, budget, resources and so on. Another example where requirements must be managed is quality. If the quality of the requirements is not regularly analysed it will quickly deteriorate, leading to requirements that have little meaning.

In short, requirements management are all activities that are necessary to bring or keep the value of the requirements on a high level after the requirements have first been elicited and documented.

5.2 Why we need Requirements Management

As has been briefly mentioned above, requirements management is necessary to ensure a high level of quality and value of the existing requirements throughout a project. But what does this actually mean? To give an impression of how complex the further management of existing requirements can become, consider only four requirements as follows.

1. the press must produce 400 car doors per hour
2. the press must have an emergency switch
3. the emergency switch must stop the press within 10 milliseconds
4. the press must have a pressing force of 50,000 kg

The above requirements are assumed to be quite representative for a press producing car doors. Once they have been specified or in other words, written down, they exist and are known to the relevant people. When the requirements are approved by the stakeholders the requirements engineering process or phase is finished.

We point out again to the fact that ideally, there is no evaluation of the requirements during the requirements engineering phase. The exclusive goal of requirements engineering is to somehow formulate the visions that are inside the heads of the stakeholders, using any language that may appear suitable. Telling whether a requirement is too expensive or not, or whether it makes sense or not, should be left to later phases. Let us now have a closer look at what could happen to these requirements after they have been engineered.

Obviously, in the light of what has been said just now, a first thing that would be very sensible to do is checking whether the requirements can be realised at all. This phase is often called the feasibility study. For example, such an analysis may reveal that it is physically impossible that the press works with a force of 50,000 kg while producing 400 doors per hour.

If the feasibility analysis is not part of the requirements development processes, then what it is a part of? Are the testers responsible for making sure that all approved requirements are testable (and thus realisable)? Does project management have to ensure that only realisable requirements are further processed? Or is realisability the domain of risk management? It is seen from these questions that once the requirements are processed any further, they start to touch upon other systems engineering disciplines.

A second thing that could happen after the above requirements have been specified is that a stakeholder wants to change a requirement. For example, it may turn out that in order for the press to be economic, it must produce 500 car doors per hour, rather than 400.

Now what should happen to this change request? Maybe the new requirement is impossible to realise due to laws of physics or a limited project budget. Should the requirement therefore be just neglected? Should we not at least document somewhere that there had been such a change request, even if it was rejected because the requirement is impossible to realise?

If we do not document this change request independent of whether it has been implemented or not, then maybe later another stakeholder or even the same proposes the same change request again. We then have to evaluate the requirement again, because we have forgotten that this has already been done before. But this case is still relatively simple, and the thing becomes more complex if the requirement is not simply impossible to realise.

If it is feasible then we must decide whether we implement it or not. Which criteria will our decisions be based on? Do we do it because we have enough resources and budget to implement the change request? Do we just like the customer and therefore do what he wants us to do? Were the criteria that govern our decisions documented and agreed on beforehand?

Let us assume that we could somehow answer all these questions and decide to go for the implementation. This will make the change affair still more complex: how do we document the change to the requirements? Do we just delete the old requirement and replace it with the new one? If so, how can we tell whether there has ever been another set of requirements? But why should it be desirable to be able to tell if there have been other requirements before?

Do we document the reasons for our decision? If not, how can we tell later why we implemented or rejected the change request? What could happen if we are not able to reproduce the reasons for our decisions?

If we keep the old versions of the requirements and the new versions, how can we distinguish between old and new? What are the advantages of being able to tell an old version of a requirement from a newer one in the first place?

Let us further assume that we somehow arrived at the conclusion that the change request is possible and should be implemented. However, say the laws of physics do not allow for the press to produce 500 car doors per hour and to be stopped within 10 milliseconds at the same time. With 400 car doors per hour, this was still possible and so there were no problems. Have we documented that there is a relationship between the working speed of the press and the time it takes to stop it in a case of emergency? Did we realise at all that this relationship exists? If yes, how did we realise it and why did we not document it? If no, could it have been possible to know?

If we did not think about these things before implementing the change request, we will afterwards find out that although the change has been successfully realised, one of the other requirements is not met any longer. If this other requirement is a killer requirement (mandetory), then all the work in connection with the change was for nothing and we have to get back to the old state, which will usually take still more work and time, or simply money.

A third scenario that is probably known to most of our readers are limited resources including limited budgets. Assume that the current project situation allows for the implementation of only three out of the four requirements as listed above. How did we find out that the budget will not suffice to implement all the requirements in the first place? When did we find this out? Was there a chance that we could have found out any earlier? What is the advantage of realising that we will not be able to implement all the requirements as early as possible? Do we have to inform anyone about the fact that the requirements will not be implemented completely? Who would that be? Do we know that it makes sense to keep on working on the project if not all requirements will be implemented? If we do, how and why do we know? If we do not, should we not try to find out? How could we possibly do this?

This is just a small sample of questions that typically arise in similar situations. Assuming that somehow we know that we will go ahead with the project, which will be the one requirement we are not going to implement? Are there any criteria for our decision? Are these criteria documented somewhere? Are there good reasons why there should be any criteria at all and why these criteria should be documented beforehand?

In such a situation, do we ask other people which requirement they think should be neglected? Who are these people and is there anything special about them? Why would we ask them and not just anyone?

Obviously, it would be sensible to leave out the one requirement that is least important. But what does this mean? Who defines importance? Based on which criteria is importance defined? Are these criteria reproducible? Are they documented? Are they known at all? Is it necessary that there are known, documented and reproducible criteria? What could possibly happen if this was not so?

A fourth thing that usually happens to requirements after they have been implemented is that the product or parts of it are tested against the requirements. This gives rise to more questions.

How can we test whether a requirement is met? What do we need in order to carry out this test? When should we carry out the test? When do we have to plan for the tests in order to keep the project on schedule? Who will carry out the tests? How much of the project budget and resources will it take to carry out the tests? Is there enough budget to test all requirements? If not, which requirements should be tested and why?

Will we document the test results? Will we also document the test procedure? Will we document which test belongs to which requirement? If we do not document these things, how can we be sure that we have carried out all necessary tests? How can we be sure that the product passes all tests? How can we be sure that we applied the correct tests?

If we document this data, where and how will we do this? If we document the relationships between the requirements and the tests and if there are changes to the requirements, how do we know if these relationships are still correct? How do we get the information that there have been changes to the requirements at all? Is it necessary to inform the testers if there are changes to the requirements they should test against?

Since usually every project tries to consume as few resources as possible to carry out each activity, it would be interesting to know whether there is any potential in testing for saving money. It may be possible for example that one test case can test more than just one requirement. It may even be possible to test the whole product with only a small number of sophisticated tests. How could we find out whether it is possible to create such test cases? If we somehow get to know that it is possible, how can we determine how the tests must look like in order to be so effective? Can we carry out the tests at any time after implementation, or are there any other preliminaries? If so, how do we know?

Let us assume that the above questions could either somehow be answered or were irrelevant, then by now we have a set of approved stakeholder requirements that are implemented and tested against. However, what do we do if one or more of the tests fail? Does this mean that the product cannot be accepted? How do we know which requirements must be met for acceptance and which are less important?

Did we realise the risks associated with unsuccessful tests? Have we documented these once they were known? During the project, have we come across other risks? Have we taken them into account or have we ignored them, hoping that the others will also ignore them? Was every project member and stakeholder aware of the risks?

In view of the risks, was there a decision to stop the project or to go ahead with it? If yes, what were the criteria for our decision and who decided? If not, why not?

If all relevant people have been aware of the project risks, have we thought of possible countermeasures? Have we assessed the possible impact of every risk? If no, why? If yes, which criteria have we used for the assessment? Who carried out this assessment? Who decided who should carry out the assessment? Why? When has this decision been made and how?

It can be seen from what has been said so far that going a little bit further into detail of what happens to requirements once they are specified immediately gives rise to quite a remarkable series of questions. In our experience, the following systems engineering disciplines have the most important interfaces to requirements engineering or development:

- project management
- quality management
- configuration management
- risk management
- test management
- version management
- change management

The above list does not claim to be complete. Depending on which different systems engineering disciplines we define it can be shorter or longer.

However, the following chapters will show that if the above disciplines and their interfaces to requirements engineering or requirements development are taken into account the corresponding requirements management processes will have a very high level of quality and will thus ensure that the requirements will also have a very high level of quality and value during a project. The following figure 5.1 is a graphical representation of what has been said so far. In the figure, the dark grey part of the circle enclosing all interfaces are the interfaces to requirements development and thus represent requirements management.

Figure 5.1: Systems engineering interfaces to requirements development

Although we have shown Quality management to be separate for the purposes of the above diagramme, in everything else we write we assert that each discipline includes the need to be correct and to achieve the necessary quality criteria and standards, that is that each systems engineering discipline includes quality management.

5.3   The benefits of a working Requirements Management

The implicit assumption that underlies all efforts in connection with the improvement of processes such as requirements development, requirements management, risk management, test management, project management and so on is that the quality of the processes is reflected in the quality of the work products or artefacts of these processes.

In other words, there is no substantial reason for having high quality processes other than the belief that high process quality will make for reproducibly high product quality. That the quality of the processes does indeed have a direct influence on whatever is created by the application of them has been shown in many different ways and is commonly accepted. If this was not so it would be hard to believe that so much money is spent for example in the automotive industry just to reach a certain level of maturity or capability within one of the process maturity models that are momentarily a quasi-standard.

Traditionally, the aeronautics and space industry has always played a crucial part in making such ideas known to the public. There are two reasons for this is: huge amounts of money involved and the danger of people being killed or injured.

The first reason, huge amounts of money involved, is usually more associated with the space industry, although the development of a new type of aircraft may also take one billion $ or more. For example, a new research satellite can easily cost one billion $, and there is usually little interest on part of all parties involved that the project fails. And whatever light a philosophical discourse may shed on the various aspects of this, it is usually true that people are more likely to make a second and third check and double check and carry out quality ensuring activities when talking about the potential loss of one billion $ instead of talking about the potential loss of one thousand $.

Of course, the corresponding project budgets will be very different, too. But having ten times more money to spend on quality assuring activities does not automatically mean that the quality will be ten times higher. And activities carried out with only one tenth of some other project's budget may create better results when carried out with heart and personal interest than when carried out with ten times more effort but without any further involvement.

The second reason for the leading role of the aeronautics and space industry in introducing new concepts of working, danger of people being killed, is mainly associated with the aeronautics industry. Although people can also be killed in space, the job of an astronaut is normally looked upon as being always somewhat dangerous, and due to nowadays space transport capacities the potential number of people getting injured or killed is very low.

An aircraft accident on the other hand frequently involves what some analysts call a "total loss", which means nothing but the death of all people on board, including the total damage of the aircraft. Apart from the project budgets, there too is a psychological aspect to this. People are normally more interested in making sure that what they have done will work under all circumstances when the health and lives of people are at stake.

And it seems as though the concepts of high quality processes and standardised ways of working have proven to be true. As is repeatedly pointed out to by advocates of aviation, travelling by air is much safer than travelling by car (at least with regard to the person mileage).

Requirements development and requirements management are two pieces of the puzzle of process areas for a modern product developing industry. While requirements development assures that what is to be developed is indeed what the customer wants, requirements management integrates the data created during requirements development into the overall project flow.

It has been shown in the previous section that if the requirements development information is not integrated with the other available project information, many questions will arise and remain unanswered after the requirements have once been specified. The result is that their quality will quickly lessen until they have no meaning. Keeping on working with such obsolete data may be more risky than starting from scratch or working.

Thus there are a number of benefits to a working requirements management. First, requirements management tries to make sure that the product under development is actually what the customer has in mind throughout the whole course of the project.

This must not be mistaken to be rather trivial. In fact, there are probably only a few projects where the initial visions of what should be invented are even approximately identical to the ideas that are formulated towards the end. The reason for this is that the ideas usually grow with the experience of the development cycles. What seemed to be a good idea at the beginning turns out to be irrelevant, and what seemed to be easily realisable at first turns out to be impossible to implement. And what has been missed at the start turns later out to be most crucial to the whole project.

Second, requirements management supports making the product to be developed manageable in terms of its lifecycle including later modifications. This means that by the way the information once available on requirements is administered, a maximum amount of continuity and usability is ensured. There are organisations for example that are quite successful with one time projects, but who could not repeat their own successes a number of times in a row. There are also projects that end successfully, but no modifications whatsoever to what has been developed can ever be carried out because everything has been engineered just to fit once and for ever.

A typical example that many readers familiar with the development of software will already have encountered themselves is "just the one additional blue 'Repeat' button in the menu bar". Changes upon changes, however small they have been, have slowly rendered the code completely unreadable and unmaintainable, for only little information has been documented in the code and associated documents. The customer shouted whenever he had a new idea and the developer responsible for the user interface implemented it on the spot, for it was always "just a few lines of code". This game goes on and on (and it does so all the time and in many projects), until finally the most trivial change like "green button instead of blue button" is just the one straw that breaks the camel's back.

With a working requirements management, all associated information remains useful and valuable for a very long time. If everything has always been properly documented, projects that have been closed even years ago can quickly be revived and up and running within little time and with little effort. We see evidence of this again and again. The documentation costs very little if done at the time, but is worth so very much for enabling changes to be made quickly and safely,

A third aspect closely related to the second benefit is reusability. Reusability means that whatever information and data are created during a project can be used by other projects. To be useful to others, information has to be prepared and documented in a certain way, and requirements management ensures that this is so. So once again, the documentation costs very little if done at the time of the change, but is worth so very much for enabling following projects and also for maintenance.

Reusability is one of the key means excessively applied nowadays especially by some industries such as automotive in order to stay alive in the never ending struggle to market products with higher quality for a lower price in a shorter amount of time. Still however, reusability manifests itself quite often in the experience of the developers only. A developer that has developed only rear view mirrors throughout the last twenty years approximately knows what he has to do when a new car product line is developed, and as long as the developer is with the company, no problems usually arise.

But once the developer changes to another department or changes his employer altogether, new colleagues have to start from scratch and make their own experiences, until they too are specialists and later also leave. Requirements management demands that relevant information be documented and safely stored away so that all people involved can retrieve this information whenever necessary. Thus requirements management tries to document the knowledge of the various people and to make it public within an organisation.

A fourth benefit of a functioning requirements management is legal safety for both the customer and the supplier. Apart from formal basics of contracts such as dates of delivery, project budget and resources and the like, the requirements are usually the only means to check whether what has been wanted by the customer is what has been actually delivered. It is quite amazing to note how many projects are still based upon informal personal talks, for example phone calls between the developers of the customer and the developers of the supplier. We have nothing against discussions between customers and suppliers, indeed we spend much of our time facilitating this, but you must document the results of the discussion. If a change is agreed it takes little to note who has agreed to what change and why. One does not have to wait long to see the benefit of this practice. Try this and find how often people have a different recollection of what was agreed. Sometimes even at the end of a meeting a summary of the meeting helps flush out how different people have concluded different things from the same discussion. The written documentation helps to create a common understanding of the (changing) requirements.

Requirements management means safety for the customer because he can always get a clear picture of what is about to be developed, how this will be done, how much this will probably cost, how long it will presumably take, which people will implement his ideas, which risks there are and so on.

For the supplier, requirements management means safety because he can always give a clear picture of what he is intending to do and what he is intending not to do, why this is so and how he is going to do what he is going to do. The supplier can justify and explain the basis for vital decisions and he is sure that all relevant project information can be looked up by the customer whenever there appears to be a need to do so.

There are many cases where towards the end of an unsuccessful project or a project with an unsatisfactory outcome the customer accuses the supplier of not having made clear what he is going to do and how he is going to do this. A common answer of the supplier is that the customer has not made clear throughout the project what he really wants and needs and left the supplier to find out for himself. With requirements management, such arguments arise with fewer consequences because the discussions happen earlier. The aim is to achieve a common understanding of the requirements before too much time and money has been invested, and if possible without aurguments and recriminations. Requirements management really means sharing information and trying to reach a common understanding.

The benefits listed so far are mainly based on a common principle that is as trivial as difficult to meet: it is the principle of having a proper communication and a common understanding between all people involved. We want to point out to the fact here that "all people involved" usually also includes the future customers or users of a system to be developed.

Thus in short, requirements management tries to make sure that everybody has all the background knowledge they need and that information is flowing properly between all parties involved. Although it is clear that only an optimum communication can produce optimum results, many organisations are still for example far from having their staff communicate with each other properly. Note that in this respect, communication means everything from a simple phone talk to a user manual with a few hundred pages.

Consequently, optimum communication gives rise to further benefits. For example, it is clear that the amount of time for development cycles can be significantly reduced due to a reduced number of misunderstandings and thus reduced rework and everything associated with this.

This aspect is very important and goes hand in hand with what has been said further above in connection with reusability. Shorter development cycles basically mean quicker time to market, which in turn means potentially more success with the product. At the same time, shorter development cycles mean that more products can be developed within the same amount of time, and so an additional factor for the success of an organisation can be that more different products can be offered as compared to competitors.

Another success factor is the proper communication with the stakeholders, including the future users or customers or buyers. Thus products based on a well-functioning requirements management do generally match the ideas and visions of the customers much more exactly than products developed secretly, assuming that whatever the developers invent is just exactly what the customers are looking for. So generally the acceptance will be higher if a product is developed with proper requirements management processes.

Besides more marketing success, shorter development cycles will usually also make for reduced costs. This alone can increase an organisation's net win, in addition to all the other benefits and aspects mentioned here. Costs are also reduced because people that have so far not been considered important during the development process are asked their needs and ideas, thus reducing the likelihood of requirements being missed. We are under no false apprehension here that getting the balance right is not easy. Simple checklists can help here to retain organisation specific knowledge about what is a successful balance. Keep the checklists and improve them over time.

For example, production, sales and the logistics departments may have most important requirements regarding some special or any new product. For productions it may be desirable to use only certain materials that are currently in stock, or it would save a lot of time and money if the housings of new products were designed according to some simple principles because this would allow for existing machine tools to be used again and again. Probably every reader could easily think of hundreds of more examples of such typical requirements which without a proper requirements management are usually not documented and thus just forgotten.

Known requirements also allow for a proper testing of the results of the development cycles. If it is not clear what functionality should be contained in a new product it is impossible to tell whether the product meets the original intentions or whether it does not.

The possibility to carry out good tests together with all other benefits makes for a higher overall product quality. But higher quality is also closely related to market success and thus net win of an organisation, and it is seen how all the positive aspects of a functioning requirements management amplify each other and open up new potentials.

Another important aspect for a better overall product and project quality are reduced risks. A more advanced requirements management process usually demands that there be an identification of possible risks and the definition of potential countermeasures. Even to simply write down possible risks is a significant improvement over not doing any risk management at all. Thinking of the possible impacts of each risk and how they could be handled creates even more awareness and will make sure that if something goes wrong, it does not do so suddenly and unexpectedly, but people are prepared and know how to react in order to get the best result under the given circumstances.

With this we close this (far from being complete!) example list of advantages of having a functioning requirements management. It may suffice to make clear that the efforts that are necessary to introduce a requirements management culture within an organisation will pay always pay off sooner or later, and our experience is that it does so sooner rather than later.

5.4   Why some people are against Requirements Management

Although we believe that there must be a sound requirements management if an organisation wants to produce high quality goods, some people are against the introduction of improvements to requirements managements. There are many reasons for this.

Generally, requirements management demands that the various project or systems engineering activities are transparent, at least to a certain degree. This is also implied by the graphical representation in figure 5.1 above. Transparency however may be regarded with apprehension by underconfident people that will take the risk that their mistakes will be built into a product perhaps causing massive costs later, rather than possibilities for improvement be discovered and improved before costs become enormous.

Let us consider a typical engineering company and the way the staff operate. We will usually be able to find senior management including the board and so on and project managers. For the sake of this example let us assume that there are no change managers, and no version and configuration managers nor requirements managers, but we may be able to find quality managers, risk managers and test managers.

Quite frequently we find, the role and responsibilities of each person are niether well-defined nor clear. Many of our readers will be familiar with the question: "What the heck does our project manager do?" I am sure that you project managers reading this may have heard something similar!

Requirements management means that all project members work hand in hand in order to ensure the highest possible quality and value of the requirements information. This implies that it is not possible for a project manager to just shut the door of his office and let all others do their work. Project management has to provide and coordinate vital information and data to all others, otherwise the idea behind requirements management will not work.

Therefore, a first reason why some people are against the introduction of requirements management is the fact that they would have to share at least some of their data and information with others. In some cultures, sharing their knowledge and information is identical to sharing power and influence, and this is unfortunately not desireable in some peoples' eyes.

We have worked for one client where information was hidden to such an extent that not only the project was unsuccessful, but the company was unsuccessful. To explain what happened we will have to disguise the the facts and use a different industry. In our example let us consider an aircraft manufacturer with various teams. The team responsible for the wings refused to share information with the team responsible for thrust (engines to you and me), and the team responsible for thrust refused to share information with the wings team. No-one would share information until they were sure that there own task was complete and error free. The engines were to be mounted on the wings. Not even the interface was agreed. Of course the tasks could not be complete without data from each other so the tasks were never complete.

But there is more to sharing data and information. Even staff that are on a relatively low level of the organisation's hierarchy might try to avoid sharing their data and information, and on such lower levels the reason is quite often not a question of power and influence. Rather, sharing their data really means that they have to publish the results of their work. This in turn is identical to publishing the quality of their work, and some underconfident people prefer to hide. This is a shame because it means that no-one can see their good work, and the complements that boost confidence are then not forthcoming.

Another reason why people may not be willing to support the introduction of requirements management is that such an introduction goes hand in hand with changes within the organisation. For example, if proper requirements management and associated processes are introduced this usually means that people have to develop a new way of working. And this is quite logical, for if no one had to change their ways of working, this would mean that everything is already as it should be and there would be no reason to change anything.

Change however is generally threatening to people. There is more to changes than just the fact that some or all staff have to change their ways of working. For example, it is possible that the hitherto ways of working with their disadvantages and inconsistencies produced some so-called company heroes whose heroism is solely based on the knowledge about how to best get around the various traps. If these ways of working are all done away with and replaced with better processes, the heroes would loose their status for their knowledge has no value any longer.

A similar situation occurs when improved processes make the work of some people redundant. One probably well-known and typical example for this is the introduction of personal computers and word processing software, which has dramatically changed the jobs for classical typists working previously on a typewriter.

Another aspect of change is insecurity caused by fear of change. Even the people who do not have to fear the loss of a hero status or the loss of their job may feel insecure when things change. For example, the planned changes may make it necessary that people use new computer programmes. This could imply that the knowledge they gathered so far about the hitherto software has no meaning any longer. Maybe the new programme is more complex to handle, maybe the new programme demands that more time is spent in front of the screen and so on.

Usually, changes also inevitably mean an increase of the number of mistakes during the initial phase. If the organisation's spirit is such that a mistake is seen as a personal failure rather than the chance for everyone to improve, then people have a very understandable reason why they would rather not change.

Thus, the readiness for changes demands a certain maturity of the organisation and its members. Change requires support and commitment from management at all levels.

5.5   How resistance can be avoided

From what has been said so far it is clear that in order to overcome the resistance against change, peoples' needs must be identified, taken seriously and addressed.

The HOOD group's philosophy has therefore always been to put the people in the centre of everything. For example, whenever new processes are necessary, the future users and other relevant people should be asked their opinion and viewpoint. In our experience however, many times this is not the case.

People need to be involved in all planned changes right from the very beginning, not just the ones who will be directly affected by it. Many organisations still believe that if someone high enough up in hierarchy commands anything, everyone will follow suit. This may be true with respect to a certain number of various subjects, but for all we know it has never worked with regard to requirements management so far.

When applied properly, requirements management is a philosophy and a way of thinking rather than just a way of working. This means that all people involved must be able to understand the basic concepts and ideas. Thus, training and coaching should always be an essential part of the introduction of requirements management in an organisation.

Experience shows that it is normally not possible to tackle requirements engineering and management with a big bang approach, trying to get from 0 to 100 within no time. Rather, requirements management has to be introduced little by little and there are a number of advantages to such a step by step approach.

First, a step-by-step approach with pilot projects leaves space for constant improvements. Whatever process or method or tool is devised, it can be tested in real life quickly and within the boundaries of one or a small number of projects. Thus the quality of the processes and associated methods and tools is as high as possible before they are introduced to all relevant departments and teams within the organisation. This in turn assures that acceptance regarding the usability and usefulness of the new concepts is high from the very beginning.

Second, a step-by-step approach makes it easier to control the progress of the requirements engineering and management introduction. The people responsible for the success of the introduction will use, amongst others, metrics to track the progress of their work. These metrics will produce results whose reliability corresponds with how narrow the focus on what they should measure is. Thus if many new subjects are introduced at the same time they will most probably influence each other and relate to each other, which makes it hard to measure one subject independent of all the others. By contrast, if new aspects are introduced one at a time it is easy to watch how one new bit changes or influences what is already there. Once it is clear that some new piece of the puzzle has been introduced successfully to fit with all other existing pieces, the next piece can be introduced and so on.

Third, the one-at-a-time philosophy exploits some human psychological traits. Everyone is familiar with the fact that some problem or task that first appears insurmountable presents itself in quite a different light when it is split up into smaller fragments that can be assessed and understood more easily. In much the same way the introduction of requirements engineering and management concepts is very much easier when the whole thing is cut into small and manageable goals that can be reached one after the other. It will be very motivating for the people involved to see the progress of their work by continuously reaching smaller or larger milestones.

People can also be motivated by the example other people give. Thus, a proven way to lessen resistance and to facilitate changes is the concept of key users or key people. Ideally, a key user is a person that is willing and able to support the planned change and that is also respected amongst his colleagues.

The key people are usually very limited in number and get special support, training and coaching by specialists. This way, the key people soon become specialists themselves and carry the knowledge and enthusiasm into the various departments and working groups. Key people are usually very important stakeholders because they really know what is going on and how it feels like to apply the new methods and tools.

The key people will usually be amongst the first within an organisation that use the new processes including methods and tools. Therefore it is good to have a forum for all key people to be able to share their experiences with each other and with external specialists that accompany the introduction of requirements engineering and management.

Such a forum is the requirements engineering and management competence centre. The competence centre provides sound and central support for projects that start with requirements engineering and management. Typically, the competence centre informs new projects, trains and coaches new users and supports in tailoring the requirements engineering and management processes, methods and tools to the specific demands of each individual proect.

At the beginning, the competence centre is usually staffed with external specialists and internal key people. In the further course of the introduction it should be a central goal that the external specialists and consultants withdraw little by litte, and that the responsibility is correspondingly handed over to internal staff. When this is done properly, the requirements engineering and management philosophy will keep on living and the organisation will be able to drive the further improvements without external help. Only when this stage is reached will the introduction have been successful.

It is our experience that without such a competence centre nobody usually feels responsible for driving the changes, except for external consultants. When they leave the organisation the efforts can come to rest and will finally be for nothing. Besides this, a competence centre will make sure that all experience and knowledge regarding requirements engineering and management are collected and stored in one central place. Thus, compared to approaches without a central institution, chances are less that all this information soon gets lost because there is no one to keep all the small pieces together and produce one big and consistent picture.

While a competence centre will mainly focus on technical aspects, the corresponding strategic counterpart is the requirements engineering and management steering committee. The steering committee plays a critical role in creating awareness and acceptance for the planned changes.

The steering committee has to look out for possible obstacles, psychological barriers and the like. It should be closely linked to the senior management of the organisation that wants to introduce requirements engineering and management. This is usually reached by members of the senior management being members of the steering committee, too. The committee should come together often to discuss the progress of the introduction, problems and possible solutions. Whenever problems appear, senior management should start countermeasures to secure and improve the acceptance of all people involved. This of course makes it necessary that the senior management are themselves convinced of the advantages and necessity of the intended changes.

Another means to motivate people and to lessen the resistance is the foundation of a requirements management and engineering academy. The intention of such an academy is not only to facilitate workshops and training, but to find out what the people need to learn in order to be successful in the new environment and to support the people in learning these things. In this sense the education process is focussed on learning rather than teaching, which makes sure that the responsibility remains with the individual. A typical collection of training offered by a requirements management and engineering academy may appear as follows:

- requirements engineering and management for senior management
- requirements engineering and management for managers
- requirements engineering and management method
- writing requirements
- requirements management tool for requirements managers
- requirements management tool for users
- workshop information modelling

The training listed above could be given by external consultants and specialists at the beginning, whereas at later stages they could be given by internal staff, for example selected key people. This has the advantage that training and coaching is absolutely fitted to the organisation, but in practice has the disadvantage that the best internal staff are normally very busy and project pressures on the key people can seem to be more urgent than supporting training.

5.6   After the introduction of Requirement Management

Some organisations believe that the introduction of requirements management and engineering is a project with a beginning and a sudden end. One common belief is that once the processes are established and working, business can get back to usual, only with some new ways of working.

Experience however shows that this is not so. Requirements engineering and management can produce many self-amplifying effects, but there must always be clear responsibilities and goals. Requirements engineering and management is like a huge engine: an almost insurmountable inertia at the beginning, and a large inertia to stop once it is running. Nevertheless, even the best engine will finally come to a rest without constant fuel supply.

One must not think that once changes are introduced, people have forgotten all there was before. There is always the temptation to fall back into old habits, even after a considerable amount of time has passed since the introduction of a new philosophy.

It sometimes appears as though requirements management and engineering conforms to modern theories of economics. It is almost impossible to remain at a certain stage of maturity or capability for a long period of time. If you do only a little bit too little, things will quickly deteriorate. If you do what is normally necessary to do it properly, you can usually not avoid to get better and better.

There is a remarkable number of organisations that have no clear vision of what they let themsleves in for when they are calling for requirements management and engineering. They are prepared to dedicate a certain amount of time and money – but please, not too much! – to some half-hearted introduction project and after that just sit back and wait for the announced wonders to come.

Without a long term commitment to embrace the improvement the advantages will be short-lived at best. It is clear from what has been said in the previous sections that there are so many aspects to the introduction of requirements management and engineering processes that it is impossible to address them properly without commitment. The real spirit of requirements management and engineering is a continuous improvement process, without a clear end. This means that an organisation must be willing to accept these boundary conditions if they want to be successful. Although it is almost certain that all efforts in terms of money will pay off realtively soon, a lot of organisations fear the initial investments and at the beginning cannot clearly see the way. All we can do is remind them of a statement made by the famous Thomas Alva Edison: "Most of life's failures are people who did not realise how close they were to success when they gave up."

5.7 Summary

The present chapter gives an introduction to requirements management and engineering . It is shown that it does not suffice to document requirements once and then leave them as they are, for a set of requirements does not usually remain stable, but go through changes.

Examples are given to illustrate how even a small number of requirements can give rise to a large number of challenges once people really start to work with them. It can be seen how all the various systems engineering disciplines such as risk management, change management, version and configuration management, test management, quality management and project management all have interfaces to requirements engineering, and the sum of all these interfaces to requirements engineering may be called requirements management.

One section lists the benefits that are associated with a functioning requirements management and engineering philosophy. Some of the main benefits for every organisation are quicker time to market, increased net profit and cashflow, products of higher quality, reduced risks, longer product lifecycle and better maintainability and reusability.

It is explained how in spite of all the benefits usually associated with requirements engineering and management processes, some people may appear to be against the introduction of corresponding processes, methods and tools.

Two of the main reasons are fear of change in general and fear of becoming transparent in terms of quality of one's own work. As requirements management and engineering , when applied properly, is a way of thinking, changes to an organisation's culture are noramlly inevitable, and people fear that it may be impossible for them to be successful in the new environment.

Therefore, a lot of effort must be dedicated to overcoming barriers and lessen resistance of the people that are affected by the introduction of the planned changes. A number of concepts are outlined in order to motivate people and make a project to introduce requirements management and engineering successful.

Some of these concepts are the building up of key people, the foundation of a requirements management and engineering academy to provide support and facilitate learning, the introduction of a requirements management and engineering steering committee to keep senior management involved and informed, and the creation of a competence centre to facilitate continuous improvement.

Finally it is shown that a living requirements management and engineering philosophy needs constant drive and must not be assumed to keep on living on its own. Introducing corresponding processes usually means to always have certain resources dedicated explicitly and solely to the further development and improvement of the existing processes. These resources may be releasing people from normal project work from time to time, having a group specifically dedicated to process improvement, or as simple as having a time of reflection and improvement at the end of each project. Once an organisation starts to neglect these needs, existing and working requirements management and engineering processes might come to a standstill after a relatively short amount of time.

6 Project Management interface

Even today projects that do not meet their initially planned time schedule and / or budget are quite common. Thus, for the relevant fields of industry it is one of the primary goals to improve the quality and predictability of their projects.

A functioning requirements management can support the project management, providing valuable data to assess the project status at any time. The creation of or access to such data relies on the existence of links between the requirements and between the requirements and other information. This chapter will show you how you can use requirements management and traceability to create relevant project management data.

6.1 What is Project Management

There are many good books about project management (for example, [Hindel2004]). Here, we will not try and give yet another definition of what project management is and is not. Rather, we try to identify the core activities that are commonly acknowledged as belonging to project management that can be supported by requirements management. In our eyes, these are:

- writing of proposals
- definition of project scope
- estimating resources and costs
- project planning and scheduling (milestones)
- project monitoring
- quality management
- reporting
- managing people

According to various other authors, activities such as risk and change management are part of project management, too. It is more accurate to say that risk and change management share interfaces to project management. Risk and change management can also be supported by requirements management, and as we cover these topics in detail in other chapters we will not take them into account here. By the end of this book you will probably share our opinion that all systems engineering disciplines share interfaces to all other systems engineering disciplines.

6.2   How Requirements Management can support the writing of proposals

As was shown in the previous chapters, a functioning requirements management will not only link say, user requirements to system requirements and system requirements to design requirements. A fully grown requirements management will also link requirements to work packages, to resources and budgets, to milestones and deliverables. With these links, even in such early stages as proposal writing, requirements management can support the project management.

There are basically two cases of boundary conditions for new development projects:

- there have been similar projects before
- there have not been similar projects before

In the first case, which we believe covers more than 95% of all development projects, information, data and knowledge from the predecessor project can be used to support the early activities.

When writing a proposal you basically make an initial estimate of the resources and budgets needed to successfully carry through the project. If there has been a similar project with a functioning requirements management, you will probably be able to identify user requirements of the old project that are similar to the known or anticipated user requirements of the current project. Using links that were drawn in predecessor projects between the user requirements, the system requirements, the design, the implementation, the project plan and the resources and budget in the old project, you will be able to quickly associate expenditures and costs with these user requirements, see figure 6.1. This will give you security when initially estimating the budgets for the current project.

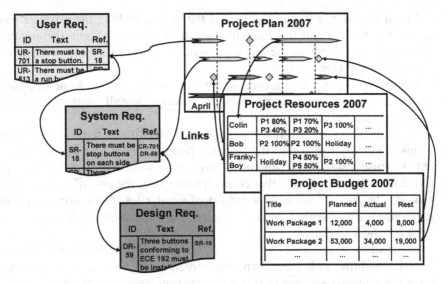

Figure 6.1: Example of linked project information

If it is not easily possible to find comparable key user requirements or if relationships (links) between user requirements and costs cannot be identified, you can still create a rough initial estimate by computing an average cost per requirement, which is very similar to the method described in section 6.5. To do so, divide the known final overall budget by all known user requirements of a similar predecessor project. You may want to do this for more than one similar predecessor project, thus giving an even better average of costs per user requirement.

This procedure should give you a very good idea of how much the implementation of one typical user requirement in your organisation will cost. Together with your initial estimate of how many user requirements there may be, you can thus arrive at an initial estimate of the overall project costs, see figure 6.2.

$$\text{Average Cost per User Req.} = \frac{\text{Total Project Budget}}{\text{Nr. of User Req.}}$$

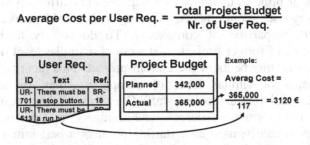

Figure 6.2: Calculation of average cost per user requirement

In our experience this works well if the person making the estimate has a lot of experience in the implementation of projects. Some differences that may seem minor to the untrained eye might make a major difference to the risks and costs of a project.

Of course, if the whole project is comparable and similar to predecessor projects, then you can simply take the known overall budgets of these similar projects as a starting point.

If the projects are similar but your estimate differs significantly, you should carefully try to find the reasons. Note however that when you are able to reuse a significant amount of work from similar projects, you could arrive at an initial estimate that is much lower than the cost of these earlier projects. In fact, if you have a project of similar level of complexity and can reuse a lot of earlier work, you should ask questions if your estimate does not show savings.

If for some reason you can identifiy similar user requirements but have no relationships (links) between requirements and costs and also cannot compute a usable average cost per typical user requirement, then still the user requirements of the predecessor projects will at least give you a good overview of what to think of when making an estimate for the project at hand, thus helping you not to forget some of the key aspects. In this case user requirements from similar projects may serve as a check list, see figure 6.3.

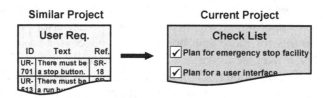

Figure 6.3: Using user requirements from similar projects as check list

If there was no similar project before, or if you feel that although there were similar projects their key user requirements differ too much from the current key user requirements, you may still be able make an estimate based on comparison of complexity. To do so, try to identify user requirements of former projects that were of a similar level of complexity as the user requirements of the current project. This identification of user requirements of similar level of complexity may be supported by developers and former project staff. Once similar key requirements are spotted, the former resources and budgets associated with these requirements can be used as a starting point or a best initial estimate for writing the proposal.

6.3   How Requirements Management can support the definition of the project scope

Writing the proposal also goes hand in hand with the definition of the project scope. You can make a sensible proposal only if the project scope is known at least roughly. For example, imagine that you should write a proposal for a robotic system. Surely it will change your estimates significantly if you knew whether you should only produce the robot, or the robot together with the power supply, or the robot and the power supply and the electronics and software controlling the robot.

Defining the project scope can be interpreted as defining the boundaries for requirements: only requirements that lie within the project scope (including project interfaces) are taken into account. If the project scope is not clear in the beginning, you will use various elicitation techniques with your customer to arrive at an agreed status. You will also elicit a number of initial user requirements. In fact, defining the scope is equal to the definition of initial user requirements with various levels of constraints and freedom to choose a solution, and various levels of detail. As a starting point you may also analyse the scope of a similar predecessor project, if there was any. Investigating competing systems is also a good start.

It is commonly known that throughout the course of a normal development project there is often a shift of scope compared to the beginning. Apart from new user requirements that may explicitly extend or change the scope of a project, this is especially true for requirements that only touch upon the boundary of the scope and are therefore harder to spot. If the requirements and thus the project scope are well documented from the beginning, it is always possible to tell which requirements were in the scope from the beginning and which requirements extended or changed the scope.

A documented change of scope may lead to re-negotiations between the project partners, as there could be additional expenditures or costs associated with the changed project scope. If the requirements or the project scope, respectively, are not so well documented, it is impossible to tell whether there is a need for re-negotiations or not. In such situations the supplier often overshoots his budget or time schedule, for he accepts and implements requirements that little by little change the scope but are not spotted as scope-changing.

When there are changes in scope a functioning requirements management will be able at any time to tell whether the system and design requirements still fit the user requirements and the scope, or whether these too have to be modified to match the changes. Without the links between the various kinds of requirements it may happen that developers at the design and implementation level are going on to plan a product that is no longer what the customer expects, or plan a product which is even more sophisticated than expected by the customer who might then not be willing to pay for such "extras" that were not ordered.

6.4   How Requirements Management can support estimating resources and costs

Estimating resources and costs is closely related to writing a proposal. For a proposal you make an initial estimate of resources and costs, as was mentioned before. However, as the project progresses and requirements are more and more developed and refined, the resources and costs needed to complete the project will be repeatedly estimated and also refined. This is one of the main activities of project management and is also related to project monitoring.

With an established requirements management it is always possible to use the links between the requirements and the work packages as identified in the project plan to relate resources and costs to requirements. This is visualised in figure 6.1 above.

The information is vital when it becomes clear that the resources and / or budget will not suffice to implement all of the requirements. In this situation decisions must be made regarding which requirements to keep and which requirements to hold for a possible later release, to waive, or reject. If the requirements are documented with an attribute for importance, the information of resources and budgets associated with each requirement or cluster of requirements can be used to identify those requirements that are of low importance but need a relatively great amount of resources and / or budget. Such requirements will be perfect candidates for waiving. However, such decisions should also be confirmed by the stakeholders, or otherwise it might for example turn out that a requirement that was prioritised low and thus waived was most important to some future users of the system who were not asked and who cannot make sensible use of the system without that requirement implemented.

We have experienced this in an organisation that created systems based on a platform electronics that provided resources to the internal customers to use to fulfil customer requirements. In order for the central platform group to meet its time and cost budgets the group decided unilaterally to not implement some the features of the platform. The platform group was judged to be successful but the other groups that relied on the platform were judged as unsuccessful because their software could not fulfil the customer requirements. The costs that resulted for the whole organisation due to lack of taking other stakeholder needs into account were enormous.

A similar situation occurs when the initial estimates and projections are constantly refined in the course of the project, revealing at some point in time that some requirements need much more resources and / or budget than were initially planned. Again, using other pieces of information such as the importance, the project management can, together with the stakeholders, decide whether they want to go on implementing those requirements or whether the requirements shall be waived.

If there are no up to date links between the requirements and the project plan with its work packages, resources and budget planning, decision as sketched above are much harder to make due to the lack of vital information. As can be seen from the scenarios described, the same is true if the requirements are not up to date: if the importance attribute for example is not properly filled in and the budget and resources will not suffice to implement all requirements, then, based only on the information on implementation costs, project management might unfortunately waive requirements which are most important to the system that is developed.

6.5 How Requirements Management can support project planning (scheduling)

The planning and scheduling of projects is closely related to the estimation of resources and costs, and both these activities will be greatly supported by a living requirements management.

Project planning usually involves an overview of available resources and the assignment of these resources to work packages. The work packages in turn stem from a work breakdown that partitions the major activities into manageable pieces.

In order to plan a project, information is needed that can be derived from the requirements. In fact, as the requirements really represent the system to be developed, they are the only source of this kind of information. If requirements management does not make these data extracted from the requirements available to project management, there is no basis to make plans.

A project plan typically includes a series of milestones and deliverables; see the following figure 6.4.

Milestones can be interpreted as end points of one development activity. If there is a defined development process, milestones may also represent end points of certain process activities. Usually, a certain result is associated with each milestone, and such a result may serve as inputs for the following activities associated with the next milestone. For example, a typical result of a milestone "user requirements analysis and review complete" is a set of agreed and confirmed user requirements.

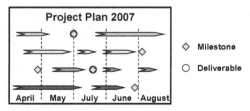

Figure 6.4: Example project plan with milestones and deliverables

Traceability is especially valuable when planning the dependencies of various results or activities within a project. Thus using the links between the requirements it is possible to tell which requirements must be implemented and which associated activities must be finished before the implementation of other requirements and the carrying out of associated activities can begin, see figure 6.5. This may save the project management from making plans that cannot be carried out in reality due to an incorrect sequence of activities.

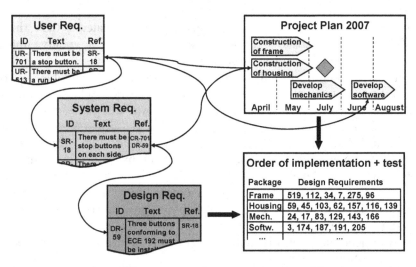

Figure 6.5: Traceability used to plan correct order of implementation

Deliverables are results that are delivered to a customer, either an internal or an external customer. Although deliverables can be delivered at any time within the project plan, they are usually associated with a milestone. A typical milestone including a deliverable could be "first prototype running".

To define the milestones, information on the work to be done is needed. From the point of view of implementation, the identification of different work packages gets easy, as each requirement or cluster of requirements can represent one work package. The detail of these work packages can be more and more refined as necessary, using traceability to step down the various levels of abstraction of requirements. For example, in practice a project manager will not plan the implementation of each single design requirement, but may define each customer requirement to be one large work package or cluster the customer requirements so as to give say, 10 main work packages. A more detailed planning can then be made by the developers responsible for each of these work packages. Here we use the terms user and customer to mean the same. Both terms are used to group together many stakeholders such as end user, Maintenance, Sales, and Production. We use customer to emphasise the difference in roles between customer and supplier, each of which may have stakeholders responsible for activities such as maintenance, sales, and production.

Apart from implementation, associated activities have to be carried out. Thus the requirements must be analysed (quality checked), reviewed, confirmed, refined, tested, integrated and so on, and all these activities must be planned and must be assigned resources and budget. With the estimates about the complexity of the requirement as provided by requirements management, it is possible to plan these associated activities and allow for a suitable amount of time.

Having defined all work packages and milestones, project management must allocate resources to work packages and estimate the time needed to complete each work package. A functioning requirements management can support this task as the overall work load can be analysed in more and more detail, going through the various levels of abstraction of the requirements as mentioned before.

For example, on the implementation level each single requirement typically may need a similar amount of time to implement, say 1 day. If the requirements differ significantly, an average time to implement can be calculated. The calculation can be made for the current project, using estimates of specialists and developers. However, it may be much more effective to take the data of previous projects and calculate an average time to implement one single requirement on the implementation level over a number of projects. This can be done for example by adding the total time needed to carry out all relevant projects and dividing the result by the sum of all requirements of these projects on the implementation level. Note that in this case the average time needed to implement each single requirement already includes the time needed to carry out all related activities, such as review and analysis, tests, implementation and so on. If the average time needed to really only implement one requirement shall be computed, then only all the time spent in all projects for implementation alone must be added and divided by the number of requirements. Valuable information can be extracted if this calculation is done for example to get the average time to test a single requirement, to review and analyse a single requirement.

These calculations or estimations can be carried out on each level of detail of requirements, but it may prove difficult to compare the level of detail of requirements. Experienced developers may provide valuable support.

By using the average time to implement a single requirement on the lowest level of detail it is possible to step back up the hierarchy of abstraction and estimate or calculate the time needed to implement for example each customer requirement. Based on this estimate and the resources allocated to each of these requirements or work packages, an estimate can be made regarding the time to finish each work package. This information can be finally used to create a project schedule.

6.6   How Requirements Management can support project monitoring

Project monitoring in general is the production of data or information about the current status of a project. As such, project monitoring may be seen as the heart of project management.

Managers need information in order to carry out their tasks. If the necessary information is either not available, incomplete or generally not reliable, the decisions will in turn be only as good as the quality of the input information. Thus managers will see to it that they have enough data at hand at any point in time. On the other hand, not every piece of information is valuable and necessary. It is thus one of the first challenges for a project manager to define the key data that shall represent or indicate the status of a concrete project.

The following list gives examples of typical key figures or data that may be tracked as indicators for the status of a project:

- budget used compared to budget available
- work packages or milestones finished and still open
- resources available compared to resources planned
- critical time path
- ...

These and more are usually used by management to get an overview of a running project. But project monitoring is not just about getting a current overview. Constant monitoring will reveal how current figures diverge from initial estimates, for example initial estimates on time and resources needed to complete the various milestones. Such initial estimates are normally inevitably incorrect, and as the project goes on and incorrect estimates are revealed, the project planning and scheduling should also constantly be reviewed and corrected according to what data is available. This may lead to later project activities being reorganised so as to take less time or to consume less resources. A simple sketch of a project management process can be seen in the following figure 6.6.

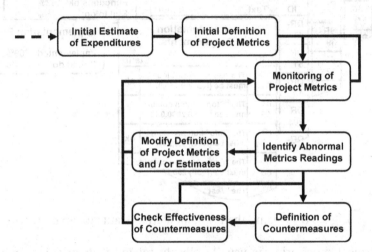

Figure 6.6: Simple project management process

Now, how can a functioning requirements management support project monitoring? We already know that the requirements represent the system to be developed. As each requirement will usually have, amongst others, an attribute indicating the status of implementation, a requirements management can quickly produce an overview of the implementation status of the project on each level of detail. This is depicted in the following figure 6.7.

Knowing the implementation status of the requirements is identical to knowing the status of the various work packages or milestones. If the project planning and scheduling has been set up using the data that requirements management can provide as described in the previous section, the requirements or work packages are also associated with budget and resources. Thus the implementation status of the requirements on a suited level of abstraction will also indicate the budget and resources consumption.

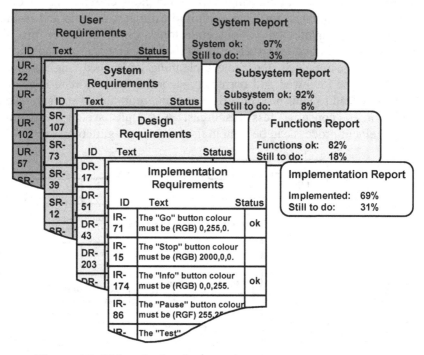

Figure 6.7: Using the implementation status to create reports

Project monitoring is usually closely related to metrics, a topic that is dealt with in detail in another chapter. The key figures that are chosen at the beginning of a project for tracking the project status are computed in regular intervals, and this is identical to producing metrics. Based on these metrics or key figures, the project management will spot deviations of actual from planned figures and will then make correcting decisions.

6.7   How Requirements Management can support quality management

Product quality is usually directly related to business success and customer satisfaction. Therefore, economically oriented organisations usually have, amongst others, the objective of providing a high level of product quality. It has been shown that a consistently high level of product quality can be achieved by installing a high level of process quality. Quality management tries to establish processes with standardised methods, tools and templates, and to constantly improve these processes, based on feedback from the various projects.

Ideally, quality management should be independent of and separated from project management. This ensures that quality aspects may not easily be compromised by project management boundary conditions such as budget or time schedule. However, since many organisations leave quality management to the project management, we cover this topic here.

Quality management covers a number of activities. These activities may be collected into two categories:

- quality framework
- quality monitoring

The quality framework is the collection of tools to support and to outline the quality management of an organisation. These tools usually include procedures, process descriptions, best practices and so on. In other words, the quality framework is the collection of all available standards and must be tailored for each individual project.

The development of such a framework usually takes a relatively large amount of time and is rather complex. Therefore, various suggestions have been made to provide a starting point. Maybe the best known such effort is the international ISO9000. This is a collection of basic standards that can be tailored to fit a wide range of organisations, for example developing and manufacturing companies.

One of the standards contained within the ISO9000 is the ISO9001, which provides an abstract quality process model. It is the task of any organisation to tailor this generic model to its needs and special boundary conditions.

The outcome of such a tailoring will be a quality management framework or manual defining all quality management processes of an organisation. It is known that in some countries there exist organisations that will certify that the process or processes as described in a quality management manual conforms to the ISO9001. Such certificates are highly valued and are demanded by some OEMs of their suppliers.

Although an organisation's quality management manual is tailored to the organisation's needs and special situation, it is usually still rather abstract and generic. For all projects it outlines the processes to be followed, the standards to be applied and the tools and methods to be used. Therefore another tailoring is usually necessary to make the basic quality management manual or framework fit the special needs and boundary conditions of any current project.

In this course of tailoring the quality manual to fit a current project, the person or persons responsible for the quality management of the project select the appropriate processes, procedures and tools and adapt these to their current needs. Also, it will be defined what sort of quality shall be achieved in the current project and how the quality may be assessed. For example, in a project to develop a new car braking system a high product quality may be defined as an extraordinary high level of reliability. In a database application development, high quality could mean optimised efficiency.

As these different characteristics can normally not be optimised all at the same time, it is mandatory to set the quality goals at the beginning of a project. This makes sure that the various developers know the points to focus their efforts onto and do not aim at opposing goals.

However, quality goals without means of checking if they are met are nearly useless. Therefore, together with the quality goals the key figures to check the quality have to be defined. This touches upon the topic of metrics that is dealt with in detail in another chapter. Getting back to the examples above, the reliability of a braking system may be measured as the number of failures during a given number of test runs. The quality goal then may be to have less than one failure in 1,000 test runs. The efficiency of the aforementioned database application may be measured as the time elapsing to process a certain number of database queries. In this case, the quality goal may be that the total elapsed time be less than or equal to 2 seconds for 100,000 queries.

Quality monitoring means checking whether the processes and standards tailored to fit a project are properly applied, and whether they are effective and helpful. In this respect quality monitoring is closely related to project monitoring. In fact, if the responsibility for quality management lies with the project management, quality monitoring is part of project monitoring.

Quality monitoring is more than just watching the figures chosen as quality indicators at the beginning of the project until they reach the target value. Quality monitoring will need repeated quality reviews and assessments to guarantee that the standards are still being followed and properly applied, and also to ensure that processes are helpful. The following figure 6.8 shows a simple example of a quality management process for projects.

Quality reviews shall contain all those aspects that were tailored using the organisation's quality manual for a project. This may mean that all internal documentation that is created in the course of the project is checked that they conform to the selected standards, that all external documentation applies the tailored templates, that for example software code is produced following the agreed coding guidelines, that system tests are performed according to a defined process and so on.

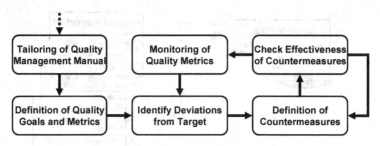

Figure 6.8: Simple quality management process for projects

The result of these reviews is a current project status with regard to the reviewed aspects of the project quality, and this can be part of project reports. In practise however, such information is often not created or not available, but it is strongly recommended to gather such information and make it accessible. The results can and should also be handed over to the people responsible for the respective aspects of quality so that they may improve their work. For example, the quality of the testing process as assessed in a review will usually be passed back to the project test manager and testers.

Requirements management is perfectly suited for supporting quality management. Two different aspects of requirements management can be identified in connection with quality management:

- requirements management for a project
- requirements management for quality management

What does this mean? The first aspect, requirements management for a project, means that all the quality requirements can properly be addressed in any project with a functioning requirements management.

For example, that certain templates must be used for any documentation that will go to the customer can be formulated in the requirements. There may be an extra section in the requirements document for quality aspects, and all of the requirements in this section may represent the organisation's quality manual as tailored to the project.

If the quality requirements are formulated, links can be drawn, for example, to the various documents created in the course of the project. This will give traceability and will thus help quality monitoring. For example, if a document meant to be sent to the customer has no links or references to the relevant quality requirements, this may mean that it does not meet these requirements yet, and must be improved before it can be delivered or published. One example is shown in the following figure 6.9.

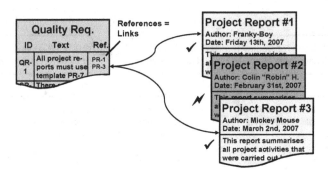

Figure 6.9: Example of using quality requirements and links to documents

Thus the quality goals can directly be incorporated into the product development process. Requirements management can make quality requirements of similar and predecessor projects available and can therefore offer a starting point for formulating the quality requirements of following projects.

The second aspect, requirements management for quality management, deals with an organisation's quality management as such. We have said before that quality management should be a dedicated process within an organisation and should therefore have dedicated resources. Ideally, there exists a quality management team that is independent from individual projects. We have also said that the development of organisation-wide quality procedures and standards is normally quite complex and can take a lot of time.

In this sense, quality management itself can be seen as one single task that goes on infinitely and that can be broken into individual projects so that progress may better be monitored. Like every other activity, quality management should be managed with requirements, too. This means that quality management projects should start with eliciting requirements from various stakeholders, for example the members of the board, the heads of the departments, developers, customers, and so on. All further actions that are taken to develop a standardised quality management process must then address these requirements.

If these requirements are kept up to date and if links are drawn between the various requirements and all related information, the advantages of requirements management can be fully utilised. Thus for example if a template shall be modified, it is easy to tell which other documents, procedures and process descriptions must also be modified. Changes to the quality management process can be assessed in terms of complexity, risk, time to implement, and costs.

The most detailed requirements that are created in such a way may finally represent the organisation's quality management manual and may therefore serve as the starting point for tailoring for the individual projects. So, the more abstract quality requirements of the organisation and the more detailed quality requirements of the projects can all be cross-linked. This allows for constant improvement of both the organisation's quality management and the projects' quality management. Also, this provides a sound foundation for any future projects to start with quality requirements.

6.8 How Requirements Management can support reporting

Project monitoring and reporting may be seen as almost identical. Project monitoring creates data that are used as the foundation for project management decisions. Reporting is the activity of compressing these data to a suitable level of abstraction and documenting this extract in a way suited for presentation.

Although a report may contain more information than can be produced with requirements – for example the number of project members that are currently ill or on holidays – most of the more important information in a report can be created using requirements management.

A report will usually include some or all of the following topics:

- budget consumption
- resources consumption
- project planning and scheduling
- milestones
- deliverables
- decisions that must be made by project management
- risks

This chapter together with other chapters of this book show how all of the necessary information may be created using requirements management. Project monitoring is closely related to metrics, and that topic is dealt with in detail in chapter 8.

6.9   How Requirements Management can support managing people

It is commonly accepted that the attitude of the people working on a project is one or the key factors for success. Thus the management of the people working on a project is mostly about motivation.

People are motivated if they are taken seriously, if they are respected and if they have a level of responsibility that corresponds with their skills. Maslow invented his theory of human needs that are arranged hierarchically ([Masl1954]). According to this theory, basic needs such as food and accommodation must be addressed first before more advanced needs such as social needs or esteem needs become important. Maslow's pyramid of human needs in depicted in figure 6.10.

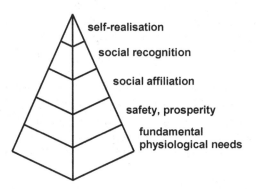

Figure 6.10: Maslow's pyramid of human needs

As it can be deemed that people working on development projects in a civilised country of western European standard do not usually suffer from hunger, thirst or deprivation of sleep, it is the more advanced needs that must be satisfied to make such people happy. Therefore, motivation of project members will aim at satisfying the social needs, esteem needs and self-realisation needs.

There are a number of ways to try and address the various needs of the people working on a project. Obviously the first means to resort to is what is usually called common sense. Common sense tells you not to insult people, to show them that they are valued and so on. However, this may not cover all open and secret needs of all project members and requirements management may help to elicit more such needs.

A project manager could have his own list of requirements or needs of his project staff. These requirements could be overtly elicited, for example by direct asking. They may also be covertly elicited, by trying to capture the atmosphere in a project and by informally talking to staff.

Another way to take peoples' needs into account is by explicitly eliciting related requirements at the beginning of a project. Depending on what kind of system is to be developed, it may be necessary that certain specialists need to work closely together, since otherwise too much deadwood is created by inefficient communications. This circumstance may mean that there should be an office large enough for all the specialists to work together in one place. If it is obvious that there are numerous experiments or simulations necessary in the course of the development, this may indicate that there is a need for a properly equipped laboratory. If some specialists are part of the project whose task is to invent new algorithms, for example for software optimisation or a control unit, this probably means that they need some quiet place for themselves where they can read related books and try out some ideas without being disturbed. When the system to be developed needs testing, this means that there must be a dedicated test space with corresponding tools to properly carry out the tests.

Thus it is seen that the more obvious and the less obvious needs of people can be realised by eliciting such requirements and by analysing the technical requirements in view of their implicit demands on the working environment, equipment and so on.

Such an approach can help ensure that regarding the working environment, project members are happy and motivated. Another key factor for happiness of project members is the progress of the project itself. Being able to see some idea growing from scratch to a fully working system is surely a powerful driver for staff. Here too, requirements management may help in a number of ways.

First, requirements management is able to give the current status of a project in terms of percentage of implementation, status of use of budget and so on. This was explained further above in connection with project planning and scheduling and project monitoring. Thus, project members always have an up to date overview of where the project is at the moment. With this, motivation of staff is increased, since everyone is able to follow the progress. This is in contrast to other ways of developing systems, where very little information is known or communicated, and where every project member only knows about his next task without being able to see the whole picture. Sadly, this kind of project management is still very common. As a side effect of requirements management being able to give a detailed status of the project, staff can adapt their next steps so as to be most efficient for the further progress of the project. This may be true for example if it turns out that some requirements are more risky or complex to implement than initially thought – in such a case the specialists may concentrate their efforts on the high-priority requirements, rather than wasting time implementing some nice-to-have functionality.

Second, the results of a functioning requirements management may be motivating in their own right. It was mentioned before that a living requirements management will usually increase the quality of the product. This is accomplished by raising the quality of all activities associated with the requirements. It is thus possible that project staff are highly motivated by one or more of the following:

- fewer requirements forgotten
- fewer implementation loops
- fewer problems with the project schedule
- fewer problems with forgotten equipment (for tests, …)
- less time to finish the project (compared to similar predecessor projects)
- fewer misunderstandings
- less unnecessary double work
- …

If these results motivate project members, they are sure to support and enhance requirements management in following projects. This will ideally lead to a self-driven, endless improvement cycle, and this really is what requirements management and engineering is all about.

6.10 Summary

This chapter deals with the interface between requirements management and project management. In particular, it is shown how requirements management can support the following activities: writing of proposals, definition of project scope, estimating resources and costs, project planning and scheduling (milestones), project monitoring, quality management, reporting, and managing people.

Other activities that can also be defined as belonging to project management are covered in detail in other chapters of this book and are therefore not taken into account here. These are change management, configuration and version management, risk management and so on.

For all of the above mentioned activities requirements management provides valuable information. The activities are very much simplified because all the requirements data and all associated information is made accessible and traceable by requirements management. Information links between the various pieces of related information stemming from the different systems engineering disciplines, such as requirements development, change management, project management, quality management and so on, make sure that all relevant information in connection with a requirement is complete and can be collected by simply following the links. As ideally, the information links build a chain or a net, all information can be gathered from any point within the chain or net. For example, if the requirements are linked to the risks and to the project management plan, the dependencies between the project planning and scheduling and the risks can easily be extracted and visualised.

In principle, project management is a constant process that lasts from the first vision of some system to be developed until the system is finally disposed of. Project management is iterative by nature, and the various process steps or activities must be repeatedly carried out. Starting with initial estimations, for example for the project scheduling and planning, these estimations are constantly refined as more and more information and data emerge and become available.

Monitoring and analysing all available data, the core task of project management is to realise when decisions become necessary and to make these decisions. For example, in the typical situation of small project budgets and few resources, project management must prioritise the activities to maximise the chance for project success. The better the information on which such analyses and decisions are based, the higher therefore the quality of the decisions and thus of the whole project.

7 Configuration Management interface

Many experts in the field of system engineering have made their collective knowledge of development processes available to the public in the form of standards and guidelines. Configuration management is identified as an important element of the development process; configuration management controls the elements of the development process.

Applied correctly, configuration management can be highly useful in product development. Some standards are applicable to specific product types and lmost all contain safety aspects, as some product types are safety-critical. Examples include medical products that need to be developed according to FDA regulations, or products in aviation. An extensive list of standards and guidelines containing configuration management information can be found in [Hass2003].

Common and well-known process assessment and quality assurance methods like CMMI (SEI) and SPiCE require configuration management in addition to requirements management to achieve a specific maturity level in the development process.

In the pharmaceutical industry, "Good Automated Manufacturing Practices" (GAMP) were developed as a guideline that provides a foundation of methods for product development in this field. For companies that require firm control of their development process in pharmaceuticals, GAMP is invaluable.

Besides several other process areas, GAMP defines CM as one component for successful product development. This raises the question: are requirements management and configuration management independent from each other, or are they closely linked? To answer this, we will look at some typical questions from the RM&E field:

1. How can configurations of requirements and relations be managed?

2. How can traceability be achieved, from customer requirements to system requirements, design models, component requirements all the way to implementation, realization and test specification?

3. How can configurations be managed that contain realization products in addition to requirements, test, and design specifications?

4. How can a release of specifications be managed that is valid, up to date, and consistent?

5. How can change requests be tracked, starting from their cause, over their effects on the specifications, and all the way to implementation and testing?

6. How can a change approval process be established, that is used as basis for decision-making for systematic assessment of change-related estimates?

7. How can tracking of the project's progress in the areas of effectively implementing requirements and executing change requests be achieved?

Can all these questions be answered in the RM&E context alone, without using configuration management? The following chapter will discuss the correlation between RM&E and configuration management to answer this question.

7.1   Of versions, configurations, and releases

Numerous standards attempt to define the terminology of configuration management [Hass2003]. However, in practice there is a lot of confusion due to different or overlapping interpretations of terms. In the following, we will create a foundation for the discussion by defining the most common terms in the area of configuration management. The selected terms and definitions were taken from the configuration management literature and represent the most commonly used terms. The selected definitions are as generic and abstract as possible, to make sure that they are free from any specific technical domain. In addition, the definitions will be defined in an order that provides a maximum of continuity and consistency. Figure 7.1 shows the different Configuration management definitions.

Configuration Unit: A configuration unit is the smallest possible building block of a configuration that can be considered "atomic" [Glin2005]. Examples include documents, specifications, source code, executable code, make files, compiler, design and test documentation. Sometimes, these configuration units are also referred to as artifacts.

Version: A version is a defined and reproducible state of a configuration unit at a specific point in time. Every version has a unique identifier to ensure that configurations can be recreated correctly. A collection of multiple configuration units is sometimes also called a version, for example to define a functioning computer program. This can lead to confusions.

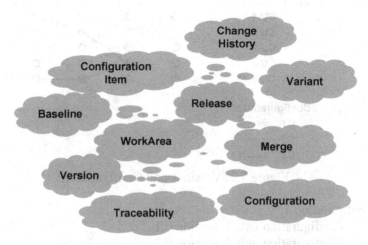

Figure 7.1: Configuration management definitions

History: The sequence of versions in time is called version history. The version history documents how the configuration unit changed over time. Another term for this documentation of all changes is "change history" or "traceability of the change history". Note the use of the important RM&E-term "traceability". Traceability is defined elsewhere in this book.

Version management: version management refers to a system that tracks all versions of a configuration unit (in other words, the version history). A configuration unit can have multiple states (versions). The various versions of a configuration unit are derived from each other. Changes on an existing version are saved as a new version, together with a unique identifier, timestamp, user identification and possibly other metadata.

Configuration: A configuration is a set of configuration units. By creating a set of configuration units, each identified by a version, a controlled configuration is formed.

The following figure 7.2 will clarify the interplay of configuration units, versions and configurations.

A configuration consists of a number of configuration units. Each configuration unit may have a number of states (versions). Each change on a configuration unit is saved as a new version, the version management takes care of this. The following representation shows one specific configuration (configuration 1), consisting of well-defined versions of configuration unit.

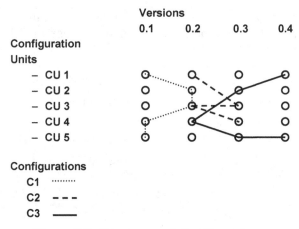

Figure 7.2: Versions and Configurations

Configuration 1:
    Configuration unit 1, version 0.1
    Configuration unit 2, version 0.2
    Configuration unit 3, version 0.2
    Configuration unit 4, version 0.1
    Configuration unit 5, version 0.1

Later on, some configuration units were changed. Configuration 2 contains unchanged artifacts from Configuration 1 and other artifacts that are different from Configuration 1. This is exemplified in the following (CU refers to configuration unit, C refers to configuration):

Configuration 2:
    Configuration unit 1, version 0.2 (contains changes to CU 1)
    Configuration unit 2, version 0.2
    Configuration unit 3, version 0.2
    Configuration unit 4, version 0.3 (contains changes to CU 4)
    Configuration unit 5, version 0.2 (contains changes to CU 5)

Likewise, configuration 3 may contain unchanged artifacts from configuration 2 and changes to configuration 2.

This is one way to represent the connection between configuration units and configurations. But there are other representations and work processes, depending on work style and the choice of tools.

BOM: The Bill of Material (BOM) is the inventory or content of a configuration, consisting of configuration units.

Version management and configuration management: To ensure that each configuration is assembled from the correct configuration units, the exact identification of the version of each configuration unit is necessary.

This task is done by the version management, which is a foundation for proper configuration management.

Baseline: A baseline is a configuration with a special meaning. Also called a snapshot, a baseline's configuration never changes, so that its content can always be referred to. A baseline is a record of a particular configuration including the specific version of its configuration items.

Release: A release is a configuration with a special meaning in the configuration management process. Typically, releasing a configuration means to make the configuration available, e.g. releasing the delivery to a customer with a special enabling process. It is a special form of baseline.

Variant: Variants are configurations with similarities in form, function or content, usually with a high content of identical components. [DIN199-1] Components in this context refer to functional parts of the system. This definition can be extended by adding that individual components of similar function, form or content are also considered variants. Variants are often confused with versions. A criterion to distinguish them is: Multiple variants can exist and be valid for the same purpose at the same point in time, while versions in a linear development chain follow each other sequentially. Variants significantly increase the complexity of the system development workflow.

Branch: A branch consists of one ore more versions of a configuration unit that exists at the same time as another version of this configuration unit and is generated through temporal parallel work on the configuration unit. It is a branch in the linear chain of versions of that configuration unit. A branch makes it possible to change a configuration unit at the same time, either by different users, or in different configurations.

The following figure 7.3 shows a version chain of one configuration unit with a parallel branch. It shows also a merge operation traced in configuration management. The changes from the parallel branch are integrated into the linear version chain.

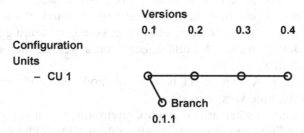

Figure 7.3: Branch

Merge: In general, merging is the joining of data. The term merging is used in two different ways:

1. It refers to the controlled merging of parallel versions (branches) into a new, valid version. In other words, the changes made in the different branches are integrated into a new version line. This case of merging can usually be traced in the version management system.

2. Merging also refers to the joining of the data from one single configuration unit, if its content in the version management system changed since editing began. This case can usually not be traced in a version management system.

Audit: Many definitions of processes for configuration management use the term audit. The term has a Latin root (audire: to hear, to attend, listen to) and means a general investigation procedure. Audits have the objective to judge processes and process results in respect to given requirements and guidelines. The objective of an audit is to ensure that the released product fulfills the requirements.

This is another important clue that shows that requirements management and configuration management are not independent from each other.

Configuration management: "Configuration management is a discipline applying technical and administrative direction and surveillance to identify and document the functional and physical characteristics of a configuration item, control changes to those characteristics, record and report change processing and implementation status, and verify compliance with specified requirements" [IEEE729]. This definition refers to individual elements of the system, but doesn't say much about the system as a whole. The following definition complements the previous one in this regard: "Configuration management (CM) is defined as the discipline of identifying the configuration of a system at discrete points in time for purposes of systematically controlling changes to this configuration and maintaining the integrity and traceability of this configuration throughout the system life cycle. " [Bers1980].

Build: A build is the creation of a configuration, putting the parts together to create a (sub)system. This term is also used in software development, a part of systems engineering. A build of software may be the result of an automatic generation process (e.g. compiling and linking in software development). A build is based on a well-defined configuration, often a baseline.

Change Set: A change set is a set of modified configuration units. It forms a unit in the version system.

Work Area: A work area is a work environment that is reserved for one editor for editing the managed configuration units. Others cannot access this area, and therefore cannot see the changes performed there (the changes that are not yet committed to the system). Editors can usually create one or more work areas for themselves.

Configuration management plan (CM plan): The configuration management plan is an element of the project documentation. There are standards and guidelines for CM-Plans. The CM-Plan contains guidelines and processes for the configuration manager, developers and other roles, regarding the use of the configuration management system. It usually describes the build process, too.

7.2   Management Disciplines and the German Government V-Modell

The German Government V Modell refers to a model known as the "Vorgehensmodell" used for German Government acquisition projects. The V-Modell is the "Development Standard for IT Systems of the Federal Republic of Germany". For a practical overview, figure 7.4 explains the management disciplines in the context of the German V-Modell. Management disciplines can be classified into the following two categories:

1. Management Disciplines that fit into the V-Modell

Management disciplines that fit into the German V-Modell include definitions of systems and subsystems, definition of components, tests of components, integration tests, system tests and release.

2. Management Disciplines that span the V-modell but do not fit into it.

There are continual accompanying disciplines that do not fit into the V-Modell, for example project management and change management.

Other members of this second category are requirement management, version management and configuration management. A common aspect of these is that they are not only applied at a specific time during the V-Modell's process execution, but that they accompany the V-Modell's process continuously from start to finish. These days, some organisations prefer to not use conventional development processes such as waterfall model and prefer instead to use iterative development. This corresponds more closely to how system development is done in practice . An iterative approach does not only support achieving a high quality of the final product, but the iterative approach also produces valid intermediate results. Iterative processes even more dependent on version and configuration management than traditional processes.

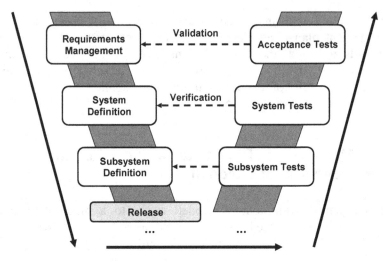

Figure 7.4: V-Model

7.3   Configurations in the Context of Requirements Management

Is it enough to consider the whole specification (consisting of requirements) as a configuration unit? What does a specification consist of in the first place? It consists of individual requirements and additional information. Each piece of information, whether it is a requirement or not, is denoted as an object in the following discussion. Objects can have properties (also called attributes) and relationships to other objects. Typically, the specification is considered as a configuration, and the objects (including their relationships to each other) are the configuration units. This perspective proved to be useful for the management of requirements information.

This organization of requirements raises a number of questions, including the following ones:

- Who "owns" the relationship between objects, the source or the target object?
- How can the relationships be taken into account in the context of configuration management?

On the other hand, a specification can also be considered a configuration unit within the configuration of the information model. This suggests an iterative process. Perhaps you prefer to consider the process as a fractal, where the closer you get to a configuration item, the more you see that it is itself a configuration of parts which each have their own identities and versions.

7.3.1 Changes of requirements and specifications in practice

Requirements and specifications might change frequently, and at specific times, baselines of specifications need to be created. Baselines define a configuration at a specific time, and record its requirements and the relationships between them. In iterative development, there can be multiple important configurations: From the initial specification through testing to the final implementation of a system, multiple versions of a requirement can be referred to in multiple configurations. The various versions of a requirement must be accessible. At least each version of a requirement that is referred to from a baseline of a specification must be reproducible.

Here is an example from real-world system development: The change of a requirement must not affect the creation of a prototype that is based on an older version of that requirement. But in order to achieve this, the old version must be accessible.

Another common situation is the development of a product for different markets. A car, for example, shall be sold in the UK, Europe and the USA. As there are different regulations in various countries, only the basic components are identical – engine, body, etc. But the details will differ for the various markets.

This is a classical example for variants. When variants were defined earlier in this chapter, we already hinted at the fact that their use can increase the complexity of the development process considerably. The development of system variants poses special challenges for both configuration management and requirements management.

Back to the previous example: While the cars for different regions differ, from the point of view of production it is desirable to maximize the number of common components. To achieve this, the car configurations must be known and understood in order to distinguish parts that can be common from parts that must differ.

This challenge applies both to requirements and the development product. When a request for the change of a requirement comes in, the affected component may or may not have variants. If the component has variants, not all of them may be affected. The change management becomes much more complicated, because all variants have to be considered for the evaluation of the change.

Let's look at the situation when in two of the three regions for which we produce cars, the regulations are made identical. To simplify production the two formerly region-specific variants of the car that were managed independently in the past shall be transferred into one product with no differences in production. There are various approaches to achieve this. One option is to start with one variant and to integrate the differences from the other one into that variant. From an abstract point of view this means: changes are necessary, thus change management is crucial.

New versions of configuration units are created, and those have to be put together into a new configuration. It is impossible to perform all these tasks without version and configuration management. A corresponding situation exists in regard to the requirements: Requirements must be changed as well, to accommodate the integration of the requirements variants.

To manage the requirement changes, version and configuration management are used – the same techniques and management disciplines that have been introduced earlier for the system changes. Configuration management for cars is much more complicated in reality; it has been simplified significantly here to get the point across. Regional differences are just one example for variants in cars. Other examples for variants include décor, similar components from different suppliers, type of car (limousine, estate) etc. all the way to engine size and type (diesel, gasoline).

The number of combinations seems endless. This leads to the situation that statistically each car consists of a unique configuration. To see an example, have a look at the car configuration tools that some car vendors offer on the Internet. Requirements for configurability production lead to highly standardized interfaces between components. Considering the complexity in the management of variants, to forget appropriate requirements management would be a big mistake. Requirements are the foundation for system development.

Problems in the foundation can lead to severe problems later on, including the collapse of the structures resting on it – just visualize a house built on sand. This danger is very real and can't be emphasized enough! This danger can be avoided by the creation of a solid foundation in systems development in the form of proper requirements and configuration management.

7.3.1.1 Solution Concept: Configuration Management for Requirements in Practice

How version and configuration management of requirements can be implemented, will be demonstrated here, using the requirements tool DOORS® from Telelogic. In DOORS, requirements are organized in containers, called Modules. A requirement cannot exist outside of its container. This distinguishes DOORS from most tools that access databases, and has implications on the usage of the tool. A requirement cannot be in two containers; instead a copy of the requirement must be stored in one of the containers. DOORS maintains a change history for each requirement, including date of change and information about who changed the requirement.

A history dialog and an API (application program interface) for scripting are provided to access old versions of objects, and to copy them to the current configuration. It is also possible to create baselines to store specific configurations of requirements. But this mechanism isn't sufficient to access different versions of a requirement concurrently. One solution would be to copy requirements on every change, together with an attribute for storing the version numbers managed manually by the user. But this creates another problem:

Now the dependencies between requirements versions that means the logical timeline relationships have to be stored and managed as well. Depending upon the method of creation of a new object, newly created DOORS Objects might have no relationship to other objects and can be moved within a container (Module) in any possible way. There are different possible solutions.

For instance, logical timeline relationships could be implemented by using links to connect objects to their successors. Another option would be the use of the hierarchy within a Module to model the logical timeline of requirements. Relationships between requirements are rarely considered for configuration management in tools. DOORS is not different in this regard. The versioning of relationships (called Links) does not exist in DOORS (version 8.0) unless you change things to make it happen. Saving the link information to an attribute gives the possibility to trace the history of changes and to denote versions link information.

The links may be automatically generated from this information within an attribute. Using standard DOORS features a link from a source requirement to a target requirement is stored together with the source requirement, but no history on link changes is kept.

If the link is deleted, it simply vanishes from the database. When a link is moved, only the final state is preserved. As stated above it is possible to archive link information by storing the link information in an attribute of the source and target requirements, which creates redundancy.

Changes on these attributes are archived together with their respective objects (as all object attributes are). This technique allows the archiving of any relationship within the database. DOORS offers another technique: Baseline Sets are groups of configurations. But before they can be used, the modules in the database have to be organized in an appropriate way. Relationships can only be archived within these groups.

In order to allow every relationship in the database to be archived, the whole database must be grouped into one Baseline Set.

7.3.2 Requirements Management – Configuration Units

The following chapter defines the adequate configuration units in requirements management, the resulting challenges and possible solutions to these challenges.

Object model for requirements: In the following, a process model for configuration management of requirements will be presented by starting with the terms that were defined earlier.

The data model used in this example has been taken from the RIF Project (Requirements Interchange Format, HIS 2005) and provides a foundation on how requirements can be broken down into data and data structures, so that they can be managed. It was specifically developed for the exchange of requirements, and provides an abstract, tool-independent view on data structures of requirements.

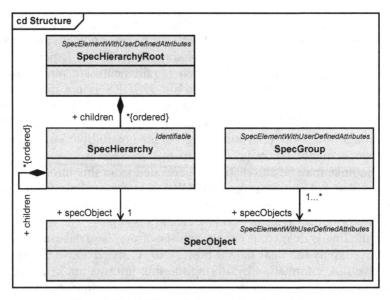

Figure 7.5: RIF model, specification object

Figure 7.5 above shows an excerpt from the RIF model the structures of specification objects. Note that the structural information of requirements (in the form of a hierarchical tree structure) is kept strictly separate from the specification objects. The root of the tree structure is an element of type SpecHierarchyRoot. This element aggregates elements of type SpecHierarchy, which recursively aggregate elements of the same type (children). This setup allows the creation of any hierarchical tree with one well-defined root. The leaves of this tree-structure have pointers to the actual specification objects.

Compared to this rather complex tree structure, the organization of specification objects into groups is trivial. The type SpecGroup refers to all the specification objects belonging to its group.

These two schemes, which can exist in parallel, allow both the hierarchical organization and grouping of requirement objects (SpecObjects). It is particularly important to note that this approach leaves the traditional document-paradigm behind, where a document was the central container for requirements, in the form of the specification document. The scheme that we just introduced allows the creation of views on the data (filtered and unfiltered), and such a view can be interpreted and exported as a document in the classical sense (see Viewpoints in [Somm98]). The model has additional structures for the modelling of dependencies.

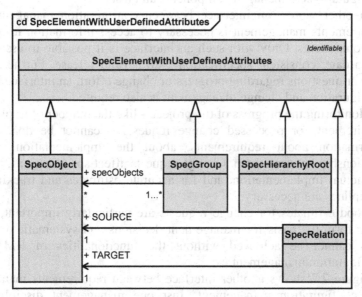

Figure 7.6: RIF model, specifcation relations

Figure 7.6 contains a schema that allows the creation of relationships between instances of SpecObject through the SpecRelation entity. As a SpecRelation has a source and a target, the relationship is directional.

RIF provides all necessary data models to represent requirement objects and their relationships, as well as the ability to export this data in a defined format. Tools in configuration management could then be used to archive requirements data, thereby applying the techniques of configuration management to this data.

7.4   Traceability in Requirement Management and Configuration Management

This Chapter opened with a number of reoccurring questions in the field of requirement management. How, for instance, can configurations and dependencies be managed, if they contain requirement specifications, test specifications, design documents, and implementation files?

Requirements management can and must cover all these, as it deals with the whole chain from customer requirements to system requirements, design models, component requirements all the way to test specifications, including their dependencies. Implementations can be included as well, but to achieve this, they have to be put in relation to everything from system configurations to managed components and tests.

In other words, an interface between configuration management and requirements management is necessary to access information in regard to all components. Only with such an interface is it possible to associate an up to date, consistent specification with a valid release. Furthermore, to answer questions regarding progress or change effort, an interface between configuration and change management is also required.

Monitoring the progress of the project – like the number of implemented requirements or processed change requests – cannot be done without information about requirements, about the implementation, and the relationship between them. Change requests affect specifications, tests and the actual implementation, and for accurate estimates and tracking, both disciplines are necessary.

Good estimates for change requests are particularly important, as they often form the basis for management decisions and systematic execution. This cannot be achieved without the functionalities of RM&E and configuration management.

Figure 7.7 shows another interface between requirements management and configuration management. Just one management discipline isn't enough to answer all these questions. The cited goals and challenges can only be fulfilled by skilled use of requirements management and version, configuration and change management, respectively. But the interlocking of the contributing processes must be planned and structured properly to take advantage of the synergies. Tool support, especially regarding the interfaces between processes, is advisable, particularly for complex projects.

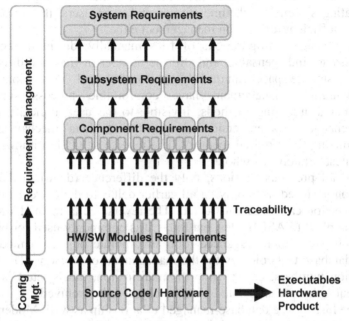

Figure 7.7: Traceability

7.5   Tool Use for Version and Configuration Management

A fundamental requirement for a version management system is the assignment of a unique identifier to each state of each configuration unit. This can even be done manually on a file system, for instance by including the relevant meta data (date, time, release state, editor) in the file name, for example: KM_Kolleg_20050505_1715_Keller_1.0.doc.

For each additional state, a copy of the file is stored with an updated time stamp. This simple scheme can be useful for documents, but fails for source code and all other files where cross-reference between file names exist. This could be fixed by moving the meta data into the files. But then the old files have to be backed up in some way to prevent overwriting. Another method is to copy each file with the time and date stamp to create a file with a general name.

This is sometimes done automatically when using a MAKE file for instance to ensure that the most up-to-date files are used to create an executable code. Another option would be to keep separate text files listing each managed file with their history. This, however, would be even more error prone than the other processes (if done manually). While some operating systems track time stamps and even users, this information is rarely sufficient for version management either.

To manage configurations of files manually, discipline and a good process are indispensable, and still the number of files and directories, as well as storage space, can quickly get out of control. Professional tools for configuration management have comfortable process support and automated archiving methods. Invisible to the user, typically they store only changes between versions using a "reverse delta" mechanism, thereby minimizing the required memory. The reverse delta algorithm stores only the latest version as a whole.

For all previous versions, only the difference (delta) to the previous version is stored. By applying all earlier deltas to the current version, any past version can be reconstructed. The reverse delta method was initially only applied to ASCII files, but today it is commonly used for binary files as well. Even more advanced tools incorporate object oriented concepts and database technologies for the management of versions. The meta data (version numbers, editor, time of modification, labels, etc.) is stored in attributes that are associated with the object to be archived.

The history is a database-managed relationship as well. Modern systems allow the storage of multiple, uniquely identified configurations without having to duplicate equal elements that happen to occur in multiple configurations. The tools also provide access control. For instance, concurrent edits on the same element may not be allowed, or the tool provides mechanisms for controlled merging. Complex projects should not be run without proper tool support in configuration management: "Modern software configuration management will contribute considerably to the success of a project - if applied correctly.

It will structure the software development and test processes, spanning the whole lifecycle to make everything predictable and traceable. Monitoring of well-defined releases is ensured, too. It aids the unambiguous definition of various configurations, both for the system and its documentation. Changes are always traceable and verifiable, when, who, what and on who's behalf the system was changed" [Kreu2004].

7.5.1 Solution Concept:Traceability in Practice

The following example will demonstrate how configuration management and traceability can be realized beyond the boundaries set by tools. Some tools allow the creation of placeholders – elements that are managed by a different tool. Telelogic DOORS®, for instance, allows the creation of placeholder (surrogate) modules that contain elements that are archived by a different tool, Telelogic Synergy™, Synergy, or Serena® PVCS® for instance.

With this configuration, a relationship between source code and requirements can be established and managed. Within DOORS, source code can now be managed inside of the surrogate Modules with additional metadata. From here, it can be linked to requirements, which establishes the traceability within the requirements management tool.

For every source code file and every version a placeholder object exists in the RM tool. Requirements, test cases and so on can have relations to these objects. For this to be useful, the tools must be synchronized on a regular basis.

Test specifications with their different versions can be archived even more comfortably by using a configuration management tool. Data can be exchanged via an API, COM interface (on Microsoft Windows), or via command line tools.

But requirements management tools like DOORS offer the option to archive test specifications and test results as well. If the artifacts from testing are stored in the requirements management tool, the test coverage of the system can be traced easier than otherwise.

Realistically, which test results should be archived? Certainly the results of system tests should be archived. It can be counterproductive to store all results of automated unit tests unless you can handle the large amounts of data effectively. If the results of a test are not important enough to store, you should question why you are performing the test.

7.6 Summary

Requirement management can be interpreted as a collection of interfaces to process areas, where the process for defining requirements forms the core [Hood2005]. These interfaces can be the starting point for an analysis, and in this chapter, we analyzed the process areas version management, configuration management, and their relationship to RM&E.

In the following figure we have chosen to place requirements definition in the centre, to show the interfaces between systems engineering disciplines and requirements development. The sum of these interfaces describes requirements management. The following figure visualizes the idea that requirements management can be interpreted as a collection of interfaces to process areas.

The process area of change and configuration management consists of the management of versions, configurations, variants and changes. To provide a foundation for further discussion, a number of key terms in configuration management were defined in this chapter.

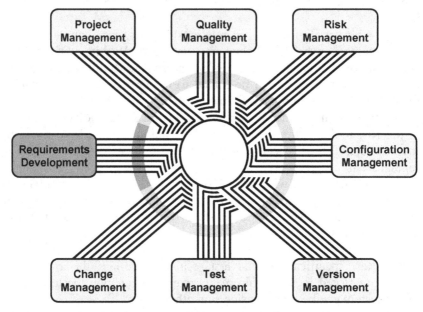

Figure 7.8: Requirementsmanagement interfaces

The RIF model provides a foundation for the management of requirements as data and data structures (rather than documents). The RM&E data model incorporates ideas and developments in configuration management. In other words, elements in RM&E are complex and so are their relationships. This complexity suggests the use of version and configuration management, to allow the recreation of earlier configurations of requirements. This is essential for proper requirements management. RIF provides the data models required for a well-defined representation of requirement objects and their relationships, which allows for their export.

An interface between requirements and configuration management is necessary to capture information regarding components that are affected by requirements management and implementation components . Configurations that not only contain specifications, tests and design documents, but also software code, can only be managed when the disciplines of requirements and configuration management are brought together. In order to cover the whole traceability chain from customer requirements to system requirements, design models, component requirements all the way to implementation (e.g. software code) and test specification. This can only be achieved with an interface between requirements management and configuration management. Systematic project monitoring and accurate change request management is only possible if requirements, version, configuration and change management are skilfully applied together. To take advantage of the resulting synergies, the interlocking of the participating processes must be planed carefully and implemented in a structured manner. In complex projects, it is highly advisable to also have tools that support the interfaces between processes.

8   Metrics and Analysis

One of the subject areas in both CMMI and SPiCE is the improvement of requirements management (or requirements management & engineering). Consequently, companies often initiate projects for introducing a standard methodology. Hence the progress of work in a project to create a system and also a project to improve a process are both of interest. This chapter describes, among other things, how both can be measured.

8.1   Metrics – general

Metric comes from Greek meaning "census or measurement". The word metric is often used within the context of measuring processes. The term has several definitions within software engineering.

The IEEE Standard 1061 describes a metric as follows:
"A software quality metric is a function that describes a software unit numerically. The value calculated can be interpreted as the degree to which quality attributes of the software unit are fulfilled."

Another definition comes from Ian Sommerville. This is:
"A software metric is any kind of measurement that relates to a software system, a process or to the corresponding documentation."

In this chapter, which is about how metrics should be used in the area of requirements management & engineering, these definitions can only be applied with difficulty. Therefore a metric can be defined here as follows:
"A metric measures the quality of results. This is achieved by defining measurement criteria and procedures by which means the degree of fulfilment of predefined goals in requirements management & engineering can be determined."

8.2   The Importance of Metrics

Measurement is a very important part of quality assurance. Here results should be measured in order to form the basis for a decision as to whether the quality standards have been met.

Measurement includes defining a benchmark by which the results are measured. Since a benchmark changes (or should change) only very rarely, this succeeds in producing a relatively "objective" evaluation of the results. Metrics are ideally the basis for drawing conclusions as to the quality of the results, and for determining what improvements are to be initiated. If no measurement is made, it can only be guessed what the results of the work are like.

J.C.Maxwell expressed this very well with the phrase "To measure is to know".

Tom de Marco articulates this point somewhat more forcefully: "You can't control what you can't measure"

Metrics are the fundamental basis for all controlling and management bodies. Whether for the classic finance department, when measuring financials and liquidity, cash flow and balance sheet totals; or the management board deciding on company strategy. Another technical example is a sensor in a vehicle, which measures the distance from the vehicle behind when parking; and by which the driver, on the basis of an acoustic tone or light signal, decides whether there is enough space.

Measurement is also of key importance in modern quality management. Hence, in terms of a continual improvement process, it is necessary to evaluate results, identify defects, and to define and implement actions for improvement. The Deming Circle is a classic example for this:

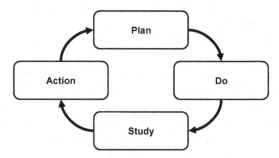

Figure 8.1: Deming Circle

For the evaluation of current results, and evidence as to the success of improvement measures, one or more metrics are required.

8.3   Attributes of Metrics

An important point is that only a part or one aspect of reality can ever be measured with a single metric. Controlling and management bodies must always be aware of this fact, in order to be able to make "correct" decisions. If the turnover of a company increases dramatically during one quarter, this metric has a completely different meaning in conjunction with another metric showing a decline in profits during the same period.

For example the effects of a discount promotion can generate significantly higher turnover. The profit margin will however at the same time be reduced so that, in the worst case, the additional turnover does not bring any increase in profits.

The values of the individual metrics are therefore normally insufficient to be able to make well-founded judgements. For this reason, metrics must be carefully selected and their attributes must be described.

Metric attributes could be the following:

- Goals supported by the metric
- Customers of the metric
- Interval of measurement
- Data or measurements used
- Unit of measurement
- Data source (Effort required to capture/reliability)
- Interpretation of results
- Strengths and weaknesses of the metric
- Prerequisites for measurement
- Presentation format of the metric

The following is a more detailed description of the individual attributes. Controlling and management bodies should be aware of each of these attributes, in order to be able to evaluate the importance of the metric.

8.3.1   Goals Supported by the Metric

When metrics are implemented for the first time in an organisation there is always a danger that too many metrics are generated, and that one loses sight of the actual objectives of a metric. Each measurement requires effort and therefore also costs money.

Consequently, when defining a new metric, it's essential to describe the goal that is to be measured as having been fulfilled.

Conversely, where no objective can be determined for a metric, it also does not make sense to define the metric.

8.3.2   Customers of the Metric

The customer of the metric is the controlling or management body, which on the basis of the metric defined, is able to intervene. As a rule this is management, which can get an idea as to the extent to which a goal has been achieved on the basis of the metrics.

Management can then also make decisions based on the results. The customer of the metric is thus a forum that can also influence the processes and methodology.

8.3.3   Interval of Measurement

The time interval in which a measurement should be undertaken is given here. An important factor surrounding this interval is the cost or effort required for measurement. A second factor is the change that can be expected between the measurements.

Generally, metrics that are implemented on the basis of reviews are significantly more time and cost intensive to implement than "automatic" measurements, which are made on the basis of an existing database. Reviews require a certain amount of preparation and follow-up work, so that a short interval makes little commercial sense.

In the case of automatic analysis of a database and automatic processing the effort is normally not so high, so that it can be worthwhile measuring in shorter intervals.

8.3.4   Measurements Used

What is to be measured should be described here. This could, for example, be a head count, the number of requirements with a particular status, or the number of discrepancies in a review.

8.3.5   Unit of Measurement

The unit of measurement is described here. This can for example be a percentage or perhaps the effort (in man days).

8.3.6   Data Source (Effort required to capture /reliability)

The data source should be described here, e.g. is it a database, review audits or training lists? Here it is important to indicate what level of effort is required to capture the data and whether this data is reliable. Thus in some circumstances it does not make any sense to conduct analysis, knowing that a database used for the analysis is only sporadically maintained.

8.3.7 Interpretation of Results

This attribute is very important in order to provide the controlling and management bodies with assistance in interpreting the analysis. This section attempts to describe how the analysis, in relation to the degree to which goals have been achieved, is to be interpreted.

8.3.8 Strengths and Weaknesses of the Metric

Because a metric can, as a rule, only describe a part of the reality, it also has weaknesses. Thus a purely statistical analysis can, without knowledge of the weaknesses, produce a "false picture" of reality. In some circumstances the reality is only clearly described in combination with other metrics.

For this reason in particular, knowledge of possible weaknesses is so important for control and management.

The strengths of a metric can equally be described here. A strength can be, for example, that it can be produced very quickly as required without a large amount of effort.

Knowledge about strengths and weaknesses is also a basis for deciding whether the metric should be used at all.

8.3.9 Prerequisites for Measurement

This attribute describes the prerequisites for a measurement making sense at all. For example, it is necessary for the data on which the measurement is based to be up-to-date, or at least regularly maintained.

8.3.10 Presentation Format for the Metric

The presentation format for the metric is described here. Normally but not necessarily, this is one or more graphics in which the analysis is presented visually.

8.4   Typical Improvement Goals with RM&E

The focus in this book is on projects that are aimed at improving requirements management & engineering within an organisation. It is therefore important for both the customer and consultants to be able to measure the success (or level of achievement) when introducing structured requirements management & engineering. To then be able to produce one or more metrics, it is important first of all to identify the goals of the organisation, or of the improvement in requirements management.

For example, there are company goals from which requirements management goals can be derived. These are goals related to quality management goals, like reaching a particular level in CMMI or SPiCE. Some typical goals are described below:

8.4.1   Reduction in Change Costs

A reduction in change costs is the main goal of introducing structured requirements management. Change costs are incurred where there are variations to an original project plan. The reasons for these variations can be, for example; that the resource situation has changed; the deadline has been altered, the market situation has changed in respect of a product development; or that errors, gaps, inconsistencies and misunderstandings are discovered.

The cost of changes generated by mistakes, gaps, inconsistencies and unclear documentation of requirements can be reduced, if these are recognised early in the development process. Structured requirements management helps in this respect.

However in practice, being able to measure the reduction in costs as a result of implementing structured requirements management, leads to several difficulties.

To be able to prove a reduction in change costs, it must first be ascertained what mistakes, gaps and inconsistencies in the respective requirements documentation there may have been in a previous project. In some organisational cultures, the then responsible project manager might not be particularly enthusiastic about additional costs being calculated from "avoidable" flawed specifications.

But when, for the reasons given above, no previous project can be considered and we restrict ourselves to the current project, it will be difficult to measure what effects a gap, discrepancy or error in the project discovered through the timely implementation of RM&E methodology would have had.

Thus a metric, which directly attempts to measure the main goal of the introducing RM&E methodology, namely the reduction in change costs, might be difficult to apply in practice. If the organisational culture is open and sees previous mistakes as an opportunity to improve, there will be little difficulty with measurement and publication of metrics.

8.4.2 Reaching CMMI Level 3 in an Assessment

This goal is generally aimed for because the customer organisation demands proof of a certain level when selecting their suppliers. Therefore this goal is extremely important for a company, to ensure that it is not excluded by these customers before even producing the offer.

In the context of reaching the appropriate level, it is very important for a supplier organisation to implement structured requirements management.

A prerequisite for Level 2 of the CMMI model is that requirements are managed and inconsistencies with the project plan and results are identified.(see Capability Maturity Model ® Integration (CMMI SM), Version 1.1 (Staged Representation)).

Requirements must be developed for Level 3 of the CMMI model. Thus stakeholder requirements must be elicited and collected. These must in turn be translated into product requirements.

8.4.3 Reaching a Specific SPiCE Level in an Assessment

SPiCE is a similar model to the CMMI model and one which some companies choose to use. As with the CMMI model, various levels are defined, which describe the level of maturity of the organisation in implementing and defining company processes. Requirements management plays a role in the following categories in the SPiCE model:

- CUS.1.1   Identify the need.
- CUS.1.2   Define the requirements.
- CUS.3.1   Obtain customer requirements and requests.
- CUS.3.2   Understand customer expectations.
- ENG.1.1   Specify system requirements.
- ENG.1.2   Describe system architecture.
- ENG.1.3   Allocate requirements.
- ENG.2.1   Determine software requirements.
- ENG.2.2   Analyze software requirements.
- ENG.2.3   Determine operating environment impact.
- ENG.2.4   Evaluate requirements with customer.

- ENG.2.5   Update requirements for next iteration.
- PRO.4.1   Agree on requirements.
- PRO.4.2   Establish customer requirements baseline.
- PRO.4.3   Manage customer requirements changes.
- PRO.4.4   Use customer requirements.
- PRO.4.5   Maintain traceability.

The following goals can be derived in the context of the above goals:

8.4.4 Introducing and Establishing RM&E Methodology in Pilot Projects

The focus here is on evaluating the introduction of predefined RM&E methodology. Thus pilot projects are designated, in which methodology is to be applied in the context of a concrete RM&E project. Employees are generally sceptical towards changes in the way they work.

It is therefore very prudent to first of all implement the changes in one or more pilot projects. The advantages are obvious. Firstly, the pilot projects can be managed very intensively by a limited number of consultants. Secondly, as a rule, adjustments to the methodology are necessary depending on company circumstances; and these are better implemented in intensively managed pilot projects.

8.4.5 Creating Basic Know-How in RM&E Amongst Employees

Here the objective is to make employees capable of using RM&E methodology in their projects.

Usually this is initially done in the form of general RM&E training sessions. As a rule, these training sessions are not sufficient, but necessary to achieve a basic understanding of RM&E methodology.

Another possibility is to brief employees on the job and thus implement knowledge transfer. This way of creating a basic level of know-how is however very time-consuming, so that this kind of know-how transfer seldom happens.

8.4.6 Improving the Quality of an RM&E Process

Business processes are dependent on several factors that are very organisation specific. These factors are, among other things, existing organisational structures, employee skills, available tools (e.g. software) for supporting the processes and company goals. Thus in every organisation there is always an RM&E process. The question is whether it is structured, documented and reproducible, and of course what results the process delivers.

Evaluating business processes alone, in respect of their quality, can then only succeed where we keep other factors (staff/ tools / etc.) constant; and only change the process flow. Next the results must then be measured before and after the change to the process flow.

Incidentally, measurements should not just be made immediately after the change. Process start-up and changeover problems alone can lead to deteriorations in the results, which are then later put into perspective.

8.4.7 Improving Customer and Supplier Specifications

The question here is how the quality of customer and supplier specifications can be measured. For example, there are quality criteria for both the overall specification and for individual requirements.
Quality criteria for an overall specification include:

- completeness
- consistency
- necessity
- free of duplication

Quality criteria for a requirement include:

- complete
- free of contradiction
- unambiguous
- feasible
- understandable
- testable
- identifiable
- atomic
- free of duplication
- correctly derived
- traceable to source

Generally these criteria can only be measured through reviews. There is also an approach implementing automatic measurement based on counting the so called weak-words. This has the advantage that it can be automated but it can also be counterproductive. (See Section 8.7)

8.5   Example of a Metric

The following shows how a metric is defined based on the example "Creating a basic level of know-how in RM&E amongst employees". The metric is used by a car manufacturer who wishes to train a large number of engineers in the use of RM&E methodology. In this case, an RM&E project manager, reporting to an RM&E steering committee, is responsible for the success of the project.

8.5.1   Creating a basic level of know-how in RM&E amongst staff

8.5.1.1   *Goals supported by the metric*

- Precise requirements for the contractor
- Early discovery and prevention of errors and inconsistencies in requirements
- Traceability of the effects of changes in requirements as far as the supplier specification.

8.5.1.2   *Customers for the metric*

- RM&E project managers
- RM&E steering committee

8.5.1.3   *Interval of measurement*

- Monthly

8.5.1.4   *Data used*

- Total number of people who should have taken part in training up to the end of 2005.
- Number of people who have taken part in training (RM&E Methodology Training or Introduction to DOORS) up to time of measurement.
- Date of taking part in training for each person

8.5.1.5   Measurements used

- Number of people who have taken part in RM&E training vs. those who, according to the plan, should have taken part.

8.5.1.6   Data source (effort required for capture /reliability)

- Forecast data from departments responsible
- Attendance lists for the respective training sessions
- Effort to obtain: moderate (with attendance lists)
- Reliability of the data: very high

8.5.1.7   Interpretation of results

- Training is the basis by which the defined RM&E methodology can be implemented.
- The earlier in the project people participate in training, the sooner they will be able to work according to the defined RM&E methodology.
- The fewer people trained during the project, the higher the risk:
- Individual coaching requirements of the engineers increases so RM&E specialists are fully occupied with support tasks

8.5.1.8   Strengths of the metric

- Objective measurement of the number of people participating in RM&E training during the period is possible
- Early indication of problems in implementing RM&E methodology possible.
- Indication as to the level of employee or section leader acceptance in respect of the introduction of RM&E methodology

8.5.1.9   Weaknesses of the metric

- Participation in the training does not allow any assessment as to the ability to implement RM&E methodology in the work place.

8.5.1.10   Prerequisites for measurement

- Forecasts of employees to be trained are made available by the departments responsible.

8.5.1.11 Presentation format for the metric

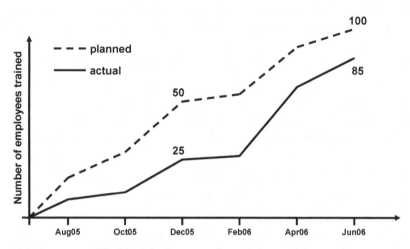

Figure 8.2: Presentation of the metric
"Creating a basic level of know-how in RM&E amongst employees"

8.6   The Evaluation of a Metric by Management

A metric is not an end in itself, but is produced as a guideline for management and provides a basis for decisions, in order to continually improve work processes and to be able to evaluate the effects of decisions.

Often the data for the metric is used as a sole basis for decisions. This can however lead to fatal misinterpretations because the following is not taken into account: A metric can normally only measure one aspect of reality.

In the above example, both the number of people participating in the training and the forecast figures are presented. When the chart is very close to the forecast chart, this implies that up to June 2006, almost all planned participants had actually participated in the training. At first glance, everything is in order. However, what the graphic does not reveal is that, up until June 2006, not all departments had submitted their forecasts as requested.

This aspect of the completeness of the forecast is not captured by this metric. When analysing metrics it is therefore very sensible to scrutinise the data collected, in order to find out about the metric's weaknesses. Management should therefore carefully read the attributes of the defined metric before making decisions, particularly "interpretation of the results" and "strengths and weaknesses of the metric".

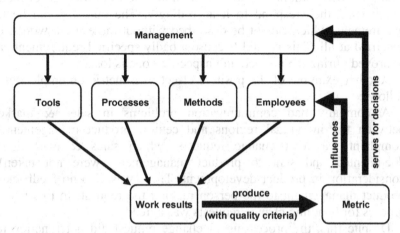

Figure 8.3: Relationship of the metric to management, results and employees

8.7 Psychological Aspects of Introducing RM&E Metrics

The previous section described the purpose of a metric as being to provide management with a basis for making decisions in respect of improving processes, methodology and tools. Another aspect of metrics is that employees, whether intentionally or unintentionally, are influenced by the measurement itself. That is providing the employees know about the measurement.

This influence can have both positive and negative effects. The positive effects are that agreed change processes are executed more quickly because their implementation is measured. A negative effect can be that the employees also recognise the limitations of a metric and then consequently exploit them.

The following example helps to explain this: A metric can be defined that counts the number of so called weak words that appear in a specification. Weak words are words that are good places to start to improve a   specification because the weak words do not describe the requirement explicitly enough. These are words like preferably, fast, automatically, cyclical...

At first glance, there is the possibility to count the number of weak words in a specification in order to be able to make an assessment about its quality. When authors of a specification are aware of this sort of metric, it can be that they respond to it accordingly. The outcome can be that a requirement, which cannot be described without these weak words, is not specified at all. This is fatal because a badly specified requirement can be improved during the project; an unspecified one is lost.

Another example of the positive effect of a metric on employees is as follows:

A company had communication problems in sales & marketing, between the individual regions and central product management. The complaint was that change requests, which sales & marketing had documented and sent to product management, were not taken into consideration in product development. There was also no feedback from product management to the person making the request. In this respect, a process for handling change requests was agreed.

Despite this, the processing of change request did not function to the satisfaction of sales & marketing. As a result, a metric was introduced that captured how many change requests were not processed or for which no feedback was given to the sales region (open requests). This was introduced for three different product lines. The result is shown in the following graph:

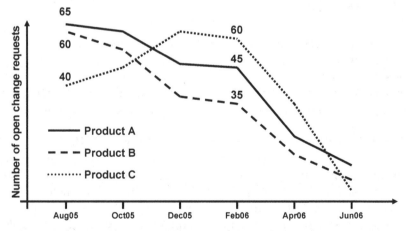

Figure 8.4: Metric "processing of change requests"

The interesting thing about the graph is that the number of change requests classified as "open" hardly changed between December 05 and February 06. This figure actually increased slightly for all three product lines. From February 06, the number of "open requests" fell dramatically.

What had happened? At the beginning December 05, a metric was approved to measure the number of open requests. The results of the metric were presented to top management sometime in January 06. Product managers responded accordingly and seemingly explicitly accepted the open change requests, which resulted in a rapid fall in these requests.

This fact alone may however, despite everything, not be sufficient to be able to make a statement as to whether the regions were happy with the processing of their change requests. After all the metric only measures whether the status of the change request has been altered from "open" to "closed". In conjunction with another metric, the number of newly made change requests, we can however draw further conclusions.

The number of newly made change requests is measured by the following metric.

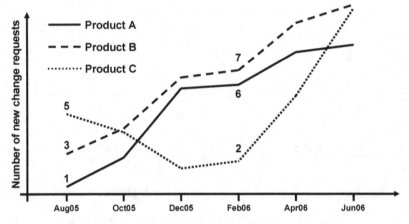

Figure 8.5: Metric "incoming change requests"

Here it is possible to see that, between February and the middle of March, the number of incoming change requests was constant. The number for all three product lines then increases rapidly from April. Evidently the sales regions were so motivated by the feedback from product managers, that they submitted more change requests. In this example the positive effects of metrics are apparent.

8.8 Summary

In summary, we can say that metrics are essential management tools and essential for motivation when implementing change processes.

When creating metrics, care must be taken to make sure that they are aligned to company goals.

When analyzing the results from metrics, it should always be remembered that a metric can only ever measure one aspect of reality; and therefore every metric has it weaknesses. Management should not make decisions based purely on the figures from a metric. A metric can only give an indication of possible problems and make management aware of potential mistakes early on. It is therefore always advisable to examine these indications in more detail, before taking management action.

Last but not least, the psychological effects of introducing a metric should not be ignored. Employees respond to metrics. When designing metrics, this can be used in a positive way.

9 Risk Management interface

One of the most important tasks of project management is the prediction of any circumstances that may be detrimental to the project in view of planning and scheduling, in view of the quality or in view of the development costs. The identification of possible risks and the definition of suitable countermeasures to minimise their impact on the project is usually called risk management ([Hall1998, Ould1999]). Risk management makes sure that all information related to risks is properly documented and accessible to the relevant project members.

9.1 What is a risk

In principle, a risk can be thought of as being a circumstance with a significant negative effect on the project, and which may or may not occur. As risks may threaten the project, the product to be developed or the organisation that carries out the development, [Somm2001] suggests to classify risks as follows:

- project risks: these are risks which may affect the project schedule or resources
- product risks: these are risks which may affect the quality or performance of the product being developed
- business risks: these are risks which may affect the organisation developing or procuring the product

This classification appears problematic, as the three categories are usually too intertwined to allow for the definition of clear-cut boundaries. [Somm2001] also points out that this is not an exclusive classification, for it is possible to think of risks that may affect the project as well as the product and the organisation.

In the following, we will therefore not use the above classification. Instead, we will give an example list of possible categories to classify the risks in chapter 9.3.

9.2   What is Risk Management

Risk management may be seen as being a part of project management or as being an independent project discipline in systems engineering. Risk management will, in some form or other, usually cover the following activities:

- identification of risks
- assessment of risks
- definition of countermeasures
- monitoring of risks

These activities together can be seen as representing a risk management process. A simple example risk management process is shown in the following figure 9.1, and this process will be described in detail in the following sections.

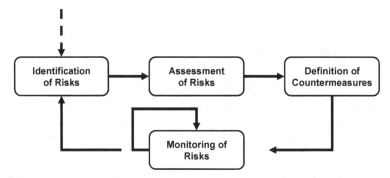

Figure 9.1: Simple example risk management process

Before the risk management process can be applied, it must be tailored to the needs of the current project and the organisation that carries out the project. In other words, the risk management needs some preparation.

9.3   Preparing a Risk Management

For every project there should be an individual preparation of the risk management process. One can think of many things to define before starting a risk management process for a project at hand, but at least the following activities should be carried out before starting the risk management process:

- define which information should be documented for risks and countermeasures
- define criteria for categorising risks and assessment of risks
- define risk management strategy

These activities set a scope for the risk management to be applied and thus make sure that the risk management related activities of all people involved will aim at the same direction.

The following list is a suggestion for a set of information (attributes) that can be documented for risks:

- identifier (ID)
- description
- short name
- probability of occurrence
- impact
- reason
- relevance with respect to time
- category
- author
- person responsible
- possible countermeasures

This list is just an example and a suggestion of how to get started. It is in no way complete.

Since risks are closely related to the corresponding countermeasures, these too have to be defined with respect to the information that should be gathered and documented. This definition should also take place before the risk management process is started. For the countermeasures we also give a typical list of valuable information (attributes):

- identifier (ID)
- kind (proactive / reactive)
- description
- estimated costs
- person responsible
- addressed risk
- probability of occurrence of risk after countermeasure was carried out
- impact of risk after countermeasure was carried out
- description of risk after countermeasure was carried out

Like the list of attributes for risks, this list of attributes for countermeasures serves as an example and is not complete. With these two example lists of information related to risks and countermeasures, we can proceed with the second preparing activity as listed above, the definition of criteria to categorise and assess risks. There are various reasons why it may prove desireable to categorise the risks. For example, it is quite common that there are different specialists for different fields of risk. Thus a controller may check the available data for financial risks only, while some engineers may check only for technical risks.

Another reason for categorising risks could be that the different kinds of risk are weighed differently in an organisation. For example, in the medical industry risks to the user (patient) may be weighed much more important than risks with regard to the time schedule.

The following list gives an initial idea of how risks could be categorised. Again, the list is not complete.

- financial risks
- risks with regard to time schedule
- technical risks
- organisational risks
- human risks
- stakeholder related risks
- process risks
- product risks

The assessment of risks helps in prioritising the risks. The risks are evaluated and can subsequently be put into an order of significance. The assessment of risks is usually carried out using the following two dimensions:

- probability of occurrence
- impact

After the information that should be elicited and documented with regard to risks and countermeasures is agreed and after the definition of the criteria to categorise and assess risks, the third activity as listed above can be carried out. The definition of a risk management strategy can be given for all risks or for each individual risk.

For example, an organisation may choose to address all risks in the same manner, or to address each individual risk in the manner that appears most promising.

A typical list of risks management strategies is given as follows:

- risk avoidance
- risk transfer
- risk minimising

- risk acceptance
- risk resolution

Risk avoidance is the strategy of making sure that the situation that gives rise to the risk cannot occur at all. For example, risks can be avoided by renouncing a deal or by abandoning a business area.

Risk transfer is the strategy of trying to ensure that if a detrimental situation actually occurs, other people or organisations will have to deal with it. A typical case of risk transfer are insurances, which get paid for taking the risks of others. Another example for risk transfer is the attempt to pass a risk on to a business partner or to even pass it back to the customer. In this sense risk transfer is also a means of risk avoidance.

A risk minimising strategy sees to it that the probability of occurrence of a risk is minimal. Examples for risk minimising are proactive countermeasures that are applied before a risk occurs, like choosing only skilled staff for a project or using a safety factor in all financial calculations.

Risk acceptance is the strategy of basically trying to "live with the risk". Quite often, special compensations go hand in hand with that strategy. For example, stuntmen in Hollywood movies may be paid almost as much as the main actors for a very short shot. This is because the risk is totally with the stuntmen and if something goes wrong, there is basically nothing that can be done.

A risk resolution strategy aims at creating a surrounding in which the risk no longer exists. For example, the risk of outdated development equipment could be resolved by buying new computer hardware and software. As sometimes a risk cannot be resolved completely but only partially, risk resolution may be seen as a special case of risk minimising.

The above list of different risk management strategies is not complete. It is quite common to initially start with the risk management strategy that appears most reasonable at the beginning and later change it, according to current needs of the projects and the available information and data.

But whatever the current strategy is, it is most important that it is documented and known to all relevant people.

9.4   The Risk Management process

A basic risk management process can be built from the activities listed in section 9.2. Before we go into details of each activity it is important to understand that the risk management process, as all other processes described in this book, is iterative.

We will therefore not have only one run through the activities. Risk management is a process that lasts as long as the project itself, from drawing the first draft project plans and eliciting the first requirements to finally disposing of the developed system.

This means that risk management starts with an initial identification and assessment of anticipated risks, possible effects and suitable countermeasures. The risks are then monitored until new information becomes available and new situations arise that alter the foundation for the initial judgements. When this happens, more risks may be identified and the risks are re-analysed, their impact on the project are re-estimated and the countermeasures are re-defined to fit the new information.

It goes without saying that all the information produced by risk management should be properly documented and made accessible to all those who may be affected by these risks. In some organisations this will give an independent risk management plan, while in others this may be a part of the project management plan.

9.4.1 Risk identification and how Requirements Management can support

The first activity in the risk management process as outlined above is the identification of possible risks. There are many risks that may exist in a wide range of businesses and thus have a universal character, for example a tight project schedule.

However, there might also be risks that are very subtle and thus harder to spot. An example of this is the risk that a system to be developed will be outdated by the time it is ready to use. Although for many developments this is probably a very small risk, for some industries this risk is quite real. Consider for example the automobile industry, which will be faced with the necessity to change from internal combustion engines to electric or fuel cell or other engines independent of gasoline in the near future. In this situation, there will come a time when it will no longer pay off to start any new developments related to combustion engines, and it will be interesting to see when this point of time will be reached or will be thought to have been reached.

The identification of risks can be facilitated in a number of different ways:

- brainstorming sessions
- personal experience
- standardised lists of common risks
- ...

The results of using brainstorming sessions, personal experience and the like are very much dependent on individual skills such as imagination and memory. This means that if these skills are not very prominent amongst the project members, the risk identification may not be very satisfying. On the other hand, a few talented people may identify more risks than were ever anticipated before within an organisation. In this connection it is interesting to note that people who are not working in the field or are not specialists might be able to provide most valuable input to risk identification, for their views are not clouded by real or would-be experience and cynicism.

Requirements management can support these subjective methods by providing the data created in the requirements engineering process. Like many other kinds of information, information on risks can be elicited with the methods as described in detail in chapter 4. For example, (mis-) use cases and (worst case) scenarios may be used to try and anticipate very different situations that can cause the project to fail, see figure 9.2.

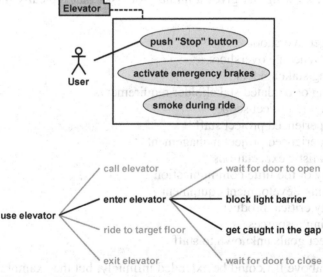

Figure 9.2: Example misuse case and accident scenario

It is important to note that usually information on possible risks – and many other valuable information – inevitably emerges in the course of requirements engineering and elicitation, even if this information is not explicitly being asked for. It is therefore mandatory to document all these pieces of information independent of whether these are directly related to the topic at hand or not. Our experience shows that all these bits of information will prove valuable sometime, and as they are offered on a plate, they should not be rejected. In this connection it may be interesting to the reader that quite frequently a requirements elicitation session will give only little information on what was defined as the actual topic, but a lot of otherwise interesting information. Thus it may happen that although many elicitation sessions might initially be called unsuccessful in a project, all necessary information is collected and documented, and the project turns out to be quite successful.

Another kind of facilitating elicitation of risks relies more on the documented and trustworthy experience of the organisation than on personal experience and imagination. Thus one of the most obvious sources for risk identification will be the lists of risks identified by past projects. Some of these risks will turn out to be similar and to occur in the majority of the relevant past projects. These can form the core of checklists and standards to be used within an organisation and thus this information is related to and valuable for the organisation's quality management as described in chapter 6.7.

The following list gives a number of risks that typically threaten every project:

- budget overshoot
- time schedule overshoot
- wrong stakeholders
- wrong or outdated stakeholder requirements
- changing project scope
- inexperienced project staff
- inexperienced project management
- unrealistic expectations
- faulty or too little communication
- missing development equipment
- safety critical product
- lacking resources
- project goals unknown to staff

The above list could be extended infinitely, but the example may suffice to give an impression of what a template risk list could look like in a specific organisation.

If risks are covered by requirements management, the information from past projects is readily available to all other projects and can be shared throughout the organisation. If risks are handled independent from requirements, there may still be some link between the requirements and the information on risks, and this link can be provided by requirements management so that the information is still accessible. These two situations are depicted in figure 9.3.

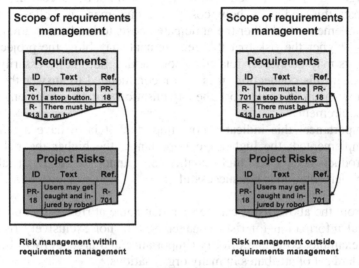

Figure 9.3: Availability of risk information in various project constellations

If the risks are not covered by requirements management, if there is no link between the requirements and the risks, and if the information on risks from old projects can not be accessed, the information must be considered lost for any following projects.

Another important contribution of requirements management to risk identification is to provide the data and information stemming from the requirements definition process. It was shown in the previous chapters that requirements are complete only if they have documented attributes. Thus typical attributes for requirements are "owner", "accepted", "implementation status" and so on.

To make the information related to the requirements most valuable for the risk management, it is recommended to define a corresponding set of attributes for the requirements engineering process as early as possible. The following is a list of typical attributes for requirements that may provide valuable information for risk management:

- volatility: this indicates how often a requirement changes; repeated changes may indicate that there is a lot of discussion regarding a requirement and this can indicate a project "hot spot" that should be monitored

- complexity: this indicates how complex the requirement is believed to be to implement; the more complex a requirement is to implement, the higher the risk that the implementation will not be successful
- cost: this indicates how costly a requirement is believed to be to implement; the higher the anticipated costs to implement a requirement, the higher the risk that this requirement may blow the project budget; costs may be closely related to complexity, but not necessarily so; note that in this connection, it is also recommended to answer the question how much it could cost the organisation *not* to implement a certain requirement
- importance: this indicates how important it is to have a requirement implemented; the higher the importance, the higher the risk that the product is not of high quality or cannot be used at all if the implementation is not successful

From the above list it can be seen that some attributes that provide very useful information for risk management are not exclusively risk related. For example, costs and priority (importance and urgency) will belong to a standard set of attributes in many organisations.

Like every other activity of requirements management, the definition of the attributes to support risk management should be carried out with common sense. This means that only one risk attribute may not suffice for monitoring and managing risks in connection with requirements. By contrast, five or even ten risk attributes are very likely not to be filled in by the developers as this would take too much time.

If all the requirements are risk attributed this will give a good overview of possible project risks in connection with the requirements. Note however that there may be more risks that have their origin outside the product requirements. Examples of such risks that may not be covered by requirements management are availability of key staff and product competition (unless of course, the key staff availability requirement or the competition requirement has been documented).

Apart from risk attributes, requirements management directly offers the development information. Thus the requirements text itself can be checked for any possible risks. This check should be carried out using the list with different kinds of risk that was introduced in section 9.3 and which has to be agreed on beforehand.

Once the kinds of risk that should be addressed are agreed, developers and other experienced staff can start to work through the requirements. An example of the result of such a check is given in the following figure 9.4, where it is assumed that the example list of different kinds of risks from section 9.3 was used.

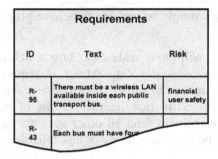

Figure 9.4: Example result of risk check of requirements

In addition to the data stored in requirements attributes, requirements management provides the information on the dependencies between the requirements and between requirements and pieces of information from the other systems engineering processes, such as project management, change management, verification and validation and so on. To this end requirements management links all the related pieces of information, so that all information can be reached from any point in the link chain.

For example, the information links between some requirements and change management information may indicate that the implementation of one change request would modify a number of key requirements. This information is most valuable to risk management, for there are a number of potential risks associated with this situation:

- the system may no longer behave as expected by the customer
- the system may not be as efficient as before
- the system may not work at all
- the implementation may not be successful
- the implementation may blow the change request budget
- ...

All these aspects (and many more) would usually have to be considered in connection with a change request, but this demands that the necessary information is available.

A second example may serve to illustrate the value of the information links between the requirements and the validation and verification process from the point of view of risk management. Assuming that the information links show that some key requirements may be very difficult to verify, this means that:

- it may be impossible to prove that the system functions correctly
- it may be unknown whether the customer will accept the system
- the budget planned for validation and verification may be overdrawn

- the system may wrongly be verified to behave properly (a false positive)
- …

These examples will have made clear how much information and how much data risk management can extract if requirements management makes sure that all related information is mutually linked and accessible. If this is not the case and if thus the various bits of information cannot be accessed, risk management (and all other systems engineering processes) will consequently be of lesser quality or less reliable.

9.4.2 Risk assessment and how Requirements Management can support

The assessment of the identified risks is sometimes closely related to their identification, but it is usually recommended to separate these two activities.

If this is not the case some risks may be dismissed immediately after identification, assuming that they are very unlikely to occur or to have only little impact on the project. There is then the danger of loosing track of such risks.

It is therefore better to list all identified risks in one document, together with the result of the assessment. It should not be allowed for anyone to delete an identified risk from the list only because it is assumed to be negligible at some point in time.

During the assessment the identified risks are analysed one by one and the possibility of their occurrence and their possible impact on the project are evaluated. This activity will usually be carried out by experienced staff together with the project manager and risk manager. There may also be other specialists and members of the organisation's senior management present.

The following figure 9.5 gives an example of how risks can be visualised in a risk graph.

With a graphical representation as given in figure 9.5, it is easy to quickly recognise whether a risk is acceptable or unacceptable. All risks that are in the upper right corner of the graph are critical, whereas risks in the lower left corner are less threatening.

A similar graphical representation of risks is given in figure 9.6 as follows. The main difference between the risk graphs in figures 9.5 and 9.6 is the fact that in figure 9.5, the risks are discretely categorised, and the number of categories along each axis can be tailored. In figure 9.6, the risks can be placed everywhere within the limits of the graph and are thus continuously categorised.

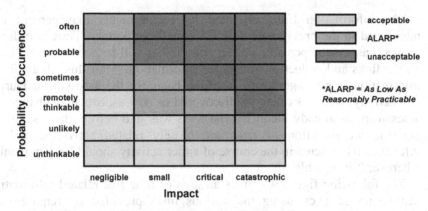

Figure 9.5: Risk graph for visualising risks (source: wikipedia)

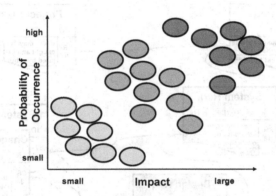

Figure 9.6: Another graphical representation of risks

It must be noted that although the assessment will aim at making judgements and predictions that are as precise as possible, the result is nonetheless arbitrary. For important and large projects some organisations therefore choose to have the list of risks assessed by two independent teams, and the list is accepted only if the results of these two independent assessments are similar.

Requirements management can support the risk assessment by providing risk related information in connection with the requirements. As was described above, a set of attributes may serve to categorise the requirements from the point of view of possible risks. The identified risks are linked with the requirements, and it is then possible to get from the risks back to single requirements and vice versa. Thus for example the customer acceptance of the system to be developed may depend on only a handful of key requirements (importance is topmost) that must be concentrated on to make the project successful.

The information links provided by requirements management and mentioned in the previous section are equally important. Thus in order to properly assess the possible impacts of a risk it will be necessary to follow all the links and collect all connected information. After this, all available information is put together to form the basis for the assessment. During this activity, new risks may be discovered or new aspects may change the assessment of already identified risks. As was said before, the assessment and the identification of risks are closely related activities, and all information extracted in the course of either activity should be documented wherever it is suitable.

The following figure 9.7 gives an idea of how risk related information can be traced back using the various links provided by requirements management.

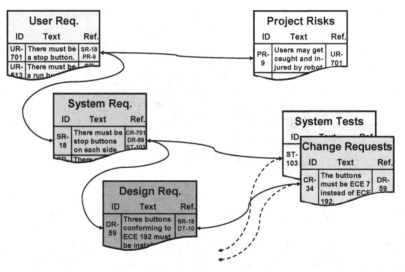

Figure 9.7: Tracing back risk related information using links

From the example in figure 9.7 it can be seen how tracing back links between different collections of data can reveal more information than would otherwise be available. Assuming that a risk was identified in connection with user requirement UR-701, the existing link chains can be run down via the system requirements (SR-18) and design requirements (DR-69). Here it will be seen that there already exist system tests (ST-103) and change requests (CR-34) that are linked to the system requirements and design requirements. The system tests and change requests may have more links to other requirements, which is indicated with the dashed links.

Thus it may turn out that although the risk was originally only identified in connection with user requirement UR-701, many more user requirements and system requirements and design requirements are affected because they are not only linked directly but also indirectly via tests and change requests.

Without requirements management, information on risks related to the requirements is usually much harder or even impossible to extract. Outdated links may present an incorrect picture of the mutual dependencies, and old versions of requirements can lead to wrong judgements in connection with risks.

After the assessment, the risks can be ordered according to their possibility and impact. It must then be decided how to further proceed. An organisation may have a standard demanding that the first say, 15 risks must be addressed by defining possible countermeasures. In other organisations, all the risks that may threaten the whole project – sometimes called catastrophic risks – have to be addressed with a plan.

If there is no standard the project manager must decide which risks to prepare for with some plan and which risks to neglect. As the assessment is repeatedly carried out, the judgements may change throughout the course of the project and the risks that are planned for may consequently change, too.

9.4.3   Definition of countermeasures and how Requirements Management can support

The first two activities in the risk management process cycle are the identification and assessment of the possible risks in a dedicated risks document or in the project management plan. After that, the next step is making up one's mind as to how these risks could possibly be addressed.

Because it is usually not possible to devise a management strategy for all risks, it was suggested before that the risks be prioritised and ordered. Similar to the assessment, the definition of countermeasures is then carried out for each individual risk whose possible impact on the project is estimated to be greater than some defined limit. It is noted that the relationship between risks and countermeasures is usually n:m.

This means that one risk may need more than one countermeasure to deal with, while one countermeasure may address more than one risk at the same time.

As the risks are best classified in view of probability of occurrence and impact on the project, possible countermeasures can, in principle, aim at minimising either of these two risk attributes. Thus a risk minimising strategy may minimise the possibility of occurrence, or the possible impact on the project, or both.

In practice, risks management plans are often of the latter kind, trying to minimise both the possibility of occurrence and the potential impact on the project. If none of the two risk attributes can significantly be minimised, a strategy may still try to think of procedures for the very worst case.

Clearly a risk management plan or strategy cannot be established using ready recipes that fit every situation. Like many other activities in the various systems engineering disciplines, risk management heavily relies on the skills and experience of the people involved.

The information provided by requirements management can support the definition of countermeasures. Following all links related to a risk one can identify a certain scope of that risk. This means that it is possible to tell in detail which aspects or parts of the system are affected by the risk and which are not. This analysis will also highlight those parts for which countermeasures will be effective.

The sum of all parts or aspects for which any countermeasures would be effective then represent the actual potential for risk management and minimisation. For the rest, not much can be done save analysing the worst case impact and hoping that it may not happen. The parts that can be addressed with countermeasures can further be prioritised and balanced in view of the associated efforts and benefits. This approach can optimise the countermeasures if there are boundary conditions in terms of budget and resources. In reality, this is usually the case.

The above descriptions may appear to be somewhat theoretical, and an example will shed more light on the various aspects of what has been said. Consider for example the risk that for some car electronic control unit the transformer may no longer be available in two years time. This risk may have been identified by using a company standard list of risks, or for example by analysing the entries in a special requirements attribute, or by analysing the role of the stakeholders identified during requirements development, with the transformer manufacturer being one of the stakeholders.

Using the information links between the project management plan and the requirements data provided by requirements management it is known that say, at least 100,000 electronic control units must be sold to make the project financially successful. The risk of not being able to get the transformers in the near future is therefore estimated to be significant, and possible countermeasures shall be identified.

Collecting all linked information it is assumed that this risk can be addressed in the following ways:

- C1: changing to another transformer type

- C2: buying so many transformers that they will last for at least 100,000 units

There may be many more possible countermeasures, but we assume that these are the most promising and realistic as found by the foregoing risk analyses and assessments. It is seen that both countermeasures would completely resolve the identified risk, and no "black spots" would remain.

Due to limited budgets it may not be possible to realise countermeasure C2. If project management decides to go for C1 in an early stage, the development can immediately be carried out taking this risk into account. Using the information provided by requirements management quickly reveals that the transfomer has an interface to the car's electric board net and to the electronic control circuit. It also has a geometrical interface to the housing and the electronic board in terms of physical dimensions.

With all this information it is now possible to plan and develop the control unit so that the original transformer and some alternative can both be used. The reason why the alternative may not immediately be used could for example be that the alternative is more expensive, and thus the original transformer should be used as long as possible. The only thing that is left to do is monitoring the risk. In the described situation this essentially means keeping contact to the transformer manufacturer and observing the deliveries. As soon as the transformer is no longer available, purchase and production must switch to the identified alternative.

9.4.4 Monitoring risks and how Requirements Management can support

The last activity in the risk management process is the monitoring of the risks. To be more precise, it is not the last activity but the one that is constantly carried out, while the other three process activities may be executed only periodically and in their logical order.

In a way, monitoring the risks is very similar to controlling a technical system of a certain degree of complexity. Taking for example a power plant, monitoring could mean to watch the various displays for pressure, temperature, voltage and so on with a defined frequency. As long as the values are within a certain range, nothing must be done save keep on reading the indicators.

If one of the indicators starts leaving the normal range and approaches a critical value, the power plant manuals must be taken off the shelf, and the relevant chapters must be read. Actions must then be taken according to the suggestions of the manuals, and it must carefully be checked if these actions can resolve the danger. If so, the operator can go back to business "as usual". If not, further actions must be taken and their result checked again. In principle, this cycle goes on until either the critical situation can be brought under control or until some catastrophe happens.

As a catastrophe is clearly not wanted in connection with a power plant, the usual security standards are very strict (hopefully!), leading quickly to the plant being switched off before some situation may occur that cannot easily be controlled. This is probably the reason why throughout the last few years there were a number of incidents where a power plant was switched off, even though according to the reports the plants were far from any really critical or dangerous state.

We choose the analogy of a power plant here, for there are some details that should not be missed. While the power plant has indicators, risk management has metrics. Metrics are dealt with in detail in another chapter, but it is important here to note that these metrics cannot naturally be derived.

Although there are some standard metrics or indicators, such as budget used versus budget still available, more specific risk indicators will usually be project specific. We stress this point to make clear that the quality of the risk management will heavily depend on the indicators or metrics chosen to represent the state of the project in terms of risk.

Just as the power plant operator might not read the voltage meter for checking the pressure, risk management estimates may be wrong if for example the "percentage of requirements implemented" metric is taken as an indicator for how much budget should approximately be already used. Let us assume for example that half of the requirements are already implemented and half of the budget is already used. If the significantly more complex half of the requirements is already implemented, risk management may miss a chance of shifting priorities to make the project more successful and quicker. If the significantly easier half of the requirements is implemented, risk management may fail to realise that there is a severe risk of not being able to implement the other half of the requirements with the remaining half of the budget.

In such a situation it may be better to use a metric giving the number of requirements already implemented and weighted with some estimated implementation effort. Such metrics and statistics are easily created with the information provided by requirements management.

9.5 Summary

This chapter deals with the interface between requirements management and risk management. Risk management is a cycle of activities constantly carried out throughout a project. The process activities are basically the identification of risks, the assessment of risks, the definition of countermeasures and the monitoring of risks.

The identification of risks is facilitated using checklists, predecessor project risk management documents and the integrated information provided by requirements management. This is a critical activity, for risks that are not discovered cannot be taken into account.

After the risks are identified, they are usually prioritised or weighted in terms of probability of occurrence and possible impact on the project. This is because normally not all risks can be addressed with a suitable plan due to budget limits. It may thus be decided to only take the ten top risks into account, or all risks that are assessed to be above some critical level.

After the risks that are further dealt with are defined, possible countermeasures are analysed and plans to address the occurrence of a risks are developed. Countermeasures may aim at minimising the probability of occurrence, or the impact on the project, or both.

Finally, the identified risks are monitored to check if the developed emergency plans must be carried out. While the identification and prioritisation of risks and the development of countermeasures may be carried out with a certain frequency and in this order, the monitoring is carried out constantly and in parallel to this.

10 Test Management (Validation and Verification) interface

Validation and verification are two of the most critical activities when developing a product. These names are given to the activities which make sure that what is being developed actually meets the customers' expectations. They are the core activities of test management. Hence validation and verification significantly contribute to ensuring the quality of the product.

As the requirements are usually the legal basis of a contract between a supplier and its customer, validation and verification check whether the contract has been fulfilled.

10.1 What are Validation and Verification?

There is a difference between validation and verification as follows: validation checks that what is being developed meets the needs of the customer that is paying for the product; verification checks that the product behaves as specified. This difference is made clear in [Boeh1979], using these two questions:

- "Are we building the right thing?" (Validation)
- "Are we building the thing right?" (Verification)

From these definitions it is seen that although validation and verification are closely related and intertwined, they are not the same. While verification tests a system against system requirements or design, validation tests a system against customer (or user) requirements to show the system can fulfil its aims; that is that the system can be used as intended.

10.2   The Validation and Verification planning process

Verification and validation must explicitly be planned for as early as possible. This is because usually, testing will need some preparation before it can be carried out.

For example, test environment hardware and software may be necessary to test a certain system. If these are not organised in due time, this may cause significant deadwood and delay in the project management schedule. If, for instance, testing requires use of a particular deep water harbour, this may have to be booked years in advance. Some testing environments are every bit as complicated to build as the system to be tested.

Also, tests may imply a significant risk from a number of different viewpoints. For example, some key requirements may be very complex to verify, and there is a risk that the customer cannot be convinced that his key requirements were correctly implemented. Some requirements may need a significant part of the resources and / or budget to verify, and this implies the risk that if the verification is carried out properly, the project may be delayed or the budget overdrawn. Note that in some projects with new technology or similar challenges, validation and verification may take up to half the total project budget.

Therefore tests should be specified as early as possible. The document that contains all the intended tests, test procedures, expected results and so on is usually called the test specification. The tests specification can be written even while the requirements are still being elicited.

The validation and verification planning process is iterative, as are all other processes in connection with requirements management.

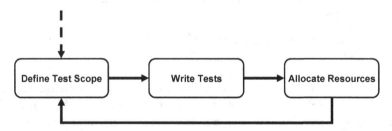

Figure 10.1: Simple example test management process

It was shown in the previous chapters that requirements are usually specified on different levels of abstraction or granularity, starting with the most abstract customer (or user) requirements and ending with the most detailed implementation requirements.

Correspondingly, tests have to be planned for each level of requirements. This relation is usually pictured with the well known V-model.

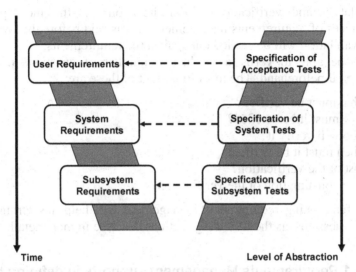

Figure 10.2: One example of the V-model

It is noted that in the above figure, the time axis is vertical from top to bottom, not from left to right. Hence the tests on each level of abstraction are planned for in parallel to the specification of the requirements on this level. On each of the various levels of abstraction, the validation and verification planning process shown further above is repeatedly executed.

However, the validation and verification planning should not only cover the writing of a test specification. A complete test plan will also make sure for example that company standards are met.

This may include the buying and application of standardised test environments, checking that company-wide (test) quality standards are conformed to and so on.

Also, a test plan will contain a test schedule that can be linked to the project management schedule. This will give an overview of the anticipated time consumption and allows for integrated project planning and scheduling.

10.3   The role of Requirements Management in Validation and Verification

Validation and verification is definitely one of the most prominent interfaces of requirements management. It was said before that verification and validation will be carried out against the requirements.

To be able to verify a product, a number of questions need to be answered beforehand. The most important of these are:

- what must be verified?
- how must it be verified?
- who will verify it?
- when must it be verified?
- cost of the verification?
- time consumption of the verification?

A functioning requirements management will help answering each of these questions, as the following sections describe in more detail.

10.3.1 Requirements Management supports in defining the test scope

The question "What must be verified?" is identical to the question "Which requirements must be tested against?". This in turn is identical to defining the scope for the verification process.

Generally, as verification checks a product's conformance to its specification, all existing requirements are candidates for testing. However, this demands that the requirements be up to date and that the specification does not contain old or wrong information. Requirements management, being the interface to all the other systems engineering disciplines, makes sure that all relevant information created in other processes is linked to the requirements.

As will be seen in chapter 11 on change management, requirements inevitably change throughout the course of a project and are not static. Thus if requirements management does not make sure that the information on changes is fed back to the requirements, the original requirements specification will sooner or later be outdated. Hence any test specification that relates to such an outdated set of requirements will also become obsolete. If the question "What must be tested?" is then answered with such an outdated test specification, the answer will be incorrect, leading to wrong assumptions regarding the project management.

Another important aspect of "What must be verified?" is configuration management. Only requirements management integrates the configuration management information with the requirements. Even if the requirements are up to date and correct, it may not be possible to extract the correct information for the test management without the information on the various planned versions and configurations. Consider the following figure.

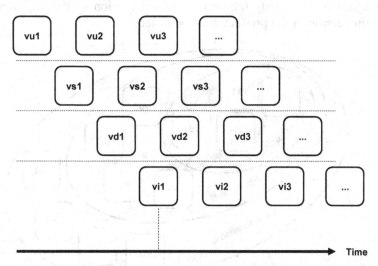

Figure 10.3: The problem of different existing versions of requirements

The above figure shows how during the requirements engineering process, the requirements are developed step by step throughout the course of the project on each level of abstraction. In parallel, configuration management will make a so-called "freeze" of the requirements at certain points in time. These freezes are basically a snapshot of the requirements on one level of abstraction and as of a certain date.

The figure shows how one initial set of user requirements (vu1) will be further developed (vu2, vu3, ...) and at the same time will be derived to give system requirements (vs1), design requirements (vd1) and finally requirements on the implementation level (vi1).

By the time a first prototype of the product can be tested against the requirements on implementation level (vi1), the requirements on the higher levels of abstraction were further developed (vu2, vu3, ...). This means that the tests on implementation level must usually be carried out against requirements that do not represent the current status of the user requirements.

If the test management has no configuration management information, it must rely on the current version of the requirements to test the system against, since this is the only version that is momentarily accessible. The figure shows that in this case, test management may test the prototype in version (vi1) against the user requirements in version (vu3), which would most probably lead to incorrect results. If requirements management links the configuration management information to the requirements, test management can easily tell against which version of the requirements a certain version of the product must be tested.

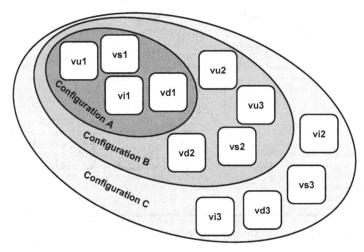

Figure 10.4: Configuration management for various requirements versions

It was said before that ideally, a product is tested against every single documented requirement. In practice however, it may not be possible or necessary to test against each single requirement on each level of abstraction. It often happens that there are no resources or no budget to test every individual requirement, and in this case requirements management can provide valuable information by making the requirements information accessible to test management. It is easy for a requirements engineer to suggest that all requirements must be tested against; but it is a skill of an experienced tester to know when to stop.

There are a number of attributes that are usually administered together with the requirements and that may help prioritising requirements for testing:

- priority
- complexity
- cost

- resources
- ...

In requirements management & engineering we discourage use of the word priority without definition; importance, urgency, both? Which do you suppose we mean here? When documenting attributes be sure that you and everyone else understands what is intended. Attributes have to be unambiguous.

If resources or budget are tight, then obviously the project manager or test manager would look for requirements that have low importance but are relatively complex or costly or resources consuming to test. Such requirements would represent good candidates for being neglected for testing.

Note however that as with many other aspects described in this book, requirements management will only support in collecting information and providing a basis for decisions – the decision itself is always with the respective people. Thus although a requirement may be judged to be very low importance, but very complex, costly and resources consuming to test, it may still be decided to go ahead with testing. One reason for example could be that the organisation developing the product uses a new technology to implement this special requirement, and wanting to gather experience it must check on the results of using that new technology for the first time.

In principle, all attribute information administered with requirements management may prove helpful when structuring or prioritising requirements for tests. Keep in mind however that too many attributes will be hard or impossible to administer, and a dedicated test management attribute for requirements may be superfluous.

A second important contribution of requirements management to defining the test scope is the validation of the requirements. Here, validating requirements means checking whether the specified customer or user requirements really represent what the customer wants. This is specific part of the analysis described in connection with the requirements definition process.

The requirements analysis is concerned with checking that the requirements conform to quality criteria that are project specific and must be defined at the beginning of the project. During requirements analysis, each individual requirement is checked on its own. We consider here requirements validation takes the whole requirements document and tries to demonstrate that it meets the customer's needs.

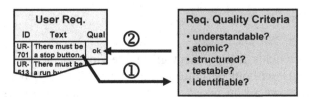

Figure 10.5: Requirements analysis example

This may often turn out to be a very complex thing to do. The basic goal is to give the customer as much information about the future system as possible, so as to enable him to imagine the future product in its future environment and with its future users in as much detail as possible. Hence requirements validation will use all the various elicitation and modelling methods described in previous chapters.

Although it may be difficult, it is nonetheless very important to validate the requirements with regard the customer's needs. Otherwise there may arise a situation where the requirements are all up to date, all requirements information is fully available to the test management and the tests are all properly planned – only the requirements do not represent what the customer really wants or needs. In this case, the tests would verify the wrong requirements, and this may be seen as an incorrect scoping.

10.3.2 Requirements Management supports in documenting the test method

After the question of what to test is answered, it must be decided how to test against the various requirements. Requirements management can make substantial contributions to solve this problem. Probably the easiest and one of the most effective ways is to introduce a suitable set of attributes to administer with the requirements. This way it is possible to document this important information even while the requirements are being elicited and specified. In our experience it is much easier to document such additional information immediately together with the requirements, rather than specifying only the requirements at one time and then try to get together all related information sometime later. In the latter case there is the danger that additional information which is in the developers head at the time of specifying the requirement will be lost if the writing down of that related information is delayed.

[HOOD2005] suggests two attributes to administer with the requirements, and which provide valuable information for the test management:

- verification method
- verification criteria

The attribute verification method describes how the developers or other specialists believe that the requirement should be verified. Typical entries for that attribute could be one or more of the following:

- inspection
- peer reviews
- simulation
- test
- analysis
- demonstration

It is seen from the example list above that requirements can be verified in many more ways than just classical testing. For example, using certain formal languages for documenting requirements, it is possible to prove the correctness or consistence of their implementation only by applying specially developed formal methods or algorithms.

User Req.			
ID	Text	Ver. Meth.	Ver. Crit.
UR-701	There must be a stop button.	Visual inspection.	Existence of at least one button.
UR-513	There must be a run button.	Visual	Existence of

Figure 10.6: Application of verification method and criteria attributes

The verification method will also contain or at least point to additional information regarding necessary verification equipment. Especially for classical testing, extended test equipment must sometimes exist to verify certain requirements. For example, the verification of the stiffness of an automobile suspension will usually take place in large test benches that can take the complete suspension and apply various loads. Such equipment must be planned for in due time to make sure it will be available when it is needed. The planning includes purchasing, setting up, becoming familiar with using the equipment and so on. All information related to these aspects should be administered as additional information for the requirements.

The attribute verification criteria documents what the verification result must be in order for the system to be successfully verified. Thus for example if the verification method for checking a system against a given software requirement was defined to be code inspection, the verification criteria may be that three programming specialists must confirm independently from each other that the code will actually do what it should do. If the verification method for one or more requirements specifying the performance of a system was chosen to be a stress test, then the verification criteria may be that the system does not exhibit more than one failure in one thousand test runs.

Having defined both the verification method and the verification criteria it is possible to document the result of the verification in another requirements attribute, or to link the requirements to this information that may be located somewhere else.

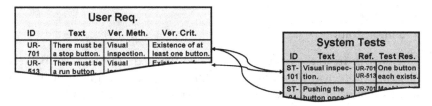

Figure 10.7: Requirements specification linked to test specification

In practice, this relation between the test management information and requirements information is often represented by links between the requirements document or database and the test specification or database. The test specification or database may then contain the test result information.

By documenting the verification method and verification result and by linking this information to the requirements it is possible in reality to demonstrate the complete verification of a product regarding its requirements. This is an enormous advantage during the development process, and even more so for the final customer acceptance tests. The developers can easily find out for which requirement test specifications must be written. The requirements definition process is supported by demonstrating that all requirements are verifiable.

Requirements management can provide the information to tell us what percentage of a system to be developed is already successfully verified. This gives a general project overview and thus closes the circle with project management.

10.3.3 Requirements Management supports in documenting who carries out the verification

In some organisations the people who are carrying out the verifications belong to dedicated test departments. They specialise in testing against the various requirements and have many years of experience in verification. In such organisation it is possible that the people who will verify against a certain set of requirements are known to be always the same, and then maybe no additional information is needed regarding who will carry out the tests.

In organisations where different people verify systems against the requirements it will normally be necessary to document which requirement will be verified against by whom. There can then be no misunderstanding regarding this responsibility. The information may be best documented immediately together with the requirement. If the developer who specifies the requirement is the one who will verify against it, then one of the usual standard attributes such as "author" or "owner" can serve this purpose.

There are also organisations where it is not defined beforehand who will verify a system against which requirements. Rather, the various test personnel take the requirements one by one and verify the system against that requirement, and a tester who is finished with some test will simply take the next requirement that is not yet covered by one of his colleagues. In such a situation it is most important to document who has verified against which requirement, for it could be anyone. In this case, the document or information data base that keeps the information on the test results will usually also contain the name of the tester and the date of the test. However, depending on the tool support available it is also possible to store that information together with the requirements and only link these to the test result information. In either case, requirements management provides the links between the various pieces of test information, thus ensuring that a test result can be traced back to the tester at any time.

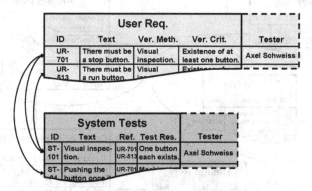

Figure 10.8: Possible places to document the name of the tester

10.3.4 Requirements Management supports in defining when to carry out verifications

It was said before that validation and verification are an essential part of a development project. In this respect validation and verification must be planned for like every other main project activity. The previous sections showed how requirements management can support in defining what to verify, how to verify and who will verify.

Another important aspect of validation and verification is the information when the system will be checked against each single requirement, and there are two ways to look at requirements in this connection. The first way to schedule the verification process uses the project management plan. This contains information on a relatively high level of abstraction, defining when each of the main activities must start and when they must be finished.

Thus the project management plan outlines a rough verification scheduling and planning. However, due to its nature and its intended readership, no detailed information about when to verify each single requirement will usually be contained in the project management plan.

The detailed information on when to verify which requirement can usually be found in the test management plan. The test management plan ensures that the verification of a system, or part of a system to prove that requirements have been satisfied, is scheduled so that the corresponding deadlines outlined in the project management plan can be met. But how can this information be extracted?

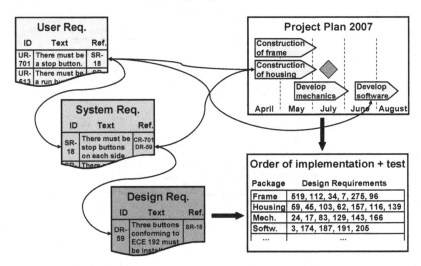

Figure 10.9: Deriving the implementation and test order from project plan

It was seen earlier that requirements management mutually connects and links all information created and stored in connection with the different systems engineering disciplines. Particularly, requirements management links and connects the requirements and associated information on the different levels of abstraction. Examples of levels of abstraction are system, sub-system, and component.

With this information the test management is very much simplified. From the V-model shown further above it is seen that verification normally begins with the requirements on the lowest and most detailed implementation level and continues level by level until finally the customer (or user) requirements level is reached. As was said before, on this level the system will not only be formally verified, but the system will be validated to demonstrate that what has been developed is actually what the customer expects and needs.

This process can outline a rough planning as to when the requirements on each of the different levels of abstraction must be verified against to keep the project schedule. However, even on each single requirements level there is usually some sequence, and this sequence must also be defined. At this point, the information on relationships between individual requirements provided by requirements management is most valuable.

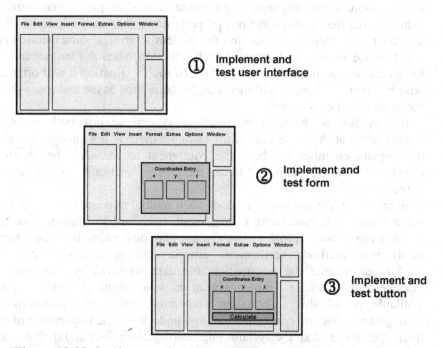

Figure 10.10: Implementation and test order for graphical user interface

By tracing the links between the requirements it is possible to tell against which requirements the system can be verified independently of any other requirements. Requirements of this kind of may be tested against as soon as they are implemented and must not be specially considered.

Many requirements however are mutually dependent, and with requirements management the nature of their interdependence can be analysed. This way it is possible to define the sequence in which the various requirements must be implemented to facilitate the system verification. For example, the various functions associated with buttons within a form on a computer display that is part of a graphical user interface can only be tested after the graphical use interface, the form and the buttons are implemented and successfully tested.

This may all sound rather trivial to the reader, but amazingly enough it is not. Experience shows that quite frequently attempts are made to test a system against requirements although the system is not ready for testing. This is true for example if requirements management does not link requirements information to change management information. In this case, a system may be tested against old versions of requirements, and the new or changed requirements may never be tested against at all.

It is also quite common that a certain test case can verify a system against more than only one requirement. For example, a requirement demands that the system functions properly down to a temperature of -50°; another requirement demands that the system's physical dimensions may not decrease more than 0.1mm in each direction when the temperature is lowered from room temperature to -50°. In such a situation it will often be possible to verify both requirements at the same time as the test cases share the same initial conditions.

It may not be possible to verify a system against both example requirements at the same time if for example there is not enough space in the climate chamber for both the equipment to measure the physical dimensions and the equipment to test the proper functioning of the system at the same time.

In any case, the documentation of such mutual dependencies is one of the domains of requirements management. It is hard to imagine how the relationship between project management plan, test cases, test equipment, verification method, verification criteria and requirements can be established without the information and data provided by requirements management. Within your organisation you might call the making available of all this information something other than requirements management. We are concerned that you understand the importance of the interdependence of all the systems engineering disciplines and their mutual interfaces. If you want to call this by another name this is fine by us. The main thing with requirements management is not the name, the main thing is that you do it.

10.3.5 Requirements Management supports in estimating the costs of verification

The full set of requirements on some given level of abstraction provides a complete representation of the system to be developed on that abstraction level. If the requirements are properly documented, estimates can be made regarding the anticipated costs to verify each requirement or units of requirements.

The result of such estimations can be documented in another attribute to go with the requirements, or it can for example be documented in the test management plan. Requirements management ensures that wherever the cost information is stored, all other relevant systems engineering disciplines will be able to access this information, together with the corresponding requirements data.

In principle, estimating the costs to verify a given set of requirements is an arbitrary act, as it relies on personal experience and skill of the people involved. However, the more information there is available on the subject, the more precise the estimates will be.

Therefore, the people responsible for the cost estimates can be significantly supported by a functioning requirements management. It will provide information on the mutual dependencies between the requirements and related information, thus presenting a view with a much wider scope than if only the requirements alone were analysed to arrive at an estimate.

For example, one of the previous sections dealt with the information on the person responsible for carrying out verification. This piece of information may indicate that a system can only be properly verified against a certain requirement or set of requirements by one single person within the whole organisation, for specialist knowledge is necessary to handle the test equipment or interpret the test results. If this specialist's daily rate is significantly higher than those of all the other developers or testers, this could influence the cost estimates.

Another example of information that was suggested to be stored in addition to the requirements was the verification method. For some requirements, this information could for example imply that very expensive test equipment or many specialists are necessary to be able to verify these requirements. If this information is accessible, it will most probably influence the cost estimates. If it is not accessible, cost estimates are prone to error.

If no substantial information is available, requirements management may still be able to support the cost estimation process by providing basic data from similar predecessor projects. If the test effort and the requirements were documented, a very simple approach could be to divide the total known test effort by the total number of known requirements. This will give an idea of how costly it is to verify one single requirement.

$$\text{Average Test Cost per User Req.} = \frac{\text{Total Test Budget}}{\text{Nr. of User Req.}}$$

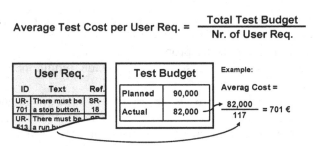

Figure 10.11: Estimating costs for testing using data from earlier projects

Doing this for a number of similar or generally representative projects may provide a good average of the cost to verify one requirement in a given organisation. This in turn may provide a starting point for the actual cost estimation, and a means to check if the cost estimates are reasonable or not.

It can be seen how all these data can feed back to provide valuable information for risk management, project management and other systems engineering disciplines. Thus, by integrating all these different aspects, requirements management provides the basis for all the other disciplines to develop further.

10.3.6 Requirements Management supports in estimating the effort needed for verification

With the information on the verification method and the verification criteria, the effort needed to verify one given requirement can be estimated. This estimate is valuable information in its own right, but is also important for example to verify the project management plan.

The project management plan contains schedules for all the main project activities, documenting when they must start and when they must be finished in order to keep the overall time schedule. As these main activity schedules are initially estimated and then constantly refined in the course of the project, additional and more detailed data on any of these subjects must immediately feed back to the project management plan.

Thus for example a more detailed planning of the verification process may reveal that the schedule initially estimated to carry out the verification of the requirements cannot be met. It may turn out that some requirements will take more time to verify than was anticipated. It is also possible that there are more dependencies between the individual requirements than was thought at the beginning, and this may lead to the effect that only relatively few requirements can be used for verification independently of any other requirements, while the major part must be verified in a certain sequence. This may also blow the estimated time schedule.

Providing all the information on the requirements and their mutual relationships, requirements management also supports in optimising the scheduling of the requirements verification. For example, requirements management may reveal that there are a number of different sub-sets of requirements that can each be tested with only one or only a few test cases. If this information is available, the test management will plan for a much smaller number of tests than if the information were not available, and a much smaller number of tests may indicate significantly less time to verify a system against all requirements.

10.4 Summary

This chapter deals with requirements verification and validation. These are the activities of checking whether a system conforms to its specification and whether it actually meets the needs and expectations of the customer.

Like all other main project activities, verification and validation must be properly planned for and should be a part of or linked to the project management plan.

There are a number of different data associated with validation and verification, and a test plan may contain some or all of the following information: What must be verified? How must it be verified? Who will carry out the verifcation? When can or must the system be verified against which requirements? How much does it cost to verify the system against requirements? How long will it take to verify the system against the requirements?

Much more information can be thought of, and the project management plan must document which additional information is to be administered together with the requirements to support the test management. Do not do this blindly, decide what makes sense and assess if the effort will be more than the resulting benefit.

Requirements management can support in answering any of the above example questions by integrating all selected related information from other systems engineering disciplines and by feeding back all this integrated information into each systems engineering process.

Like many other processes described in this book, the verification and validation planning process is iterative. Therefore, some initial estimates will be established to roughly plan for the validation and verification. As the project goes on, more detailed information will emerge and become available, and this information feeds back to the verification and validation planning process.

11 Change Management interface

11.1 General

Change management is one of the most important aspects of requirements engineering. The subject is closely related to other areas such as configuration management, variant management and also project management. Change management theory is essentially not very complicated.

Unfortunately, in practice it is often not so easy to implement. The following chapter explains the basics of change management, the relationships with RM&E and also the problems of turning the theory into practice.

11.2 Basics of Change Management

"Changes always happen in a project and at every project phase."

This is a premise that applies to almost every project. Unfortunately, time and time again attempts are made to simply disallow changes made after a "certain point in time". The reason for this is that changes, particularly in later project phases, can be very uncomfortable. Development departments in particular insist on keeping the requirements as static as possible. During the project, project members are then continually surprised that the above mentioned "certain point in time" ultimately coincides with the end of the project.

A further indication of the above mentioned premise lies in the fact that, as a rule, there is always a project manager. If no changes were allowed after a particular point in time, there would also be no need for a project manager after this point in time. That is to say, the project plan would exist and everything would run like clockwork until the end of the project. One would simply need a project planner instead of a project manager.

11.3 Factors Influencing Change

The reasons for change are varied. Hence, there are factors that themselves cannot be influenced by optimal RM&E in project analysis. These may be for example:

- Cost or budget levels
- Resource situation (e.g. staffing levels)
- Scheduling
- Conceptual changes (system-/ architecture)
- Strategic changes in marketing and sales

There are however further factors that, with structured RM&E methodology, reduce the risk of changes:

- Forgotten requirements
- Incorrect/contradictory requirements
- Requirements so formulated that they can be misunderstood

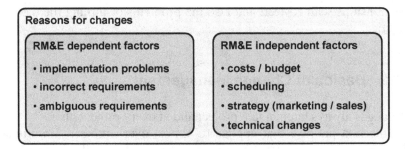

Figure 11.1: Reasons for change

For example, if cost or budget levels are reduced or, what happens much less frequently, the budget is increased, this naturally has an effect on the project implementation. It can equally happen that the project resources are increased or reduced. Relatively often, one can observe a project milestone being brought forward, or put back.

In the course of the development, the development department can realise that an architectural concept or use of new technology is not sustainable, and therefore a general redesign is necessary.

The market situation of the product to be developed can also fundamentally change. For example, a competitor launches a more efficient product first. This can make it necessary to implement additional functionality, or to launch one's own product earlier, so as not to lose market share.

Good requirements management & engineering only has limited effect on the above mentioned factors.

There are, however, factors that generate changes during the project that can influence well-structured RM&E.

Changes can be generated because the specifications have not been defined carefully enough. Requirements may unfortunately be, among other things, contradictory, not testable, incomplete, not explicit enough, or open to misunderstanding.

Specifically in this case, structured RM&E helps to reduce the number of changes in the later development phases.

11.4   Number of Changes during Development

Irrespective of the previously mentioned premise, that changes will occur during the entire project, one goal must be to reduce the negative influences which generate changes.

This is because implementing a large number of necessary changes towards the end of the project actually damages the success of the project. In this respect, it is very problematic for a development manager when many changes have to be implemented towards the end of a project. Unfortunately, organisations are still putting too little effort into producing good, well thought through specifications.

For the most part, at the start of a project, customer specifications are copied from a previous product and adapted or extended in a makeshift way, to as to be able to start a request for tender as soon as possible. The inconsistencies and mistakes will then only be recognised towards the end of the project - at a time when the costs of rectifying them are greatest!

Although there can be no generalisation about what the scale of changes during a project should be, there are however levels that can become critical to a project.

Here, we mean changes to the specification and not to the ultimate system being developed. Good change management requires that changes are first of all documented. Relying on two or more people sharing a common recollection of a telephone conversation is not enough.

If only a few changes are specified at the beginning of the project, this might indicate that the definition of requirements was uncharacteristically successful. Or more commonly this can indicate that the elicitation of the requirements, analysis and requirements modelling has not been carried out carefully enough. Mistakes, gaps and inconsistencies will then first be recognised during implementation and above all when testing. This often considerably increases the number of changes necessary towards the end of the project where the repercussions are most extreme.

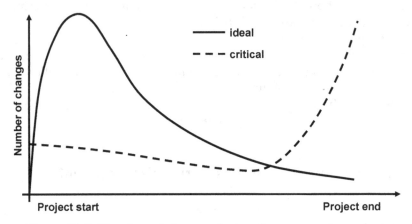

Figure 11.2: Number of changes during the course of a project

It is also important to note that, even in a project with exemplary elicitation, analysis, modelling and reviews, the number of changes can suddenly increase considerably: for example, if the resources or budget situation changes dramatically, or a solution proves not to be feasible.

In order to prevent misunderstandings and despite appearing to argue in favour of a "waterfall model": It is necessary and important to be clear about the scope of the system to be developed at the start of the project. The amount of effort invested in a "good" specification is definitely worthwhile, because correcting inconsistencies, errors or ambiguities is cheapest when they are discovered and rectified at the start of the project, i.e. when there's nothing more than documentation available.

Nevertheless, based on findings and experience during the project and the above mentioned factors, changes will continue to occur

11.5 Two Phases of Change Management: Informing and Approval-based

How do I now deal with changes during the project? As already shown above, most changes at the start of a project are to specifications. This is normal, because the actual process of producing the specification takes place here. The author of a specification first of all gets a understanding of the other stakeholders' expectations.

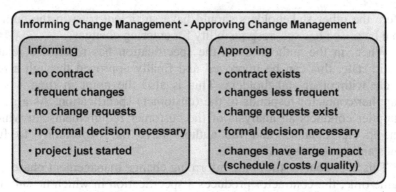

Figure 11.3: Differemces between informing
and approving Change Managment

This phase is characterised by a lot of work on the requirements document and therefore the number of changes and adjustments is high. After some time, a consolidation phase should occur, in which decisions are taken with regard to what the system to be developed must provide. Lastly, an agreement is made with the supplier/contractor. From then on, the number of changes should no longer be so high. From this phase onwards, approval-based change management applies.

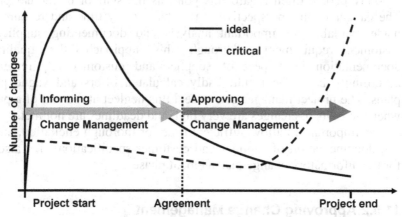

Figure 11.4: Two phases of Change Managment

11.5.1 Informing Change Management

In this phase there is no sense in defining a bureaucratic and elaborate process in which every change is followed by a large number of actions.

Here the other stakeholders should have sufficient trust in the author, so that he or she has sole responsibility for entering changes.

When, in the author's eyes, the specification has reached a relatively static state, this can be improved and finally approved through a review cycle with other stakeholders. This is also the point in time when the supplier/contactor responds to the (customer) specification. As a rule, the supplier conducts an analysis of the customer requirements, in which he checks the contents and the authors have the opportunity to further substantiate these specifications.

This is of course still in the informing change management phase. At the same time, the contractor produces a specification in which he submits an offer to the customer in respect of the customer specifications. Adjustments to both customer and supplier specifications are made during the negotiations.

Project management personnel are also heavily involved during this phase, because, at the very least, rough milestone planning and cost estimates should be made here to establish sound project planning. Once the customer and supplier are agreed on the scope (documented in the customer and supplier specifications), the remuneration and schedule, informing change management is at an end and release-based change management has begun.

Many people often regard this point as the start of the actual project. The danger of this perspective is that hardly any time and resources are made available for important analysis and documenting supplier and customer requirements. Through this approach, the quality of documentation in respect of supplier and customer requirements is accordingly bad. The result: badly calculated offers and vague project plans. The project manager gets to feel this neglect at the end of a project, when the costs of changes are very high and deadlines are not met.

It is important to allow sufficient time for thorough elicitation, analysis and documentation of supplier and customer specifications, i.e. also plan for the informatory change management phase.

11.5.2 Approving Change Management

Normally at a certain point in time, the customer and supplier will agree what the system to be developed should provide and what it will cost. This point in time is the completion of an agreement/ contract between both parties. Because others are relying on the published specifications, ad-hoch changes are no longer acceptable.

Often, the fact that changes are necessary after this point in time is suppressed. Therefore there is also no agreement about how to proceed in this case. It should be clear to each party that changes after signing the contract are legitimate. There should be an agreed process of dealing with changes.

Incidentally, this customer-supplier relationship does not always have to be between two organisations. It can also be between two departments of the same organisation e.g. between the product management and development departments.

Thus a process should be agreed, which deals with changes in a structured way. Of course, this is not possible without a certain minimum level of bureaucracy. The effort required is kept to a reasonable level when no large numbers of changes have to be dealt. Here the quality of the elicitation, analysis and specification in the informing change management phase will prove itself.

The state of the specification is adhered to in the agreement. Each change, irrespective of from which side it comes, is now no longer immediately entered in the specification, as was the case with informing change management. The change is initially documented as a change request.

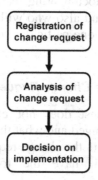

Figure 11.5: Activities of approving change management

11.5.2.1 Documenting Change Requests

Every project member (stakeholder in the list of stakeholders) should first of all be acquainted with how change requests in the project are documented and made. This should definitely be a central function. Furthermore, every stakeholder should have access to the current version of the customer and supplier specifications.

Exceptions to this global access are to be expected with commercially sensitive or security relevant information. The valid versions are those versions of the specifications agreed between the customer and supplier.

When the development of the system has already started, these are also the versions from which development is done.

Stakeholders from both the supplier and customer must be able to make change requests.

It is sensible to provide every stakeholder with a clear insight; not only into the current valid versions of the specifications, but also into all relevant change requests made. Care must be taken to protect people from information overload by choosing who should receive which information. Generally there is a role that is informed about everything with the task to decide who needs to know what. Keeping stakeholders updated with relevant information can reduce the risk of one and the same requests being made and processed several times. In addition, the decisions that have lead to a request being accepted or rejected are also documented here.

The person receiving change requests (Request Administrator) has the task of supporting the requestor in producing the change request, so that analysis of the change request can be quickly addressed.

The Request Administrator then assigns the requests to people who then analyse the implications. Depending on how complex the system to be developed is, the person documenting the request must decide whom the change request concerns and also who will analyse it. The change request may possibly relate to just one particular configuration in the system to be developed.

11.5.2.2 Attributes of the Change Request

Normally a change request does not comprise just information that something needs to be changed and what that change is, but also additional information that is filed with the change request.

A change request can have the following attributes (additional information):

- Change request identification number
- Date of recording the change request
- Priority of the change request
- Identity of Requestor
- Short description of the change request
- Reason for the change request
- Status of the change request
- Date of the decision about the change request
- Reason for the decision
- Owner of the change request
- Results of analysis (Implications for the entire project)

- Reference to requirements in the specification that are likely to be changed

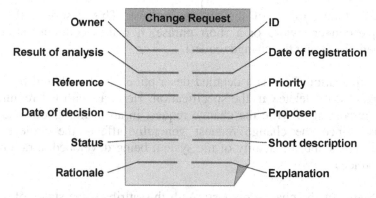

Figure 11.6: Possible attributes of a change request

This is just a selection of possible attributes for a change request. Which attributes are particularly meaningful must be decided on an individual basis. Amongst other things, this depends on the specific process for handling the change request, the structure of the system being developed and the structure of the organisations involved. Now to the attributes in detail.

Change request identification number: This attribute serves as a way of being able to uniquely identify a change request in communication with other project members. The attribute may be used for uniquely capturing the request in a database and so that it can be referenced to other information (e.g. requirements).

Date of recording the change request (registration): With this attribute, the person dealing with the request can, in conjunction with the status, assess performance in processing the change request.

Priority of the change request: An initial classification of the change request according to its importance can be made here. Where an error or conflict in a specification is identified that could generate significant costs, the estimated priority (importance or urgency) must be higher than for an additional improvement recommendation. The priority then represents a criterion that is important in the subsequent change request analysis phase, when all new change requests must be considered in terms of their effects on the entire system.

Proposer: The name of the person making the request is recorded here. This is important so as to be able to query the change request.

Short description of the change request: This describes the change request in one word or a short phrase. It makes communication easier when discussing the change request.

Explanation: This is a detailed description of what should be changed, expanded or deleted in the specification. Here, as with the requirements, it's important to write the change request in an unambiguous and logical way. Since the change request generally affects the project budget, milestones and the quality of the system being developed, a rationale is a good idea.

Status of the change request: With this attribute the status of a change request can be identified. This helps with processing and making decisions about change requests. Typical status are "new", "under analysis", "to be decided", "approved", "incorporated" or "rejected". Incidentally, these are only examples of status. In certain cases, more or even less classifications may be a good idea. This depends entirely on how the change requests are processed.

Date of the decision about the change request: When a decision about a change request has been made, it's sensible to record the date of the decision. A similar change request could be made at a later date. Then it makes sense to have documented the sequence of the decisions.

Rationale for the decision: As a rule, every decision has advantages and disadvantages. Very often, sometime after a decision for or against a change request, the disadvantages of the decision will become apparent. If the reason has not been documented, then a new discussion will start.

Owner of the change request: The owner of a change request is the person who performs the analysis and is responsible for bringing about a decision regarding the change request. It is also their responsibility to inform the requestor about the status of his or her change request.

Results of analysis (implications for the entire projects): The "owner of the change request" enters the results of the analysis here, i.e. the likely effects on cost, scheduling and quality of implementing the change request. This provides the working group deciding on the change request with a basis on which to make their decision.

Reference to requirements in the specification affected or likely to be changed: Here it is a good idea to reference test areas in the specifications, which need to be customized in the event of the change request being approved. Where it's possible to search according to references, any consolidation problems with other change requests can be identified in good time.

11.5.2.3 Analysis of Change Requests

The aim of this part of the process is to evaluate the effects of the change request, in order to create a basis for deciding whether the changes can also be implemented.

This task must be performed by people who are also able to assess the effects on scheduling, cost and system quality. As a rule, this is a project manager or an experienced developer.

The analysis can also be split between several people, depending on how many areas are affected be the request. The important thing is to nominate someone with overall responsibility who coordinates the entire analysis. Depending on the specific process, this coordinating person can also be the person named in the attribute "owner of the change request".

It may become necessary to undertake change request analysis in several stages. This is the case where one single individual can no longer assess the effects of the change request.

The "owner of the change request" must present the effects of the change in a way that the decision makers can understand. Often, when describing the qualitative effects, the mistake is made of formulating them in a too technical fashion, so that decision makers have great difficulty understanding them.

11.5.2.4 Decision to Implement the Change Request

The decision whether to accept a change request is generally made in one or more forums. The decision making process is highly individual and can also be conducted at various levels. However, it can generally be said that the following factors influence the decision making process:

- Results of the analysis (in particular effects on costs and schedule)
- Technical structure of the system to be developed
- Organisational structures of the customer and supplier

The results of the analysis are important since normally, depending on estimated additional costs, reduction in quality or shifts in the schedules, another level of management might have to be involved in the decision.

It is important to consider the technical structure because the risks of side effects increase with complex system structures; and those responsible for each subsystem should take an appropriate part in the decision making.

Ultimately the organisational structures of the participating organisations are also important, in order to involve all stakeholders as appropriate.

The working group meets often to decide on change request that already been analysed. It is up to the coordinator to decide on the priority in which change requests should be decided. The analysed change requests are usually collected together and discussed in one session.

The important thing about the composition of the working group is the participation of personnel from both the customer and supplier.

The final decision of the working group determines whether a change request should be implemented or rejected. Here it is very important that the decision is documented.

If the decision is to approve the change and its consequences (changes to costs, milestones and product quality), the change must firstly be entered in the customer and supplier specifications. Then, a new version of the customer and supplier specification documentation is produced. From then on, development takes place on the basis of these new specifications. In the process, it is important to ensure that every department affected by the changes is informed about the new versions of the documentation as soon as possible.

It is important to group changes into releases and to plan the releases. If a project is constantly changing it is possible that nothing gets delivered. In our experience it is better to plan for a number of releases, each consisting of a viable system. In this way, depending on the type of project, some experience can be gleaned from use of an early release

11.6 Turning Change Management theory into practice

Section 11.5 describes theoretical approaches to dealing with change. If these were to be implemented in organisations, a lot of time, conflict and, above all, costs could be saved. Unfortunately this is often not the case in practice. The following section is concerned with the factors that make effective change management so difficult.

Preventing bureaucracy in change management: When an agreement is first made between a customer and supplier concerning the scope of the system to be developed, normally everyone involved is satisfied. As a rule, reaching a consensus is not that easy. A change at a later date restarts the agreement process. This "extra work" is avoided by all concerned, particularly where a change is seemingly not particularly time-consuming to implement.

Nondisclosure of changes: Changes after the agreement are interpreted by some colleagues and superiors as carelessness by the authors of the customer and supplier specifications. That is, "if the work had been done more carefully, this change would not have been necessary". The change itself is regarded as negative. The result is that changes are often not communicated openly and kept as secret as possible.

No transition from Informing to Approval-based change management: There are projects, particularly internal ones, where no explicit transition is agreed. The reasons for this are that the customer is unsure whether he has actually described all requirements in his specification; and might often want to keep things open to incorporate changes "free of charge" at a later stage.

However understandable this strategy may be, it does not allow the supplier to do any reliable project planning and makes it more difficult to develop a feasible technical concept or architecture. In addition, a permanently smouldering conflict exists between the customer and supplier concerning the services to be provided. Ultimately the customer lays the foundation for failure, because the chance of actually getting what is stipulated in unapproved changes is relatively small.

Due to time constraints, changes just before the end of the project are no longer documented.

This is a quite a favourite problem. As the project end approaches, the project manager tries to save time by no longer documenting changes in the specifications, but by implementing them straightaway. This is fatal in so far as getting approval for a live system requires an up-to-date specification of the requirements. The negative effects of this behaviour then materialize in the follow-up project. As a rule, after the seemingly successful development of a system, a follow-up system will be proposed. The customer and supplier specifications for the previous system are normally used as a template for this. However, when this has not been updated completely, uncomfortable déjà-vu feelings can arise. In short, a malfunction previously fixed by changes will repeat itself, because the customer and supplier specifications have not been updated.

11.6.1 Effects of a Lack of Change Management

Poor and unstructured change management can sometimes have serious consequences for project cost and scheduling. The greater the division of labour: the more serious the effects. Where several development teams do not have the same information about the status of changes, implementation will be on the basis of out-dated customer and/or supplier specifications. Discrepancies in the level of information will eventually become apparent; in the worst case, not until a subsystem has to be integrated and does not function as originally planned. As a rule, it can then be established that development has been incorrectly conceived due to lack of information, for example about interfaces.

In an actual case, a contract developer made a small change to a programme to be delivered, at the request of a customer developer. This programme was a module of a larger system, which had already been approved and tested. The cost of the regression test, which had to follow, was more than €100,000.

It is particularly important from the psychological point of view that the customer is always informed about changes and involved in the decisions regarding a change. If this doesn't happen, the trust between the customer and supplier is destroyed. In some circumstances, customer expectations are not fulfilled. This can even lead to the customer feeling deceived and the acceptance of the system being refused.

Customer acceptance of the system is also a situation that can become very difficult when no structured change management has been implemented. The bases of acceptance tests are in themselves consistent and current requirements. Where these are nonexistent, there is no possibility to generate test cases with which to conduct tests. Where only out of date customer specifications are available, it is difficult and often actually impossible to incorporate "approved" changes and therefore produce an up to dated customer specification. No reliable test cases can be generated without it, and without test results a definite system acceptance is not possible.

11.6.2 Management support for introducing processes

Management plays a key role in the successful introduction of structured change management. Sufficient time should be allowed for producing the first version of the customer and supplier specifications. Unfortunately in practice, this is relatively seldom allowed for.

Here it is important to remember that the implementation has not yet started during this phase and that developers are not yet working on the project. So as not to have developers "sitting around" doing nothing, attempts are often made to shorten informatory change management as far as possible. Since normally the most experienced and productive developers are required to produce customer and supplier specifications, it is very difficult to remove them from previous projects in order to specify the follow-on project.

But, in the event of a deadline crisis, these very people are required to bring the previous project to a close as planned. This is actually a vicious circle, for which management needs to find solutions by implementing important decisions and not just giving priority to seemingly urgent situations.

Furthermore, it must be ensured that customer and supplier specifications are reviewed accordingly to previously defined criteria, and that the results of the review are incorporated in the customer and supplier specifications. This is extremely important prior to an agreement between the customer and supplier (at the end of the informing change management).

Of course, every review costs time, which management must approve. But in any case, this time is well invested and has a definite pay-off in the implementation and test phases. Management must create a climate in which timely recognized mistakes have no negative consequences for the authors of the specifications or project manager. Finding mistakes is good. Find them before you build the wrong product.

Management should in any case ensure that a process is defined for approval-based change management between the customer and supplier, which takes up the theme of change management.

It's important to inform staff about the process and to ensure that they have adequate support when questions or uncertainties arise. Change requests should be easy to submit and (for the stakeholder) easy to follow up.

11.7 Procedure for Introducing Structured Change Management

As a rule, one should firstly check how changes are normally dealt with in an organisation, whether processes have already been defined and, more importantly, whether these processes being followed in reality. If that is the case, these projects can be structured upon the processes.

If no structured change management processes have been defined or implemented, they can be defined and implemented in a typical pilot project. As a pilot project, a project should be chosen in which accepted staff work, who support the goal of introducing structured processes.

Firstly it should be ensured that all staff involved in the project work on all requirements based on a standard information base. This standard information base can be a document or a database. The important thing is that all stakeholders have access to up-to-date information from this database. A "mini"-process is initially sufficient for an update when changes occur. This will be tailored depending on the size of the project. This can be defined as follows:

There is one owner of the database, whose task it is to enter all changes into the database. It must be made clear to all project members that no agreements about changes are valid unless they have been entered in this database. Developers may only implement what is in the database.

In this way an important milestone is created which is the prerequisite for a structured system approval.

Then one addresses the further development of the change management process. This includes considering the following factors:

- Organisational structure of the organisation
- Product or system structure
- Configuration management
- Product development process
- Sales process
- Supplier selection

As can be seen, there are numerous factors that affect the final change management process.

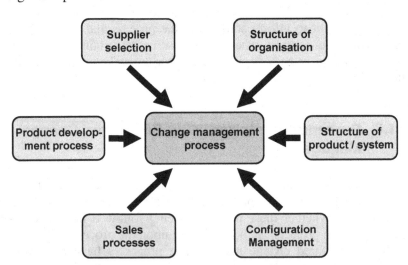

Figure 11.7: Factors influencing the change management process

11.8 Summary

In summary, the responsibility for change management must rest with management. Change requests during development should not be a taboo subject, but should be decided openly and communicated to all affected stakeholders.

Above all, careful documentation of the changes, from which customer and supplier specifications can be updated, before (!) the changes are implemented, are important in order to provide a basis for system acceptance. These customer and supplier specifications can represent an important basis for follow-on systems.

12 Advanced Requirements Management: the complete specification

So far we have learned about the interfaces of the most prominent systems engineering disciplines with requirements. These interfaces are described in detail in chapters 6 through 11. We have explained the meaning of linking the various kinds of requirements with each other and of linking requirements with other information. We know how requirements support the activities of project management, risk management, test management and so on.

In these previous chapters we have frequently referred to requirements management as though it was something readily provided, preferrably by divine providence. Thus the reader may feel that the question is still not completely anwered: what exactly is requirements management?

The short answer to this question is: requirements management is the sum of all systems engineering disciplines when applied to requirements. A somewhat more detailed answer will be given in the following, which, to a certain extent, is inevitably a repetition and a summary of what has been said previously in this book.

12.1 Interfaces between other Systems Engineering disciplines and Requirements

Previously, we have identified the following systems engineering disciplines to be most important with regard to their interface to requirements:

- project management
- quality management
- configuration management
- risk management
- test management
- version management
- change management

It has been shown that if these systems engineering disciplines are not applied to requirements, the quality of the information as provided by requirements development will soon deteriorate.

For example, without change management the requirements will soon be outdated, thus giving an obsolete and even incorrect picture. Without configuration management, after a few months or so nobody will be able to tell which requirements belong to which version or release of the product.

And the same is true the other way round: the systems engineering disciplines will not grow to their full strength if they do not make use of the requirements information. For example, a project management that has no overview of the current status of implementation will be unable to relate the budget used so far to the actual project progress. Thus there will be no reliable comment on whether the project needs correcting actions or not.

The following figure 12.1 gives an overview of the various interfaces analysed so far.

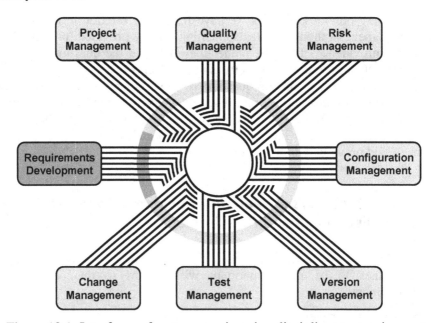

Figure 12.1: Interfaces of systems engineering disciplines to requirements

In figure 12.1, the light grey circle encloses all the various system engineering disciplines interfaces, while the dark grey part of this circle symbolises the interface of all the systems engineering disciplines as described in this book to requirements development or requirements engineering. We use these two terms requirements development and requirements engineering to mean the same thing. Thus, the dark grey part of all interfaces *is* requirements management, the sum of all interfaces between requirements engineering and the other systems engineering discplines.

Note that figure 12.1 could be greatly extended, depending on the organisation and the specific goals defined for requirements management. For example, in organisations that use dedicated software tools to support the requirements management and engineering activities, there could be another bubble "RM&E Tools". In the above figure, this would mean that any RM&E tool must not be assumed to be completely detached from the other aspects. The tool would have to be able to handle all necessary interfaces, and might in turn, due to its nature, restrict some of the ways in which people work. In other words, there would be interfaces to the tool.

As a second example, there could be an organisation that heavily uses simulations. This could be a supplier in the aircraft industry, where many products have to be checked by simulation, amongst others. In such an organisation, the above figure might contain another bubble "Simulations", implying that requirements management will assume a specific form to deal with the information in connection with simulations.

It is also possible to think of organisations where one or more of the interfaces shown in figure 12.1 are missing. Take the producer of roller coasters, for example. Typically, roller coasters are individually developed and therefore exist only once. In such an environment change and version management will presumably play a lesser role than for example in software producing organisations, where many software modules are written to be used again and again in many products and many releases.

Every organisation has to define their individual version of figure 12.1. Apart from what is more or less important to this specific organisation, its version of figure 12.1 will also imply how far people want to go with regard to requirements management. This is a very important point. Do not blindly follow the ideas in this book. You must work out how much effort to invest in each area in order to get the best return.

12.2 Getting away from the document view

12.2.1 The document view

Traditionally, requirements are still seen in many organisations as being part of special documents. Typical names of such documents are for example "customer requirements specification", "system requirements specification" and "design requirements specification".

One or more such documents are usually the legal basis of a contract between a customer and a supplier. In other words, the question whether the supplier actually delivers what the customer pays for is answered by comparing what is delivered against what should be delivered according to the respective documents. Figure 12.2 shows some typical associations in connection with requirements.

Therefore, requirements are recognised by some people as being associated with mainly legal stuff and as having little to do with "real" development work. At least, once the contract is won and the specialists are able to start doing what they really want, the specification is soon forgotten.

Figure 12.2: Typical associations of requirements documents

This way of thinking is often encouraged by such simple but nonetheless existing problems like document structure: the documents are often arranged so as to best fit their legal or contractual purposes. As such, a typical developer does not feel comfortable with the way the information may be presented there. And other groups of people might have still other ideas of an ideal structure. For example, someone belonging to the change management group could sort the information with regard to the change cycles that were carried out.

12.2.2 The information view

For the successful introduction and implementation of a requirements management way of thinking it is most important to help people change the way they look at requirements. They must understand that requirements are a vital part of all project information, and that the individual fractions of the project information are inevitably intertwined and related to each other. By contrast to the typical cliché shown in figure 12.2, the following figure 12.3 shows a document independent view of the various people involved in a project upon all available information.

A figure like 12.3 might help people to start realising that even though everyone uses a slightly different part of it, it is indeed the same pot of information they are all sharing.

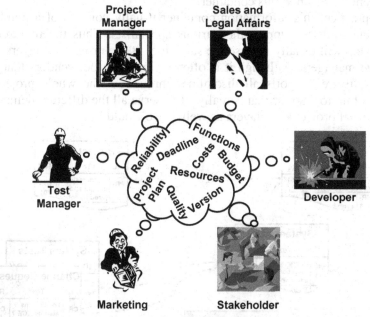

Figure 12.3: Document independent view upon project information

Once people have grasped this concept, they will change the way they look upon the other parts of the information. For example, the test management will begin to understand that if the requirements are reliable there could be no better source of information for their test activities. As another example, a risk manager will be happy to have access to so rich a source of information on possible product, technical and other risks.

Ideally, the various people involved then begin to have their own special interest in the management of the requirements. Thus for example the risk manager will support any activities to keep the requirements up to date, so as to always have reliable risk information. The test managers will see to it that the change managers put the requirements into the scope of their activities, so that test management can access information on changes of requirements. This will enable the testers to always carry out suitable tests that are not outdated or wrong.

12.3 Implementing Requirements Management

Figure 12.3 suggests that all project information may bee seen as one big container, and the different people involved in a project simply have their different views upon this container.

In practice, this information container usually consists of a number of different tools to support the various specialists. Thus the requirements managers will usually not use the same tool as the project managers or the change managers. Although it is often claimed by tool vendors that some new software supports all disciplines throughout the whole project, we know of no tool so far that is really fit to serve all the different demands of the normal project key players as well as we would like.

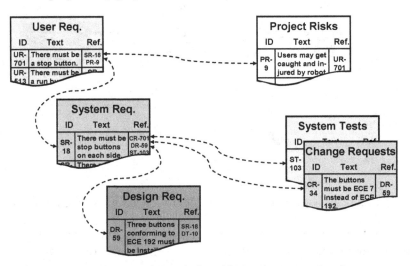

Figure 12.4: Documenting relationships using textual references

For the different tools to form one consistent information container it is most important that all tool and process interfaces are engineered to seamlessly mesh with each other. And indeed, it is one of the main challenges of requirements management to make sure that this is so.

It has been repeatedly pointed out that requirements information will develop its full strength only when the relations between the individual parts of the information are documented and can be traced back and forth. Thus the tool and process interfaces must assure that relations can be documented even between the data stored in two or more different tools. And do not forget that the relations will need change management etc.

In a simple case, relations could be documented as textual references in natural language, as for example shown in figure 12.4. In a more advanced environment, such relations could be realised using hyperlinks or similar techniques. This allows for easy navigation from one information sub-container (tool) to another and vice versa, as shown in figure 12.5.

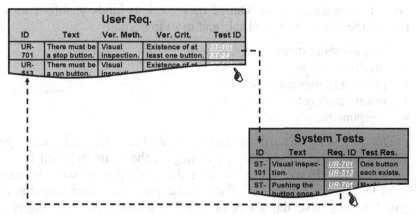

Figure 12.5: Documenting relationships using hyperlinks or similar

While the tool interfaces will provide the different project members with easy access to each relevant part of the project information, the processes and their interfaces must define the way these different pieces of information are

- created
- maintained
- used
- owned

With regard to requirements management, the respective processes must define how and when requirements are elicited, specified, analysed, reviewed, changed, released, implemented and tested.

In parallel, the processes representing requirements management must define the relevant parts of the requirements information for all systems engineering disciplines, and how and when each discipline will access their relevant information.

The following sections show how the each of the above listed interfaces can be implemented. It is important to note that these suggestions are neither complete nor absolute. They are meant to provide a draft or a starting point, and the readers are encouraged to further improve and tailor these drafts and templates as needed.

12.3.1 Implementing the interface to Project Management and Quality Management

Chapter 6 shows what kind of information requirements can provide a project management with. Out of these various kinds of information, we believe the following to be basic and most important:

- requirements status
- implementation status
- planned implementation
- resources / costs
- responsible

The following discussion details possibilities for understanding and documenting the information pertaining to the status relevant to project management. In each case we need the possibility to show whether an entry has been made or not. Each of the above attributes would have the possibility to have the status of "To be defined" or more normally in practice "TBD".

Also it might be possible that not every entry in a requirements database will require a defined status. To avoid confusion this needs to be documented and as mostly done by defining a status of "not applicable" or more normally in practice "NA". The use of NA and TBD is assumed and is not repeated in each of the following sections describing each attribute.

12.3.1.1 Requirements status

This information or column (in a spreadsheet sense) or attribute (in a database sense) should indicate the current work status of each individual requirement. The requirements status information will usually be maintained by developers and quality managers or requirements managers.

It is good practice to restrict the number of possible entries for the requirements status. A typical list of such entries could look as follows:

- new
- for review
- rework
- accepted
- put back
- deleted

The above list is engineered to be as short as possible, while all vital information can be extracted. The process using this information or attribute could be as follows.

Every new requirement would start with the status "new". This allows for a quick overview of which parts of a specification have come into existence only recently.

Once the first version of a requirement is finished, the author sets its status to "for review". This is the signal for the people responsible for the quality of the requirements. They can then start with the requirements analysis and review.

The result of this could then either be "rework" or "accepted". If rework is necessary, an additional attribute or text information could provide more information on what aspect of the requirement must be improved or modified before it can be accepted.

If rework was necessary and the responsible author has corrected the requirement accordingly, he or she sets the status back to "for review". Now the requirement can be reviewed again. Once the review and correction cycle is over, the status of the requirement is "accepted". The same procedure applies when a requirement has to be changed. We will go into more detail on the change management interface in a following section.

At any point of time during this development cycle the requirement could also be put back or deleted. Putting a requirement back could mean that it is not meant to be deleted, but its further development is postponed, for example because some discussions with stakeholders are necessary.

It is good practice to use the requirements status to indicate whether a requirements has been deleted, rather than deleting the requirement from the respective view or even physically. This is because the deleted requirements tell a certain story and thus provide an additional context or some background information. If the deleted requirements are not visible in the normal working view or if they are physically deleted, it might be unclear why the current collection of requirements is just as it is.

12.3.1.2 Implementation status

This information shows how far the implementation of a requirement has got. As there are normally only two possibilities, the typical entries for this field or attribute are "not implemented" and "implemented".

This attribute will help all relevant people to gather a quick overview of how much work has already been finished and how much still remains.

Most tools allow filtering and creation of reports based on the information contained in the database.   Using attributes such as Implementation Status the creation of an overview can be automated.

12.3.1.3 Planned implementation

This information indicates when some requirement should be implemented, and it can be maintained for example by project management.

The attribute helps the developers to plan their work packages; it helps the testers to plan for tests in due time; it helps project management to check how much work is delayed or is on time.

12.3.1.4 Resources / costs

This information can be maintained by experienced developers or other staff that have to do with the estimation of costs in projects, for example project managers or project controllers. It gives an estimate of how much resources or costs are associated with the implementation of a requirement.

Typical entries in this attribute could be for example "3 man days" or "1500 €". This information helps the project management to estimate how much work has already been carried out and how much is still waiting. If requirements must be prioritised due to limited resources or budget this attribute together with some attribute "importance" or similar will prove most valuable. They support in selecting the requirements that are best suited for neglecting, such as requirements that are of relatively low importance but relatively expensive to implement.

12.3.1.5 Responsible

This information is necessary to know who is responsible for the requirement. Sometimes this attribute is called "Owner". Who may change the requirement? Who shall we contact if we have questions regarding understanding what is meant? When we need to compromise and move the implementation of a requirement to a later release, who should best understand the implications of this? Without someone being responsible for a requirement, without the sense of ownership, we might easily delete something necessary or spend huge amounts of effort or resources implementing something that was not very important. Who is responsible for ensuring that the attributes of a requirement are filled out and filled out correctly? Someone has to be responsible and we need to know who it is.

12.3.2 Implementing the interface to Version Management and Configuration Management

It has been shown in the previous chapter on configuration management and version management that these two topics cannot be separated from each other. Rather, they are two different aspects of the same problem.

Regarding requirements, version management is concerned with the question of archiving and managing one set of requirements at different stages and points in time. For example, the first draft of user requirements could be called "user requirements V1.0". During their further development, the user requirements might advance to version 3.0, at which point a branch is created to account for the fact that the system under development can exist in two basic forms, for example a premium and a standard version. The two respective branches of user requirements could be called "user requirements V1.0 P (premium)" and "user requirements V1.0 S (standard)". Figure 12.6 shows this situation.

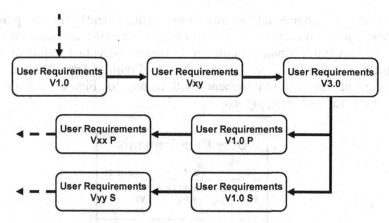

Figure 12.6: Example of different versions of user requirements

Configuration management is concerned with the administration of the different versions of all pieces of necessary project information. For example, the user requirements V2.3 and the system requirements V2.1 and the design requirements V2.7 together could be called "standard configuration V1.4". This is shown in figure 12.7.

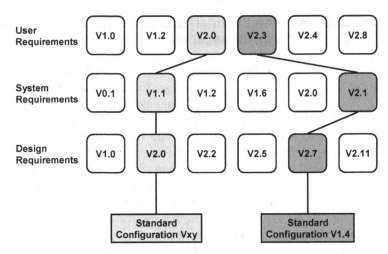

Figure 12.7: Example configuration with different requirements versions

With a commercial requirements management tool, a pragmatic approach to requirements version management is the introduction of only one additional attribute or column. For each individual requirement, this attribute would list all versions of the set of requirements or requirements document that this requirement shall belong to. Figure 12.8 shows an example for such an approach.

User Requirements		
ID	**Text**	**Version**
UR-701	There must be a stop button.	V1 V2 V3
UR-702	The stop button must be red (RGB 255-0-0).	V1 V2 V3
UR-703	The stop button must always be sensitive.	V1 V2 V3
UR-	The light mu~ be su~	

Figure 12.8: Example of using a version attribute for requirements

When using the approach as shown in figure 12.8, it is also necessary to create a new requirement each time an existing requirement should be modified for less than all existing versions.

For example, a specific requirement has so far belonged to all existing versions 1, 2 and 3 of the system requirements. Now the requirement needs to be changed, but only for version 3, not for versions 1 and 2. In this situation, the requirement must be copied and modified. The old requirement would then only be relevant for versions 1 and 2, and the new requirement only for version 3. Figure 12.9 pictures this example.

User Requirements		
ID	Text	Version
UR-701	There must be a stop button.	V1 V2 V3
UR-702	The stop button must be red (RGB 255-0-0).	V1 V2
UR-924	The stop button must be blue (RGB 0-0-255).	V3
UR-	The stop but must a	

Figure 12.9: Changing a requirement when using a version attribute

In figure 12.9 the attribute "Version" refers to the version or release of the set of requirements such as a document containing the requirements. For the sake of simplicity we have not shown here the version numbers of the individual requirements. There is a relationship between UR-702 and UR-924 that is not shown in figure 12.9. The relationship is that UR-702 is version 1 of the requirement, and UR-924 is version 2 of the same requirement. Versions of requirements are mentioned here for completeness but are not shown due to space constrictions and to enable us to produce simple diagrammes. In a real project we document the versions of requirements and also versions of configurations of requirements such as a versions of a document that will contain particular versions of requirements.

Although it may seem quite obvious to the reader that in the above example the modified requirement is actually a new requirement, our experience shows that quite frequently people would change requirements and have no way of viewing the older version. Requirements that have been relevant for release versions 1 and 2 of a document are unfortunately often overwritten like this, even if the change is only relevant for version 3 of a document.

Practices like this are the source of many confusions and inefficient ways or working. For the example at hand, a typical reason for such practices is the assumption by some people that versions 1 and 2 of the document are obsolete, because version 3 of the document is the most recent. They forget that there might be products that use version 1 or 2 of the set of the requirements, and that there must be corresponding tests. Thus it is important always to be able to recover older versions of a set of requirements, even if these older versions are currently not used or appear to be outdated.

With respect to requirements, the version management interface can also satisfy many of the needs of the configuration management interface. If all different versions of each set of requirements are known as a result of an effective version management, then with regard to requirements, configuration management only has to make sure that the various versions of each set of requirements are put together correctly.

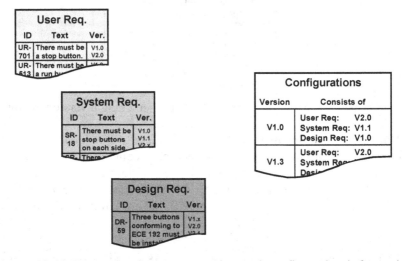

Figure 12.10: Example of separate version and configuration information

Unlike the version management information, configuration management information for configuration of sets of documents is quite often not maintained together with the requirements. This is because while every single requirement is normally relevant for at least one version of the set of requirements it belongs to, a configuration of a set of documents usually contains many requirements from one specific requirements set. In other words, the version information must be maintained for each individual requirement, but the configuration information must only be maintained for sets of versions of different kind of requirements.

Therefore, the version information for sets of requirements is well suited to be maintained using a specific attribute or column for each requirement, but it would normally be far too much work and redundancy to also introduce an attribute for configurations of sets of documents. Figure 12.10 sketches how version and configuration information for sets of requirements can be maintained separately. The attribute "Ver." In Figure 12.10 refers to the version of the set of requirements that each requirement is a member of.

12.3.3 Implementing the interface to Risk Management

From the requirements point of view, the implementation of the interface to risk management is relatively simple. As the relation between risks and requirements is generally n:m, the risks are usually maintained separately from the requirements.

This is especially true since risks usually have their own special set of additional information or attributes, which has been described in detail in chapter 9 on risk management. Thus the risk management information can be thought of as being orthogonal to the requirements information.

We therefore suggest to add only one attribute or column to the requirements information, and to use this attribute to list all risks that relate to each individual requirement. In order to be able to navigate in both directions, a corresponding attribute or column would have to be introduced also in the risk information container or risk document. Figure 12.11 shows what has been said so far.

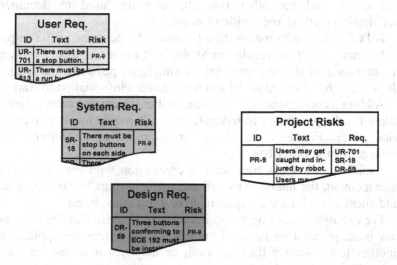

Figure 12.11: Example interface to risk management using a risk attribute

As can be seen from figure 12.11, each time a requirement or risk information is changed, the interface must be taken into account. Thus for example, changing a requirement could mean that some risk no longer applies to this requirement, or that a risk that has so far been irrelevant for the requirement at hand now becomes relevant, or that a new risk comes into existence.

In turn, changing the risk information could mean that this risk no longer applies to one or more of the requirements it has applied to so far, or that it applies to more requirements than before, or that it applies to other requirements now.

In both cases, the interface attribute must be checked and maintained accordingly to make sure that the information and relationships (links) are always up to date.

12.3.4 Implementing the interface to Test Management

The interface to test management is similar to the interface to risk management in that the test management information is orthogonal to the requirements information, as the relationship between these two is n:m in general.

Referring to the detailed discussion on test management in chapter 10, we suggest the use of three attributes to be added to the requirements information. In this approach, one attribute is used to reference the relevant test cases, and the other two attributes are used to document the verification method and verification criteria.

All other test information, like for example the name of the responsible tester and the test result, must be documented, too. To keep the maintenance of the requirements as simple as possible, we suggest that these data are all stored in the test management information to start with.

Adding a corresponding reference attribute to the test information would allow for the possibility to navigate from the requirements to the tests and vice versa. Figure 12.12 shows an example of an interface to test management as described.

Similar to what has been said in connection with the interface to risk management, the interface to test management must be taken into account and checked each time a requirement or a test is modified.

For example, changing a requirement could mean that the test case that has been planned to be used so far can no longer be applied. Maybe another test case can then be used, or maybe a new test case must be created.

Changing a test case on the other hand could mean that some of the requirements that should be tested with this test case are no longer covered, or that more requirements than before can now be tested with this one test case.

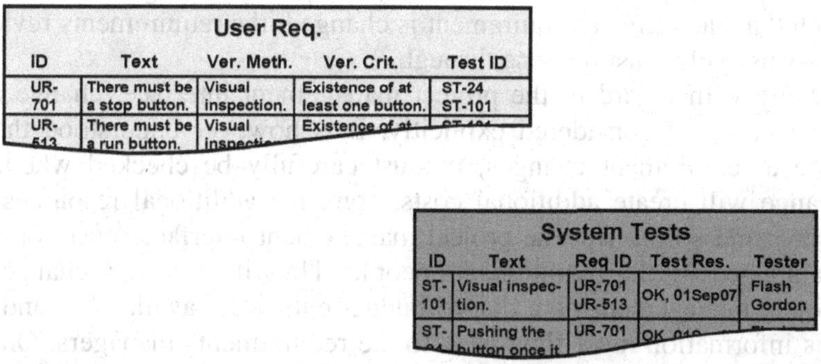

User Req.				
ID	Text	Ver. Meth.	Ver. Crit.	Test ID
UR-701	There must be a stop button.	Visual inspection.	Existence of at least one button.	ST-24 ST-101
UR-513	There must be a run button.	Visual inspecti...	Existence of at...	...

System Tests				
ID	Text	Req ID	Test Res.	Tester
ST-101	Visual inspection.	UR-701 UR-513	OK, 01Sep07	Flash Gordon
ST-...	Pushing the button once it...	UR-701	OK, 01...	...

Figure 12.12: Example interface to test management using a test attribute

Due to the interface between requirements and tests, and the interface between requirements and risks, the risks may be taken into account when deciding on a test strategy. For instance high risks might lead to a decision to test the system against the requirements to a higher level of assurance. We see that risks, for example are common to requirements, risk management, and test management. In reality all systems engineering disciplines are interrelated. Requirements management is the sum of the disciplines of systems engineering applied to requirements. The interface between requirements and all other systems engineering disciplines is the sum of the interfaces between requirements and each individual systems engineering discipline.

12.3.5 Implementing the interface to Change Management

In connection with the maintenance of the interfaces to the various systems engineering disciplines the previous sections already touched upon the topic of change management.

In particular, it has been pointed out that each time a requirement is changed the impact on its relation to risk and test information must carefully be checked. In turn, changing a risk or test information must go hand in hand with checking the impact on the relationships between risks and requirements or tests and requirements, respectively.

In connection with the version and configuration management interfaces we have shown that changes to requirements necessitate a check on the valid versions and configurations, and vice versa. Thus if a new version of one set of requirements or a new configuration of more than one set of requirements is to be created, or an existing one is to be modified, it must be carefully defined which requirements shall belong and which shall not.

It has been briefly mentioned that the quality management interface is such that each time a requirement is changed, the requirements review and analysis cycle must be gone through.

Only with regard to the project management interface, change aspects have not been considered explicitly. It is however understood that each time a requirement changes, it must carefully be checked whether this change will create additional costs, consume additional resources, cause delays and so on. But the project management interface must not only be maintained by the requirements people. Thus if there is a change in the project management plan due to budget cuts, staff availability and so on, this information must flow back to the requirements managers. Only then will it be possible to decide whether some requirements must be neglected for implementation and which ones these should be.

Apart from this, the changes to the requirements themselves have to be documented in order to be able to reproduce the current version, any previous versions and the history of changes. If special requirements management and engineering tools are used, these should provide a history mechanism to trace back any changes that have been made to any part of the available information, which basically is the complete set of attributes or columns and associations. Note however that the versioning and configuration mechanisms provided by such professional and commercial software are normally found to be insufficient without customisation when things become only a little bit more complex.

Many organisations simply use common office software such as WORD or Excel when they start introducing dedicated requirements management and engineering processes, and nobody should underestimate such approaches. There are organisations that are brilliant in using named software even in rather complex projects, and there are organisations that although they have access to the finest state of the art software, will probably never manage to get things right.

Besides, using the history mechanism of professional software is not always straightforward and the relevant information can only be extracted with many mouse clicks. This is often found to be rather ineffective. Therefore, and in view of users of standard office tools as mentioned before, a relatively simple but quite effective solution is the use of one history attribute or column.

After the initial version of a requirement has been created, all changes to this requirement are documented using the history attribute. The procedure would then be as follows: copy the current version of the requirement into the history attribute (or append it to any existing entries) and formulate the new requirements version in the normal text attribute. Figure 12.13 shows an example of the result of this procedure.

User Req.			
ID	Text	Author	History
UR-701	There must be 5 stop buttons.	U. Looser, 01Apr2007	There must be 3 stop buttons. (John Johnssonson, 3Mar2007)
UR-513	There must be a run button.	C. Side, 12Dec200̸	

Figure 12.13: Example of using a history attribute

Of course, a similar approach could be used to document changes to the other interface attributes, for example the three suggested test attributes. It is also possible to document any changes to the requirement or any associated attribute or column in the history attribute only. However, this may lead to problems with large chunks of text in some standard software tools.

Alternatively, the requirements text could simply be extended by entering the new version. If the software used for requirements engineering and management is limited in view of length of text entries, then a new row or object might be inserted in the right place. To support the reader of the document in telling history from the current version of a requirement, the previous entries could be struck through. Figure 12.14 sketches this alternative approach.

User Req.		
ID	Text	Author
UR-701	~~There must be 3 stop buttons.~~	J. Johnssonson, 03Mar2007
	There must be 5 stop buttons.	U. Looser, 01Apr2007
UR-513	There must be a run butt̸	C. Ø̸

Figure 12.14: Documenting the history together with the requirement

The solution shown in 12.14 can easily be applied to any other attributes or columns if they are also subject to changes. This has the advantage that changes are immediately visible. Some authors do not use any technique even though it costs nothing to implement and nothing to introduce. There are unfortunately some authors that still deliver 150 page requirements documents with no documentation of what has changed since the previous version.

12.3.6 Overview

The previous sections showed how requirements management, which is the sum of the interfaces of requirements development or requirements engineering to all the other systems engineering disciplines, can initially be implemented.

It has been described how all project information related to requirements can be managed if all the systems engineering disciplines work together to this common end. For a basic requirements management, we suggest the following set of attributes or columns to maintain together with the requirements:

- reqiurements status
- implementation status
- planned implementation
- resources / costs
- responsible
- version
- risk
- test id
- verification method
- verification criteria
- history

Thus with only 11 attributes or columns (in addition to the attributes and columns that have been suggested in connection with requirements engineering in general, such as references or links, author, ID and so on), it is possible to multiply the power of requirements information.

We have pointed out that requirements management will only be effective if the interfaces are maintained not only by the requirements people, but also by the people responsible for all the other systems engineering disciplines.

Therefore, in addition to the attributes suggested above, the test managers, risk managers and project managers must maintain their parts of the project information, too, and share their information with the requirements managers. Ideally, all the pieces of information of each systems engineering discipline mesh with all the others, so as to give one complete set of data.

12.4 Summary

This chapter summarises and completes all the previous chapters on the various interfaces of requirements engineering to all the other systems engineering disciplines analysed in this book.

The chapter shows that in fact, requirements management is not an independent systems engineering discipline. Rather, requirements management is the sum of all systems engineering disciplines when applied to requirements.

The requirements management philosophy is shown to be most effective when a documents based view upon the available project information is abandoned in favour of an information based view. Changing their point of view this way, the people involved in a project will soon start to realise that they actually all use and need the same information container. The only things that might be different from case to case are the individual portions of this information that are relevant for each project member. Thus for example the requirements engineers might mainly be interested in the requirements texts, while the risk managers are mainly interested in the risks associated with requirements, and the project manager could be mainly interested in the resources and budget consumption due to the requirements.

In the following sections of this chapter, a suggestion is made for a basic initial approach to requirements management. In short, it is shown how using just a few attributes or columns for requirements (in addition to those that should be part of requirements information anyways, such as identifier, author, date and so on) can already address many of the problems described in earlier chapters.

These attributes are the requirements engineering part of requirements management, and they represent the interface to project management, quality management, configuration management, risk management, test management, version management and change management.

Examples and recommendations of how to use these attributes are given, and alternative approaches are described for users of professional requirements engineering and management tools and users of standard office software.

This said, the authors hope that the reader feels a little bit more familiar with the philosophy and aims of requirements management now. We encourage everybody to just start introducing dedicated requirements engineering and management activities and thus get a feeling for what is more applicable and what is less, and which needs and situations a specific organisation must address in order to be successful.

Requirements management is an adventure in its own right, and like all true adventures there will be obstacles and times of doubt. However, a happy end usually waits for those who go through all the efforts to overcome the obstacles. As with everything, the beginning is the hardest – once the mechanism is set in gear and running more or less smoothly, it will be hard to stop it.

Finally, do not forget: according to our own viewpoint, things just have to be started, no matter how sophisticated this is to begin with. You can always improve things as necessary as you carry on. It will never be too late to improve.

13 The HOOD Capability Models

This chapter gives a brief introduction to and overview of capability models in general, presents a few of the currently widely used capability models for requirements engineering and management in some detail and introduces the HOOD capability models for requirements definition and requirements management. These two models will be dealt with in detail in the following two chapters.

13.1 The meaning of capability models

In principle, capability models shall support organisations in estimating their current status with regard to certain abilities, and they have experienced an ever increasing interest throughout the last two or three decades.

Usually, capability models try to measure the maturity of various processes within an organisation. For example, a certain capability model could classify an organisation's abilities with respect to developing software code, while some other capability model specialises in determining the effectivity of an organisation's administration.

The basic idea behind capability models is the assumption that a high quality of processes will be reflected in a high quality of the results or artefacts of these processes. In connection with requirements engineering and management, the processes that are involved in developing a product are of special interest. It is the common belief of almost all industries that if the development processes are of high quality, the final products will inherit a fair portion of that quality. This is thought to be true of practically all products including services, be it software, hardware, mechanical parts or anything else.

Many hours of work have been spent with the effort to come up with consistent capability models that cover almost all aspects of an organisation, rather than specialising in only one or a few fields of typical activities. Two very well-known results of such efforts are the Capability Maturity Model Integration, or CMMI, and the model for Software Process

Improvement and Capability Determination, or SPICE. We will look at these two models in some detail later in chapter 13.3.

By offering methods for estimating how far advanced an organisation is with respect to its processes, capability models automatically provide a basis for improving the processes. Quite frequently, the evaluation patterns go hand in hand with checklists or tables of contents to support the user of the model in setting up appropriate processes or in improving existing processes.

However, there are drawbacks to this, too. Many people think that what they have to do is strictly follow the rules and recommendations of the specific capability model they chose to use. Such an attitude is often reinforced by the fact that the organisation does not want to work with capability models at all, but is forced to do so by industry partners. For example, the big automobile manufacturers expect their suppliers to be certified according to some capability model. If a supplier refuses to become certified, this frequently means that he will no longer be able to win any contracts.

But in an ideal world, it would be the other way round. An organisation would seek to improve its processes on its own account. Only after having established appropriate and effective processes, the organisation could then check whether their processes are in agreement with what is considered to be the current standard or state of the art. Obviously this should be an iterative improvement effort, and not just done once and for all. Every long journey starts with one step.

In our experience, organisations that choose the second approach usually fulfil the requirements of the common capability models easily, while organisations that choose the first approach frequently fail because they only follow what is written, not the spirit of the model.

13.2   Why we need capability models

Since capability models support in evaluating the status of an organisation with respect to the maturity of its processes, such models are strongly connected to measurement and metrics. An organisation needs the possibility to judge its status at any time and to measure its progress from one evaluation to the next for many reasons.

One reason is the need to relate expenditures to benefits. What is an improvement of process quality good for if the organisation spends all its money for these process improvements and is finally ruined. On the other hand, how much improvement does an organisation expect when it is prepared to spend only say, 0.1% of its net profit.

Another equally important reason is the psychological side of process improvements. It is well known that an organisation usually has to overcome severe barriers when introducing new processes, methods and tools. This is due to those people within the organisation that are affected by these changes. They will usually resist changes, for changes inevitably mean saying goodbye to some old ways of thinking and working, having to learn new things, feeling insecure and so on. Amongst other things, one very strong and reliable means to lessen such resistance is the ability to clearly show what has been achieved so far and to outline the next steps. If people can see a possibility of success then they generally have less anxiety than if the task seems insurmountable.

Since capability models normally follow a little-by-little philosophy with increasing levels of maturity, they provide numerous milestones of more and less importance. This is perfectly suited to help motivate people within an organisation to change. Instead of trying to reach some rather virtual and far-off goal, people can thus experience little successes all the way long.

The third reason for why we may need capability models is the fact that the models approximately outline how improvements may be accomplished. Each model does this implicitly, and some do explicitly. They thus give an idea of how to get started with improvements.

For example, when we use a model's checklist for our software development process and the evaluation comes up with the result that the change management is missing or inadequate, then we know at least that we must go into further details with our change management processes, if they exist or are documented at all. In this case the checklist and the result of the evaluation are implicit hints at what to do to improve. The more detailed the evaluation process of the chosen capability model is, the more detailed we will implicitly be told what to concentrate on to become better.

A framework to be tailored to individual needs is an example of an explicit capability model. For example, a specific model could demand that requirements be managed in terms of changes and tests to reach a certain level. We then know beforehand that if we want to achieve that maturity level, we must have change management and test management processes. Depending on how far the model goes into details, we may also be able to tell what aspects these processes must cover and which level of quality they must conform to.

A fourth reason to use capability models is the need for standardisation. Although generally all efforts of an organisation to improve its own processes must be acknowledged and encouraged, a comparison between different organisations becomes hard or impossible if everyone uses their own individual plans for process improvements and evaluations. For example, it is very common that the large original equipment manufacturers demand of their suppliers to be qualified and certified to work according to a certain level of maturity of one of the well known capability models.

Using tested and proven concepts avoids the problem of every organisation reinventing the wheel again and again. This also means that inefficient experimenting stemming from inexperience is minimised, and the improvement measures will become effective much quicker than otherwise. The framework that such standards offer should however not be mistaken to be inflexible, and the suggestions must not be assumed to be rigid laws.

With the main reasons for using capability models described, we will now go into some detail with two proven and frequently used models, SPICE and CMMI.

13.3   Two example capability models

13.3.1 SPICE

The abbreviation SPICE was originally created as the short form of Software Process Improvement and Capability Evaluation, but was later changed to mean Software Process Improvement and Capability dEtermination, due to concerns about the word "evaluation".

SPICE basically represents a framework to assess software processes and was created by the International Organisation for Standardisation, ISO, and the International Electrotechnical Commission, IEC. It therefore carries the identifier ISO 15504 ([wikipedia]).

The technical report of SPICE is divided into a number of parts. Some of the most important of these are:

- part 1: concept and overview
- part 2: reference model
- part 3: performing assessments
- part 4: improving processes
- part 5: assessment model
- part 6: assessors

SPICE is usually used to improve processes and to determine the maturity of existing processes. Organisations can become assessed through the evaluation of their processes by certified and trained SPICE assessors. SPICE uses 6 levels of maturity to classify processes ([wikipedia]):

- level 0: incomplete

- level 1: performed
- level 2: managed
- level 3: established
- level 4: predictable
- level 5: optimised

In order to arrive at a result, the processes that are assessed with SPICE are analysed with respect to 9 process attributes. These are:

- performance
- performance management
- work product management
- definition
- deployment
- measurement
- control
- innovation
- optimisation

Each of these process attributes is rated on the following scale with four points:

- 0 – 15%:   not   (N)
- 15 – 50%: partially   (P)
- 50 – 85%: largely   (L)
- +85%:   fully   (F)

Originally, SPICE focussed exclusively on software development processes. But as the model was more and more applied it became clear that the processes that interface with software development must also match a certain level of maturity, otherwise the effect of well-established software development processes alone must remain limited.

Therefore, SPICE has continuously been expanded and at the moment covers the following business areas:

- organisational
- management
- engineering
- acquisition
- support
- operations

SPICE has been widely used in industry since it has been first drafted out in 1993/1994. There was a major revision in 2004, and amongst others the process reference model was removed then. SPICE has influenced the development of the CMMI capability model and vice versa.

13.3.2 CMMI

CMMI stands for Capability Maturity Model Integration. It is the successor of the Capability Maturity Model, or CMM. The latter was developed from about 1987 until 1997, and CMMI was first released in 2002.

CMM and CMMI were developed by the by the Software Engineering Institute (SEI) of the Carnegie Mellon university and have been sponsored by the US Department of Defense, amongst others([wikipedia]).

The basic aim of the CMM and CMMI is to support organisations in improving their processes. To this end, CMMI makes suggestions as to which processes to establish for 22 different process areas. The CMMI model strongly recommends that it be tailored to the needs and boundary conditions of each individual organisation. Therefore, there is no standardised way to rate an organisation on the CMMI scale, but there are appraisals based on methods such as SCAMPI ([wikipedia]).

CMMI focusses on which processes should exist in each process area, rather than how to implement or organise these processes. CMMI wants to improve the usability of capability models for various engineering disciplines. It is a collection of a number of different maturity models, integrating these into a common framework.

The 22 process areas momentarily covered by CMMI are:

- CMMI Causal Analysis and Resolution
- CMMI Configuration Management
- CMMI Decision Analysis and Resolution
- CMMI Integrated Project Management
- CMMI Measurement and Analysis
- CMMI Organizational Innovation and Deployment
- CMMI Organizational Process Definition
- CMMI Organizational Process Focus
- CMMI Organizational Process Performance
- CMMI Organizational Training
- CMMI Product Integration
- CMMI Project Monitoring and Control
- CMMI Project Planning
- CMMI Process and Product Quality Assurance
- CMMI Quantitative Project Management

- CMMI Requirements Development
- CMMI Requirements Management
- CMMI Risk Management
- CMMI Supplier Agreement Management
- CMMI Technical Solution
- CMMI Validation
- CMMI Verification

By contrast to the SPICE model, CMMI is freely available, for example from the SEI homepage. This is one of the reason why compared to SPICE, CMMI appears to have been more successful.

Usually, capability models that cover a number of process areas, like SPICE and CMMI, do not go into very much detail with respect to each individual process. This is due to the amount of information that appears suited in connection with a model.

For this reason, models like SPICE and CMMI go hand in hand with other models that patch up gaps and black holes of certain detailed aspects in the high level models.

Two of such models that can complete the high level models are the HOOD capability models for requirements definition and HOOD capability model for requirements management. They will now be briefly introduced and are dealt with in detail in the following two chapters.

13.4 HOOD Capability Model for Requirements Definition

The HOOD capability model for requirements definition (HCM-RD) represents the HOOD Group's suggestion for how to evaluate the quality of the processes. This may also be used for a guide for stepwise introduce and to improve requirements definition processes in an organisation.

The model goes into very much detail with respect to the information that should be documented along with requirements. This covers for example stakeholder lists, project scope, and interfaces. Thus, the model can be used to extend or complete more general capability models such as SPICE or CMMI regarding the elicitation of requirements and all necessary information in connection with requirements.

The HCM classifies the maturity of an organisation with respect to requirements definition on a scale with 3 levels (apart from level 0: no processes at all). However, this classification is not rigid and should be adapted to meet the needs of an individual organisation. As we said earlier, an organisation needs to decide for itself what scope for its process is necessary.

This flexibility is one of the main advantages of the HCM-RD over other existing models. Another advantage is the fact that the model goes into so much detail of requirements development that in principle, everyone can start introducing and improving their processes and methods on the spot.

13.5 HOOD Capability Model for Requirements Management

Along with the HOOD capability model for requirements definition, there is also the HOOD capability model for requirements management (HCM-RM). These two belong closely together, for one will not be effective without the other.

The model is similar to the requirements definition model and shows how requirements management can be evaluated. HCM-RM can also be used to guide requirements management as it is introduced and improved step by step. Again, three levels of maturity are defined (apart from level 0, no requirements management at all).

To reach a certain level, various aspects of interfaces to the other systems engineering disciplines have to be taken into account.

13.6 Summary

This chapter gives an overview of what capability models are in general, how a capability model is used and when and why the use of capability models can be advantageous.

Two well-known models that are currently widely used in industry, the Capability Maturity Model Integration (CMMI) and the Software Process Improvement and Capability Determination (SPICE), are described in some detail.

The HOOD capability model for requirements definition (HCM-RD) and the HOOD capability model for requirements management (HCM-RM) are introduced. It is shown how due to their very fine level of detail, these two models can supplement and complete existing high level capability models such as SPICE and CMMI with respect to all process areas associated with requirements.

The HCM-RD and the HCM-RM will be discussed in great detail in the following chapters.

14 The HOOD Capability Model for Requirements Definition

In the previous chapters numerous references have been made to various capability or maturity models. Examples for some well known such models are the Rational Unified Process (RUP) and the Capability Maturity Model Integration (CMMI), and both are also applied in connection with requirements management and engineering. Capability models are generally used to assess how advanced some organisation is with regard to a certain field of expertise. To this end, such models usually offer various means to classify all the processes underlying the development cycle on a certain scale.

The HOOD capability model for requirements definition (HCM-RD) is the HOOD Group's standard capability model for assessing the maturity of an organisation's requirements definition process. The HOOD requirements definition process was introduced in the first chapters of this book and can also be found in [Hood2005], but will be briefly referenced here.

14.1 Brief repetition of the HOOD Requirements Definition Process

The previous chapters showed in detail the various activities that are necessary for the definition of requirements, and the HOOD requirements definition process was presented. We recall that in summary, the requirements definition process consists of the following activities.

Definition of scope:
- identify interfaces
- define interfaces
- define stakeholders and roles

Definition of requirements:
- elicitation

- specification
- analysis
- review

We also recall that modelling was the one activity that can support any other activity, and that all activities can take place at the same time. The HOOD requirements definition process is shown in figure 14.1.

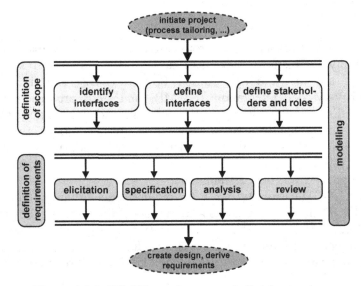

Figure 14.1: HOOD requirements definition process

The following sections will show how the quality of the requirements definition process and its activities can be measured using the HCM-RD.

14.2 The idea behind the HOOD capability model for requirements definition

It is a commonplace that success in an organisation depends almost solely on the people working for it. This has been true, it still is true, and it will remain true for quite some time. It appears as though this is so fundamentally true that nobody consciously tries to recall what this actually means.

Phrases like "Our people are our best asset" are ten a penny, and many companies try to ride this would-be human wave. However, observing the world around us will sometimes make you wonder whether those in charge of the relevant decisions do care about the people at all.

The HOOD Group's philosophy has always put the people in the centre of all efforts. (OH NO! we here you cry, not another platitude! But we mean it). From the very beginning of every project to introduce requirements management and engineering and associated processes, those who will be affected are taken into account, and their needs and fears are taken seriously. Many years of experience in different industries show that quite often, ideas that are basically good cannot be made work because the people who should implement the idea were not considered properly.

The introduction of requirements management and engineering in an organisation is usually not a simple thing to do. Developers have to adapt to a new development philosophy, to new processes, methods and tools. This is often associated with resistance caused by anxiety or fear of the unknown.

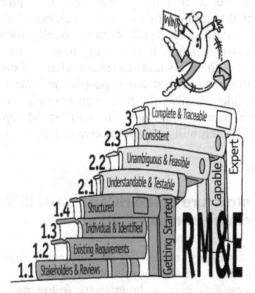

Figure 14.2: Overview of the different levels of the HCM-RD

To lessen that resistance, many different means must be applied. Amongst those are for example interviews, workshops, questionnaires and the like. The nature of the resistance is manifold, ranging for example from fear of becoming redundant to hate because the intended processes would make the development processes more transparent.

The HOOD capability model for requirements definition addresses many of these problems by chopping what is called "introduction of requirements management and engineering" into manageable pieces. Thus it is not necessary to go for the big bang introduction, which is usually doomed to fail.

Rather, small steps of improvement are taken one by one and with the speed that fits the organisation. The following figure 14.2 shows the single HCM-RD levels leading to the final expert level 3.

The underlying assumption of such an approach is that small steps of improvement are very much easier to implement than the complete thing. This assumption is supported by the experience of many requirements management and engineering introduction projects.

The monitoring of the progress and success goes hand in hand with the small implementation steps. Hence smaller and larger milestones are placed all along the way to the planned quality of the development process. This is very motivating for the people implementing the improvements, for there are smaller and larger successes in a relatively high frequency. Cases are known where after having overcome the initial problems, new successes in quality improvement could be celebrated almost weekly.

Also, an approach with small steps is usually more attractive to the organisation's management. It makes the project easier to track, and the risks associated with each small step are smaller and can be assessed more precisely. If the management has a positive attitude towards the project and shows confidence, this will serve as an example, motivating the people involved even more. This in turn will speed up the progress of improvements, which will be more motivating and so on, thus closing the circle.

14.3 The structure of the HOOD capability model for requirements definition

The HOOD capability model for requirements definition is basically organised as a matrix, relating levels of maturity to the single requirements definition process activities as shown in the following figure 14.3.

It is important here to note that the above figure is only a suggestion, based on good practices and experience. It shall serve as a starting point, but can be customised in whichever way appears suitable. The sequence for introduction is not suggested by the above table. An organisation might prefer to for instance not use modelling, or perhaps review is out of scope as this is done by others.

	Level 1	Level 2	Level 3
scope	- list of interfaces - stakeholders & roles - functions / objects	definition of interfaces	
modelling	scope	- sequence, states, data, algorithms - fit for intended readers	
elicitation	requirements are taken from existing specifications	requirements are prioritised	proper elicitation technique
specification	- atomic - identifiable - structured	- understandable - testable - ...	- complete - traceable - correct abstraction level
analysis	- atomic - identifiable - structured	- understandable - testable - ...	- complete - traceable - correct abstraction level
review	reviews are - carried out - documented	- all roles - each iteration - criteria	- explicitly with regard to quality criteria - participants

Figure 14.3: HOOD capability model
for requirements definition (HCM-RD)

	Level 1.1	Level 1.2	Level 1.3	Level 1.4
scope	- list of interfaces - stakeholders & roles - functions/objects			
modelling	scope			
elicitation		requirements are taken from existing specifications		
specification			- atomic - identifiable	- structured
analysis			- atomic - identifiable	- structured
review	reviews are - carried out - documented			

Figure 14.4: HCM-RD Level 1, broken down into more detailed sublevels

What is important is that a specific organisation analyses their needs and resources, and then creates a plan to introduce requirements management and engineering in manageable and suitable portions. Analogous to every management plan, the single levels of maturity shown in figure 14.3 can be further broken down into more detailed sublevels as shown in figure 14.4. Note again that this is not an inflexible and set plan, but can be tailored according to an organisation's individual needs and visions.

14.4   How to use the HOOD capability model for requirements definition

In the following, we will show how to apply the HCM-RD, and what its various levels actually mean. It is important to understand that the different levels as suggested in figure 14.3 are neither a suggestion nor requirement for a sequence for introduction in an orgainisation.

For instance, you do not have to complete one level before you tackle the next. It would be very unwise for example not to work on requirements traceability if you already could, only because you have not yet reached level 3.

The improvement progress must continuously be monitored with suitable metrics, and significant advances must be made visible and communicated to the people involved. People will be motivated only if they know and understand what they have already achieved. They may then want more on their own, thus starting a chain reaction.

14.4.1 Level 1: Getting started

As with everything else, getting started is always the hardest thing. This is true because at that point in time some old habits must be thrown aside, and as everyone knows, old habits die hard. For instance we know of one organisation where a development engineer was capable of writing computer programmes in Hexadecimal code (a very low level computer language) and he recently found the switch to more modern computer languages that younger engineers could read to be very hard.

With level 1, it becomes necessary to consciously identify requirements and to separate these from additional information. The requirements must match a certain level of quality, and to this end they must be analysed (checked against quality criteria) and reviewed. To prepare for later requirements elicitations, possible stakeholders and their roles must be identified.

All these activities must constantly be focussed by defining the scope of the system to be developed.

14.4.1.1 *Scoping*

The definition of the system boundaries as shown in figure 14.5 is the beginning of all structured requirements management and engineering.

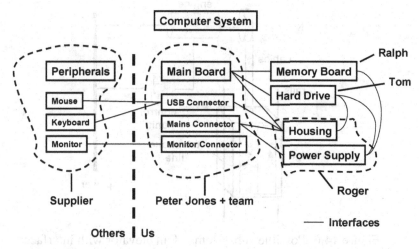

Figure 14.5: Example scoping of a computer system with interfaces

It is amazing what a simple picture as shown in figure 14.5, drawn at the beginning of a development project, or a few lines of text can accomplish. It is equally amazing what effects it can sometimes have not to draw such a picture or not to jot down these few lines of text.

For example, consider a control unit controlling an automobile's engine. Or, more dramatically, consider the unit controlling one aspect of a nuclear power plant. There has been a trend throughout the last decade or so to software becoming cheaper and cheaper. What has been hardware before, for example special control circuits, can now be realised with software code and standard micro controllers. And yet there are still applications where the hardware version is mandatory because it is still faster than the software version.

In our example, the software engineers must know whether they have to implement the control logic as software or whether the hardware engineers will create a special circuit. If there was no communication at all between these two groups of engineers the final system may turn out to have two controllers, one in software and one in hardware. More probably, the system would have no controller at all, for each group relies on the other to implement it.

When you build an elevator system, it must be clear whether you only build the elevator cage or whether you will also build the rail system to guide the cage or whether you will also build the engine or motor that will drive the whole system. This example is depicted in figure 14.6.

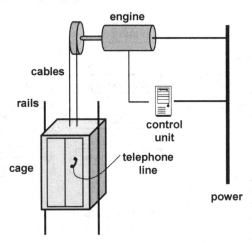

Figure 14.6: Possible subsystems of an elevator with interfaces

Although this may all seem rather obvious, it appears to be forgotten many times once a project has started. From many years of experience we know that quite often, promising projects lift off in quite a respectable manner, with all staff motivated and efficient. When some time has elapsed however, people start concentrating on their own little subsystem and begin to forget about the others. Still later, the interfaces between the various subsystems become no longer clear at all, and there is a lot of confusion about who is implementing which parts. Some interfaces may then exist more than once, and some not at all.

We therefore suggest starting every project with a proper scoping, however simple this may be. Neglecting the need to set the scope is a good way to run into severe problems in the later course of a project.

14.4.1.2 *Stakeholder and Roles*

Once the scope is defined for the project at hand, the key persons must be identified and their roles documented. We call such people that have "a justified interest in the project" the stakeholders. What a justified interest is depends of course on the situation and the judgement of the people responsible for carrying out the stakeholder identification. A more practical definition may simply call a person a stakeholder if his or her requirements are taken into account.

In many cases, the project management or the customer lists a number of persons that must be taken into account. However, such lists do not have to be complete – in fact, quite often they are not and are a suggestion rather than some set condition. Whether there is an initial stakeholder list or not, a good requirements manager will always consult his own judgment and experience. The following questions may help to arrive at a suitable stakeholder list:

- Who pays for the system?
- Who uses the system?
- Who maintains the system?
- Who is against the system?
- Who needs the system?
- Who specifies the system?
- Who develops the system?
- Who buys the system?
- Who disposes of the system?
- Who delivers the system?
- Who installs the system?
- Who develops a competitor system?
- Who controls the system?

Even if the customer or the project management believe their stakeholder list to be complete, it is always good practice to point out possible shortcomings and to make additional suggestions. If such suggestions are waived, then at least this can be documented, together with a rationale, and there will be no questions later in the project why some persons have not been asked for their needs and wishes. In any case, the stakeholder list needs periodical review and is usually changed throughout a project.

It has proven helpful to document not only the stakeholder but also his or her role. To make clear the difference: the stakeholder is the person, for example "Peter D. Seast" or "Colin Hood-Lum"; the role is the same as the job description of this person, for example "member of the board" or "project manager". An example stakeholder list is shown in figure 14.7.

Whenever we deal with a stakeholder, his role or roles will be a guide for our aims and actions. For example, a technical director or the CEO may have a requirement regarding the software to be used, and this requirement should be checked. There could be company standards, a central development platform and the like. However, it may turn out that the technical director has no opinion of the software to be used, and maybe by proposing such a requirement he only wants to conceal the fact that he does not know about the details of the company's development process.

Stakeholder List				
ID	Name	Role	Importance	Interviewed
SH-7	Ian M. Barrasing	Project Manager	low	- -
SH-3	Tom Jones	Sales	mid	04 Sep 2006
SH-13	Susan Summer	Public Relations	mid	12 Oct 2006
SH-2	Albert Onestone	Developer	high	30 Feb 2007
SH-11	Flash Gordon	Saver of Universe	high	23 Mar 2632
SH-6	Roger Rapid	Customer		

Figure 14.7: Example stakeholder list

To know this will help spotting this requirement as very low importance or even as irrelevant. Another example could be a first level help desk support officer, who would like some information system to be developed to tell him the rough schedules of the development department so as to be able to tell the customers on the hotline when they can expect the new version of some software. After this requirement is documented and handed over to the analysis and review board it may be decided that the hotline staff should have no insight into the development department's activities, and the requirement is thus neglected. On the other hand, if the head of the development department wants the future system to give him more information on schedules of the development department, this requirement may have to be taken into account.

Thus in summary, the role of a stakeholder gives us an idea of which kind of requirements that stakeholder may have a right to propose and where the limits of his competence and authority are.

14.4.1.3 Engineering Requirements

For level 1 of the HCM-RD it is recommended to collect requirements from existing specifications, see figures 14.3 and 14.4. It is part of our experience that since requirements engineering is the critical activity, the developers should slowly become familiar with the new philosophy of how to look at requirements.

It is normally a good idea to take existing requirements from similar projects to provide a very good starting point to lift off from. Even in companies with a very advanced and established requirements management and engineering process this is often the first thing to do, for almost all systems that are developed today have some predecessor and only extend and improve what already exists.

Also, development staff must learn to distinguish between requirements and other pieces of information. Existing specifications are perfectly suited for this, for they usually contain a multitude of information. Figure 14.8 shows an example of a specification, which is fictitious but otherwise believed to be quite typical.

> ... The flight passenger transportation system shall conform to the regulations for safety critical airport equipment. According to ASR 1492, this means that the system must recognise passengers that are not totally within the carriage. This will give rise to the need to have light barriers. Children must be seated during the ride, while adults may also be standing. No extra compartment for the train guard is needed as the train is controlled completely automatically. The doors must close within 2 seconds. The train does not need a power collector because it runs on batteries. There will be at least 6 of these automatic trains running at Bloody Hell's airport. About 2000 passengers will use these trains every day ...

Figure 14.8: Fictitious example specification with typical style

If people are told what to look for, they will quickly learn and understand how to tell a true requirement from supporting information. Also, reading specifications that were probably written by others will give an impression of how easy or hard it can be to follow someone else's ways of thinking just by what has been documented. This will in turn motivate people to try and write better requirements that are more clearly also to other possible readers.

14.4.1.4 Managing Requirements

When the people involved start engineering requirements using existing specifications, this is a perfectly suited moment to introduce more of the basic requirements management and engineering concepts. For example, the developers will soon find that their requirements need some structure, just like a good book needs a table of contents and different chapters and sections. A structure will make the requirements more readable, and also some interesting piece of information can be extracted very much quicker than without any structure.

Another important thing to show is the need for requirements attributes. When the developers learn to tell requirements from additional information, they may want to mark some bits as requirements and others as information. For example if they already decided to introduce requirements structures, they may want to indicate headings as opposed to requirements.

A very prominent example for attributes is a unique identifier for each requirement and maybe also for additional information. It will soon dawn on most of the people that talking in terms of "the last but two sentences on page number 17, middle section" is not very efficient but ambiguous and can cause many time-consuming misunderstandings. Showing them that a unique identifier will save trouble and time will motivate them to apply this concept wherever sensible.

This will automatically lead to the idea that the requirements should be best formulated as singular entities. This is what we call atomic requirements. After the developers have started using structures, attributes, identifiers and so on, they may still find that too much information is contained in one identifier. For example, one long sentence containing three requirements could be given an identifier, but it would still not be possible to talk unambiguously about one single requirement when talking about this one sentence. This will motivate to try and apply a good rule of thumb: one sentence, one requirement. A possible result of the application of these practices to the specification in figure 14.8 is shown in figure 14.9.

ID	Text	Type
SR-23	**3.1 Legal regulations**	Heading
SR-82	The system must conform to ASR 1492.	Req.
SR-83	The system must recognise people standing in the doors.	Req.
SR-24	**3.2 Passenger Safety**	Heading
SR-85	The system must use light barriers to recognise people standing in the doors.	Req.

Figure 14.9: Improving existing specifications applying good practices

Thus if people are trained, introduced and guided properly, this can start a chain reaction of needs and desires which when addressed, automatically improve the quality of the requirements management and engineering process. This can be very motivating to people, and ideally they start wanting more and more.

14.4.1.5 Requirements Reviews

It is one of the fundamental principles of the requirements management and engineering philosophy to quality check every relevant piece of work that has been carried out.

For example, in some organisations all pieces of work that are put under configuration management must be quality checked. In other organisations there exist lists to tell which outputs must be quality checked.

But whatever the relevant work products in an organisation are, the principle of quality checks should be made clear right from the beginning.

It is therefore necessary even in early stages of the introduction of requirements management and engineering processes in an organisation to plan for analyses and reviews. The members of staff should be explicitly told that what they create will be checked by others. This needs a lot of social competence, for people will at first suspect that they are being controlled. In fact, to establish the understanding and the desire for quality reviews is probably one of the hardest parts of introducing requirements management processes.

The following figure 14.10 shows a simple requirements analysis and review process.

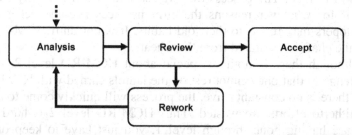

Figure 14.10: Simple requirements analysis and review process

Reviews loop back on quality attributes, for it is only possible to check for quality aspects that were agreed on beforehand. For example, we should not check the requirements for atomicity if it has never been mentioned before that requirements should be formulated atomically. Also, we should not check whether the documented requirements are testable if we never told the developers to consider this while formulating requirements. The following figure 14.11 shows what a requirements analysis could look like in reality.

Although it is obvious, the requirements process would come to an end if after the review nothing more happened. Thus every review automatically implies that the defects spotted during the review process must be removed and the new work results must again be quality checked.

Only then will the circle close and we started a continuous requirements quality improvement process.

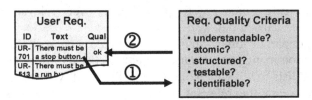

Figure 14.11: Example requirements analysis

14.4.2 Level 2: Capable

The previous sections showed how we can initiate a requirements management and engineering process based on continuous improvement. We explained how especially the first work results can motivate people to go ahead with the new philosophy and thus keep the process alive.

While HCM-RD level 1 is a very important milestone indicating the beginning of new ways of thinking and of seeing things, its (visible) results are still limited. The process that was started is still not fully established, and if for whatever reasons the circumstances become detrimental, the developers may revert to their old habits. It is not until HCM-RD level 2 that the chaff is separated from the wheat.

Although there is nothing special about HCM-RD level 2, it is a big challenge in that one cannot rest on the laurels earned with HCM-RD level 1. If there is no constant drive, the process will quickly come to a rest, and all hitherto efforts are wasted. Thus HCM-RD level 2 is hard to tackle because having gone through level 1, you just have to keep on running without having a rest. Organisations that master level 2 are very well working. It is clear that all criteria to reach level 1 automatically apply to level 2, and thus we only have a closer look at the additional criteria to reach level 2.

14.4.2.1 Engineering Requirements

For HCM-RD level 1, requirements must be atomic and identifiable. To reach level 2, the requirements must conform to more quality attributes. First, they must be understandable and unambiguous, which means that during the specification of requirements, the developers consciously check whether their requirements are understandable and clear to other possible readers.

This implies that the requirements are formulated so that the anticipated readers will have a maximum chance to understand what is going on. It means that requirements are not only specified in plain text, but will also use pictures, use case diagrams, flow charts, mind maps and whatever appears to be best suited for the various readers. Note that it could also be a video tape with the developers demonstrating some system workflow, or a music tape giving an idea of how some acoustic signal may sound.

Second, requirements on level 2 must be testable and realisable. Realisability may be proven in many different ways, one of the most common being the experience of the developers. By introducing the idea of realisability, we try to separate requirements that will probably be implemented from those that can and will not be implemented. This information will later help saving time, for no effort is wasted to deal with requirements that are irrelevant in this respect.

Testability is best proven by documenting the test that will check if a requirement is fulfilled. The test may be documented right along with the requirement, or in a separate test document. Whichever way is chosen, this aspect is very important because we start to link the requirements to the tests. An example of requirements linked to tests is shown in the following figure 14.12.

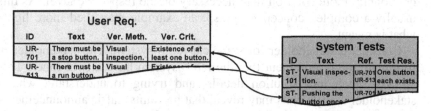

Figure 14.12: Requirements linked to tests

This traceability between requirements and tests makes it possible to extract valuable information. For example, by checking which requirement has no link to a test we may find requirements that are not testable. Or it may turn out that a test has been forgotten. Also if a test has no link to at least one requirement, this may mean that either a link has been forgotten to be drawn, or that this test is superfluous, for no actual requirement is affected.

Test management or verification and validation is dealt with in detail in chapter 10, where more information can be found. Here, it should be noted that traceability is one of the most important gains of requirements management and engineering.

Third, requirements on HCM-RD level 2 must be consistent, free of redundancies and correctly derived. Consistent means that the requirements do not contradict each other. For example, no specification should have a requirement A stating that "The button must be blue" and at the same time have a requirement B which says that "The button must be red".

Consistency is closely related to redundancy. It may be desirable not to have two or more requirements that in principle formulate the same desire. To stick with the above example, there should be no requirement A demanding that "The button must be blue" and some requirement C defining that "All user interface elements must be blue". The danger comes mainly here with changes, when one requirement might be changed and the other missed thus causing the set of requirements to become inconsistent.

It is important to remove inconsistencies and redundancies because inconsistencies will lead to inconsistent behaviour of the system to be developed, and redundancies would have to be synchronised each time one of the respective requirements is changed or otherwise become inconsistent. The activity of removing inconsistencies and redundancies is often called consolidation.

If a requirement has been correctly derived it is formulated on the proper level of detail or abstraction. This means that the requirement does not contain more solution than necessary on the respective level. As this is usually a complex concept to grasp, an example may shed more light on what is meant.

Consider a stakeholder for some car radio system. The stakeholder may formulate the requirement that the radio system have a twin tuner. This is already much into solution details, and trying to understand what the stakeholder really wants may reveal that he wants traffic announcements to be automatically checked in the background, and the only way he thinks this is possible is by using a twin tuner.

Once this is known the requirement would then demand that traffic announcements be automatically checked in the background, and there could still be any solution to this requirement. Note however that it is also possible that the stakeholder wants a twin tuner because all his friends have a twin tuner, too. In this case, it may mean that in fact we must implement a twin tuner, or at least stick a label to the radio that suggests that it has a twin tuner. Not all requirements are based on technology, some requirements have other roots.

This concept also means that on the implementation level a requirement must be all solution and there should be no space left for interpretation. If for the implementation a requirement states that "The colours of the buttons must be easily distinguishable from the colour of the display" this indicates that we are still on a level of too much abstraction. Depending on the owner of this requirement we might call this requirement incorrectly derived, and for someone that has to implement the requirement it should better read something like "The colours of the buttons must be in RGB colour code: 132 (red), 34 (green), 202 (blue)".

It is possible that there are only two levels of abstraction, customer requirements and implementation requirements, but if there are more levels as is usually the case then requirements on these intermediate levels should have a corresponding level of abstraction. Practical doing will soon give the necessary experience.

14.4.2.2 Managing Requirements

In addition to the criteria to reach HCM-RD level 1, the requirements must now also be prioritised. This lays the foundation for making many pieces of the valuable information described in the previous chapters accessible.

Once the requirements are prioritised, we can focus limited resources and budgets on the most important aspects of a system under development, rather than wasting time implementing mostly requirements that are only nice to have. We dealt with these aspects in detail in the previous chapters, especially in chapters 6 and 9, and will thus not go any further here.

14.4.2.3 Requirements Reviews

As was explained in connection with the HCM-RD level 1, all relevant work results must be checked against the quality criteria agreed on. On level 2, the requirements must be checked to conform to the above mentioned quality criteria, in addition to those from level 1.

14.4.3 Level 3: Expert

HCM-RD level 3 is as good as it gets. Level 3 represents a way of thinking that is represented by the maturity of the processes. When you have reached level 3, your people will automatically push for continuous quality improvement, and as long as you can address their needs and desires, this way of thinking will stay alive. You will have measurable successes compared to past development approaches, and your customers will be more satisfied with your products.

Although level 3 is almost identical to level 2, one little difference will lay open the full power of a grown requirements management and engineering process. The magic word here is traceability between requirements. The step from level 2 to level 3 is not easy to achieve in practice. Here you have to be good in detail.

14.4.3.1 Engineering Requirements

Only two additional quality criteria are waiting for you on HCM-RD level 3, but these are the hardest to achieve. They are completeness and traceability to the source.

Completeness means that your technical specification be complete in terms of the requirements. In fact, this may seem to be an impossible goal, for we know no means to check a specification for absolute completeness. But we can check for completeness within the needs at certain stages. The question is "Is it complete enough". Incompleteness can sometimes be found out the hard way, for example if important requirements were forgotten.

However, the goal is that an organisation tries consciously to get their specifications as complete as is practically possible and sensible so that the requirements are fit for purpose. Although this is probably aimed at every time requirements are documented, our experience tells us that setting this as an explicit goal makes a huge difference to the way the developers specify their requirements.

The other level 3 criteria is traceability to the source. We have already come across traceability on level 2, where we demanded that the requirements must be linked to the tests. Now we demand that the requirements on each level of abstraction be also linked to the requirements on the level above. For example, all derived system requirements must have a link to the customer requirements, and all design requirements must have a link to the system requirements. The following figure 14.13 shows an example where the links are created using textual references in a dedicated attribute.

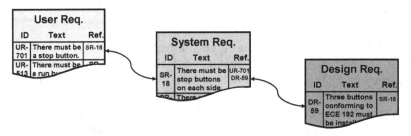

Figure 14.13: Linking between different kinds of requirements

Of course, as has been shown in previous chapters, traceability and referencing (linking) goes far beyond only documenting the relationships between the different kinds of requirements (user requirements, system requirements, ...). We have seen that we can and should link requirements also to project management, change management, risk management and so on. A more complete picture is shown in the following figure 14.14.

Why does this open the door to so many positive effects of requirements management and engineering? For example, this kind of traceability allows for the check whether some user requirements have been forgotten. If they have no link to at least one system requirement, this may mean that the link has not been drawn or that this user requirement has not been derived and taken into account yet. On the other hand, if a system requirement has no link to at least one user requirement this may mean that the system requirement is superfluous and has no justification.

As all of these advantages have been discussed in detail in the previous chapters, we will not go into more detail here, but want to stress a point that has already been mentioned before. The HCM-RD is no rigid law or model layout to introduce requirements management and engineering in an organisation, but is based on our many years of experience. It is explicitly meant to be tailored to your individual situation and abilities. You do not have to start with atomic requirements if the aspect of ambiguity is more important to you. Also you do and should not wait to begin introducing the quality criteria of higher HCM-RD levels before you have fully completed a lower level. We repeat this very important aspect here because if you can link requirements right from the beginning, do so. Do not wait until you formally reach HCM-RD level 3.

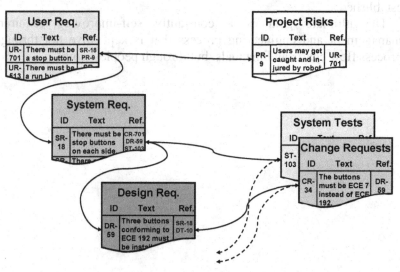

Figure 14.14: More linked project information

14.5 Summary

This chapter introduces the HOOD capability model for requirements definition (HCM-RD) and explains how to use it. The model is a suggestion of how to introduce requirements management and engineering in an organisation, applying a step-by-step philosophy rather than a big-bang approach. It is organised with three levels ranging from getting started to expert.

Criteria are given to assess which level an organisation has already reached. These criteria are a suggestion based on many years of experience in the introduction of requirements management and engineering processes in organisations of all sizes. The criteria are not defined as being fixed but can be tailored to the special situation and needs of any organisation.

By defining small goals people can monitor their advances. Many milestones are all along the way and have a motivating effect on the developers. Usually people are initially trained and then slowly made familiar with the new development philosophy by practical doing. If they get the necessary support, they will soon see the advantages and become more comfortable and cooperative. Ideally, this will start a chain reaction of more successes, more drive, faster pace, more successes and so on. Once the inertia has been overcome, it is important not to have a rest on things but to keep on pushing until the processes and ideas are firmly established.

The ultimate goal is a constantly self-improving requirements management and engineering process that is kept alive not through the process flow charts and manuals, but through peoples' spirit.

15 The HOOD Capability Model for Requirements Management

The previous chapter on the HOOD capability model for requirements definition (HCM-RD) described in detail how the processes in connection with the development of requirements can be introduced and improved step by step.

This chapter explains how requirements that have been created can be managed, so that the information they represent is always up to date throughout a project and so that the information created in the course of a project can be used and reused in following projects.

Like the HOOD capability model for requirements definition, the HOOD capability model for requirements management is the HOOD Group's standard to evaluate the maturity of an organisation with respect to its abilities in connection with the management of requirements.

The following sections show the basics of the model and its proper use. It is noted here that the two HOOD capability models really belong together, for the value of requirements that are developed will quickly deteriorate if they are not managed during the course of a project.

It is thus recommended to start the introduction and improvement of processes in connection with requirements using both capability models right from the beginning, rather than starting with only one of the two models.

15.1 The structure of the HOOD capability model for requirements management

Similar to the HOOD capability model for requirements definition, the requirements management model can be visualised as a matrix, see figure 15.1. The matrix consists of the three levels of the HCM-RM and the processes and information that must exist to reach a certain level.

Like before, it is noted that the following is a standard suggestion for the focus of each level, but the model is not rigid. If an organisation needs change management processes for requirements more urgently than version management processes, then it would be stupid to wait until level 1 as shown in the following figure has been reached before proceeding any further with the change management subject.

	level 1	level 2	level 3
risk management	risks are identified	risks are linked to requirements	risks are assessed and prioritised, and counter-measures are defined
change management	changes are explicitly documented	changes are documented so that they can be traced back	impacts of changes on risks, configurations, versions, tests, project and quality are documented
configuration and version management	requirements are freezed (baselined) as necessary, freezes can be identified	the various freezes are put together to give configurations as needed	configuration and version plan is created including rules for baselining
test management	key requirements are tested and the results are documented	verification method and verification criteria are documented for agreed subset of requirements	a complete test plan with work packages, costs and dates is created and linked to requirements
quality management	requirements are analysed and reviewed at least once	regular review and analysis of requirements	regular review and analysis of requirements
project management	requirements are prioritised	work packages are defined and controlled	costs are estimated, resources are estimated, defined and assigned

Figure 15.1: HOOD capability model for
requirements management (HCM-RM)

15.2 How to use the HOOD capability model for requirements management

This section will make suggestions of how to use the HOOD capability model for requirements management and will detail each level. Similar to what has been said in connection with the HOOD capability model for requirements definition, the different levels of the HOOD capability model for requirements management shown in figure 15.1 can and shall not be strictly separated from each other.

Also, as mentioned before, the model is not rigid in view of the contents of each level. For example, an organisation that produces only two kinds of ball pens, one standard ball pen and an exclusive ball pen of high quality for businessmen, will have less to do with risk management than an organisation producing explosives. Thus the model can and should be tailored to the needs and specific situation of each individual organisation.

This implies that different organisations may not be directly comparable by their HCM-RM level, for the same level may contain different subjects and mean different things in each organisation. However, the overall maturity remains very well comparable using the HCM-RM, for normally the levels are tailored such that they approximately demand the same effort to be reached.

15.2.1 Level 1: Getting started

Although level 1 of the HOOD capability model for requirements management demands only activities which most organisations already carry out, it formalises these activities and thus takes out possible randomness.

This is especially true since the model naturally depends on every result to be properly documented, and this little detail makes all the difference to the way organisations usually work.

15.2.1.1 *Risk management interface*

To reach HCM-RM level 1 with regard to the interface to risk management it is sufficient to identify possible risks. The risks are documented in a suitable way, for example with an identifier, a short name and a description, see figure 15.2.

Risks			
ID	**Description**	**Short Name**	**Author, Date**
R - 12	In manual control mode, the operator may move the robot so that it hits other objects including people.	Robot operation	Steve Miller, 21 Aug 2005
R - 5	There may be high voltage in the cables when the oper		

Figure 15.2: Risk management information to reach HCM-RM level 1

Besides the information suggested above, there should also be of course such information like author and date of creation as shown in figure 15.2. These data are basic standard and are not specifically associated with risk management, but they are always assumed to exist even when not mentioned explicitly.

There are many organisations that have a good feeling for possible risks, and this feeling is usually based on sound experience from many projects. Often, this feeling or experience is concentrated onto only a few or even only one developer or senior staff, and there exists nothing reproducable apart from the intuition of these key people.

This is quite typical, and starting a risk documentation even as simple as shown in figure 15.2 starts to make the knowledge accessible and reproducable. For example, with a simple list as shown above, it is possible to create a checklist for future projects, thus making sure that none of the most important possible risks may be forgotten in a current project.

Such a checklist can then be continuously improved, making it more and more complete and valuable from project to project. If the above mentioned key persons having the risk knowledge then leave the organisation, other people have something to take over and to start with, rather than having to begin from scratch.

15.2.1.2 *Change management interface*

Level 1 of the HOOD capability model for requirements management demands that each change be explicitly documented. This means that a change must be identifiable as a change, and in our experience this is in contrast to the established way in which many organisations work.

It is quite common that people change such things as requirements texts, names or dates according to current needs. They make changes just like this and leave it to the reader to find out if and when they have changed something. Without such a concept like baselining and freezing, it is often impossible to trace back changes.

For example, a Powerpoint file could contain vital project information such as an electronic schematic. If the file is changed by some user and saved with the same name, nobody can recover its old state.

In this connection it is interesting to note that even if the people that make changes in such a way get confused themselves because they cannot keep all the changes they have made and their effects in mind, they usually still refuse to adopt a more efficient way of working. And it is also interesting how quickly one can loose track even of a very small number of changes if nothing is documented.

Therefore, level 1 of the HCM-RM demands explicit change documentation, rather than implicit change information which could for example be a more recent file time stamp in your operating system. Remember that there are quite a few people who would point you to such things as a new file time stamp to prove that the changes they have made are obvious.

Explicit change documentation can be very simple to start with, but it will be very effective nonetheless. With regard to requirements, one could start a change documentation by striking out the current version of a requirement and adding a new version with author and date, see figure 15.3. The same concept is applicable for changes in the risk management data, the configuration and version management data, the test management data, the quality management data and the project management data. If software tools are used that automatically document changes, then the explicit documentation of changes may be superfluous, but sometimes an automatic change documentation is so intricate to use that it is still desirable to document changes as proposed.

User Req.		
ID	Text	Author
UR-701	~~There must be 3 stop buttons.~~	J. Johnssonson, 03 Mar 2007
	There must be 5 stop buttons.	U. Looser, 01 Apr 2007
UR-543	There must be a run butt...	C. ...

Figure 15.3: Explicit change documentation to reach HCM-RM level 1

Although the effort for documenting changes in the proposed way is very small compared to the benefits this will create, it is our experience that the documentation is often neglected and vital change information gets lost.

15.2.1.3 Configuration and version management interface

To reach the HCM-RM level 1, configuration and version management only has to make sure that freezes or baselines of vital information are drawn as necessary and can be identified.

This means that for the most important milestones, the project data are copied and stored away so that they can be recovered if necessary. For example, the first set of approved user requirements should be carefully frozen before the user requirements are developed further, using a typical name such as "user requirements approved V1.0" or the like. Thus level 1 really aims at introducing a version management, while the configuration aspect is put back until level 2.

To many readers it may seem natural to do this, but quite frequently vital information gets lost because data are changed, improved and further developed without having made a freeze in between. Getting back on the above example, the "user requirements approved V1.0" can never be recovered if they are not stored away immediately, or still worse, people do not even know that there has once existed or that there should exist something like a first version of approved user requirements.

It can be seen from this that configuration and version management is closely related to change management. While change management tries to ensure that the evolution of information can be traced back through all stages to the origin, configuration and version management tries to ensure that every piece of information, including the various instances of changed data, belongs to at least one entity with an individual version and configuration identifier.

Level 1 of the HOOD capability model for requirements management initially creates awareness of the necessity to have freezes or baselines at various stages during a project. The benefits of having freezes usually start to show rather quickly, especially when there are more than only a few people involved in the project so that it cannot be assumed that everyone always knows what all the others are doing.

The following figure 15.4 sketches how a simple version management to reach HCM-RM level 1 could look like.

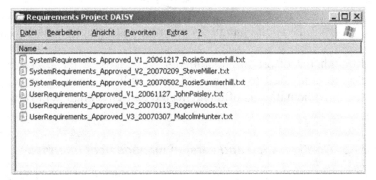

Figure 15.4: Simple version management to reach HCM-RM level 1

It is seen from the above figure that a lot of information can already be put into a good file name. Together with a short description of what each file actually means, the example shows how a simple but nonetheless working version management can be set up.

15.2.1.4 *Test management interface*

Regarding the interface of requirements definition to test management, level 1 of the HOOD capability model for requirements management is reached if "key requirements are tested and the results are documented".

This phrase is rather vague, and deliberately so. A test manager who is faced with the task to reach level 1 must answer a couple of questions before he can proceed any further:

- What is a key requirement?
- How must a requirement be tested?
- How and where shall the results be documented?

The first question makes it necessary that the requirements be classified in view of their importance and / or urgency. Although a requirement could be a key requirement with regard to tests only and otherwise just a normal requirement, this assessment will usually be related to the classification of the requirements from the viewpoint of project management.

From figure 15.1 and the above explanation it can thus be seen that HCM-RM level 1 for the test management interface goes hand in hand with level 1 for the project management interface, which demands that requirements be prioritised.

The second question given above creates awareness for the fact that tests must be planned for in a number of different ways. The "how" not only indicates that for example test equipment must be purchased if necessary. What is more important is the fact that a test manager must decide what to do in order to find out whether a requirement is met or not, even if all necessary equipment is already there. For example, a software module could be tested to work according to the specification by letting it run 10 hours without a break and see whether there would be any errors. Thus the "how" also implies that people already think of the verification method and the verification criteria, without explicitly saying so.

The third question of the above list could be assumed to be quite simple to answer, but once people start to document their tests they usually find out that this is not at all a trivial thing to do. In a first approach to HCM-RM level 1, the documentation could be as simple as "passed" or "failed" in a test column or attribute within the requirements document.

But as the documentation of the verification method and verification criteria is left to level 2, it will soon be realised that such a result really has little meaning on its own. Just by reading the result one cannot know what exactly it was that was tested, or how.

One way to meet this problem is to document the tester together with the result. It is then possible at least to address the respective tester if any questions arise and ask him or her what has been done and how and why and use their specific knowledge. However, this is only possible if the organisation aiming to reach HCM-RM level 1 acknowledges that tester is a role to be assigned to someone, rather than a job that must be done by anyone who can momentarily spend a few minutes.

This in turn prepares the stage for the suitable definition and assignment of work packages, which is necessary to reach HCM-RM level 2 for the project management interface. Again, it can be seen how all the different interfaces on all the various HCM-RM levels mesh with each other.

The following figure 15.5 shows an example of a test management interface for HCM-RM level 1.

User Req.				
ID	Text	IsKey	Res.	Tester, Date
UR-701	There must be a stop button.	Yes	Pass	John Wine, 12 Aug 2005
UR-4	The current must be 15A.	No		
UR-34	There must be a run button.	Yes	Pass	Richard Nickson, 7 July 2005
UR-35	The run button must be green.	No		
UR-	The noise must be < 40dB.	Yes		

Figure 15.5: Example test management interface for HCM-RM level 1

The "IsKey" attribute or column in the above figure could be waived if there is the agreement that the column "Res." is only filled in for the key requirements (which makes sense), but there may be situations when it is good to have these two pieces of information separated. Note also that the test information could also be stored separated from the requirements, as shown for example in figure 10.7.

15.2.1.5 Quality management interface

Level 1 of the HOOD capability model for requirements management is reached by at least once analysing and reviewing all relevant (valid) requirements.

It is our experience that although the task sounds simple enough and although the result of a requirements analysis and review is clearly desirable, many organisations fail at this point. One possible reason for this is the fact that practically nobody wants to be corrected. Therefore people try to find a way to avoid having to put their work to the test. Another quite popular reason is the lack of resources. There are a lot of organisations that are happy if the requirements are specified at all, let alone analysed and reviewed.

If resources are available and people are open for improvements on their pieces of work, organisations can still fail because of the lack of knowledge to properly carry out requirements analyses and reviews. From what has been said in the previous chapters on the interface to quality management it is clear that a proper analysis and review cycle is far from being a trivial thing.

To allow for a proper analysis and review, an organisation or project must first assign resources. That means that time and / or money must explicitly be planned for right from the beginning. In parallel to or shortly after this, the quality criteria to be checked for must be agreed on. It was mentioned before that it makes no sense to carry out a review with both the author of the requirements and the reviewer not knowing what to check for.

When the quality criteria are agreed on and made known to all people involved, the authors of the requirements can start their work. As the requirements are specified one by one, the people responsible for the analysis can start to check them with respect to the quality criteria.

After the analysis, the members of the review team have to decide what to do with each requirement. In our experience it will then soon become clear that it is usually impossible to improve every single requirement, as this would consume too much time and money. Rather, only those requirements that are more important than the rest are looked at in more detail. In other words, it must be decided whether a requirement is so important that the extra work to improve its quality is acceptable or whether it is not.

This touches again on the HCM-RM level 1 for the project management interface, or more precisely, the fact that requirements must be prioritised to reach level 1. Like before, it is seen how all pieces of the requirements management puzzle come together to give one single consistent picture.

Figure 15.6 sketches an example of how the quality management interface for reaching HCM-RM level 1 may look like in a requirements specification.

User Req.			
ID	Text	Analysis	Review
UR-701	There must be a stop button.		Accepted
UR-4	The current must be 15A.	Not clear: which current is meant?	Rework
UR-34	There must be a run button.		Accepted
UR-35	The run button must be green.	Not precise: what does "green" mean?	Accepted
UR-	The noise must be ≤ 40dB.		

Figure 15.6: Example quality management interface for HCM-RM level 1

15.2.1.6 Project management interface

The most important contribution of the interface to project management to reaching level 1 of the HOOD capability model for requirements management is that the requirements are prioritised.

It was shown in the previous sections how the interfaces to other systems engineering disciplines or other parts of the requirements management rely on the requirements to be classified with regard to their importance and / or urgency. If this information is missing, it is hard or impossible for example to choose the requirements that should be tested or to decide whether a requirement is worth reworking or whether it is not.

Prioritising requirements is one of the most simple and at the same time one of the most difficult things to do. It is very simple because in principle everyone can rush through a set of requirements and put a "low", "mid" or "high" mark to it in a relatively short amount of time. Then again it is very difficult because the result of such a classification is different for each different assessor.

It will thus be necessary to have a team of reviewers with similar viewpoints and opinions, and to allow for discussions to find compromises. There may also be a psychological aspect to the classification, for authors of requirements could feel pleased to have as many of their requirements classified as being of high importance as possible. Cases are known where soon after the introduction of an importance attribute, all requirements were classified as being of high importance. It was then decided to change to the three categories "high", "very high" and "extremely high" in order to get more sensible results.

The fact that many activities of requirements management rely on the requirements to be prioritised should remind everyone of the importance of this activity. Prioritising requirements should not be mistaken for putting some sign on them which may make them look more or less interesting. Rather, the success of a project can depend on a sensible classification of the requirements.

It is no use to mark every requirement as being of high importance, just like it is no good to have no highly important requirement at all. There are organisations that work with a rough percentage for each category. For example, there must be no more than 5% of all requirements that are classified highly important.

We rely on common sense to arrive at a due distribution. For example, if only requirements are marked highly important that are absolutely vital and without which the system under development will not properly work, then the number of highly important requirements should automatically approach a sensible value. If it does not, there may be some misunderstanding on part of the reviewers or the project managers, and this needs clarification.

15.2.2 Level 2: Capable

Similar to the HOOD capability model for requirements definition, HCM-RD, the HOOD capability model for requirements management may appear to produce only very limited visible results on level 1.

However, starting to document all relevant information in a suitable way is a milestone in many organisations. If people feel that there is a benefit in working that way the step to level 2 will be small, but nonetheless challenging.

15.2.2.1 Risk management interface

On level 2 of the HCM-RM, the risk management interface must provide links to the requirements. Although linking is a simple concept as such, the creation and maintenance of links turns out to be one of the most challenging activities in requirements management in practice.

One possible reason for this could be the time it takes to properly create and maintain the links. It is usually not sufficient to create the links once and never touch them again. Every time something has been changed or created anew, existing links must be checked for whether they are still valid, and new links may have to be drawn between new pieces of information. This problem also depends on the tools that are used to manage requirements. For example, some tools offer functionality to support the linking of pieces of information. But a number of tools such as WORD or Excel, which are also frequently used for requirements management, cannot provide such functions, and the only practical way to draw and maintain links is using textual references. This may take more time than drawing links for example in a graphical drag-and-drop way.

Another possible reason is the fact that quite frequently there is no clear concept within an organisation of how to draw links between the various pieces of project information. Simply linking everything to everything can soon turn out to be counterproductive, and people could get lost in the flood of information.

As no more details of how the linking between risks and requirements should look like are given in the HCM-RM for level 2, one example of how this can be achieved is given in figure 15.7. It is noted that in the figure the link could either be the textual references as shown, or the arrow representing some tool supported way to link the two sets of data.

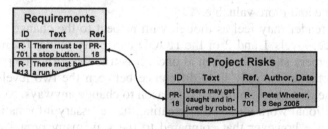

Figure 15.7: Example risk management interface on HCM-RM level 2

15.2.2.2 Change management interface

To get from HCM-RM level 1 to level 2 with respect to the interface to change management, changes must not only be explicitly documented, but they must be documented so that they can be traced back.

The most important impact of this is that in contrast to level 1, there must now be a documented reason for a change. As can be seen from figure 15.3, changes are identifiable as changes on HCM-RM level 1, but there is no justification as to why the change was made at all. The following figure 15.8 will therefore look more complete than figure 15.3, and the information provided here is definitely more valuable than before.

User Req.			
ID	Text	Author	Change rationale
UR-701	~~There must be 3 stop buttons.~~	J. Johnssonson, 03 Mar 2007	
	There must be 5 stop buttons.	U. Looser, 01 Apr 2007	Standard EU-7031c demands 5 buttons.
UR-~~542~~	There must be a run button.	C. Sidwell, 07 M...	

Figure 15.8: Example change documentation on HCM-RM level 2

Further aspects of the change traceability could be thought of. For example, having a change rationale you are only one step away from also having an additional column or attribute "approved" or similar. This implies the existence of something like a change control board, people who are competent to approve or reject a change request (which could of course be the authors of the requirements themselves).

Another possible impact of the change rationale column or attribute is a more complete linking of the different pieces of project information. For example, a reason for a change could be the fact that somewhere else something has changed, say a new possible risk has been discovered. The rationale would then point at the change in the risk management document to justify the change in the requirements document, thus linking these two otherwise dissociated pieces of information and making the data more complete and more valuable.

The reader may feel as though with respect to the change management interface, levels 1 and 2 of the HOOD capability model for requirements management should be taken at once. It is true that from the point of view of effort, there is only little difference between the two levels. And it is also true that people must have a reason to change anyways, so that there is no additional work involved in creating the necessary information. It is our experience however that compared to the way many organisations work today, meeting the requirements of HCM-RM level 1 for the change management interface would already be a significant improvement.

15.2.2.3 Configuration and version management interface

It has been mentioned further above that HCM-RM level 1 for the configuration and version management interface focusses on introducing a version management, while the configuration aspect is addressed at level 2.

The following figure 15.9 gives a rough idea of what your project information could look like after you have met the requirements of HCM-RM level 1.

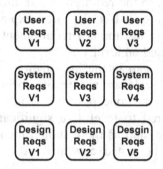

Figure 15.9: Version management information on HCM-RM level 1

It can seen from the above figure that the different versions of project data exist and can be identified and recovered, but have otherwise nothing to do with each other. It is on level 2 that the relationships between these sets of data are established and maintained and given a name or label. One such name or label is then called a configuration. Figure 15.10 sketches the step from versions to configurations.

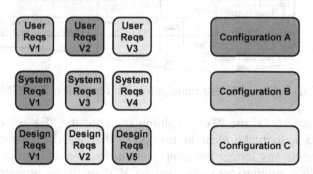

Figure 15.10: Configuration management on HCM-RM level 2

As one or more versions of each set of requirements are put together to form a logical entity called a configuration, they are no longer isolated from each other. Thus for example changes within one version of a set of requirements may mean changes to other sets of requirements belonging to the same configuration. Again, it can be seen how closely change management and configuration and version management are related.

15.2.2.4 Test management interface

With respect to the interface to test management, level 2 of the HCM-RM is the logical extension to level 1. It has been shown before how the test people have to prioritise the requirements in order to be able to mark key requirements for testing. It has also been explained that the testers must have an idea of how to test the key requirements, even if this information must not be documented on level 1.

Level 2 closes this gap in the information. At first, there must be an agreement between all relevant project members on which requirements to test. This is similar to the concept of key requirements on level 1, but it is assumed that compared to level 1, a significantly higher percentage of requirements is tested, and as there should then be nothing special about the requirements to be tested any more, they are no more called key requirements.

After the requirements to be tested are defined and agreed on by the relevant people, the verification method and verification criteria must be documented for each of these requirements. The result of this process could look similar to the example presented in the following figure 15.11.

User Req.						
ID	Text	Test	Res.	Tester, Date	Ver. Meth.	Ver. Crit.
UR-701	There must be a stop button.	Yes	Pass	John Wine, 12 Aug 2005	Visual inspection.	Existence of at least one button.
UR-4	The current must be 15A.	No				
UR-34	There must be a run button.	Yes	Pass	Richard Nickson, 7 July 2005	Visual inspection.	Existence of at least one button.
UR-35	The run button must be green.	No				
UR-	The noise must < 40dB.	Yes	Fail	Patricia Mu...		

Figure 15.11: Example test management information on HCM-RM level 2

In figure 15.11, the "Test" column replaced the "IsKey" column from figure 15.5, to make clear at this point that we do not talk about key requirements any longer but simply about requirements to be tested. Like before, this column could be waived if there is an agreement that the "Res." Column is only filled in for the requirements that must be tested, but there could be reasons why it would be desirable to have these pieces of information separated.

As already mentioned in connection with figure 15.5, the test management information shown in the above figure could of course also be stored and maintained separated from the requirements data, see for example figure 10.7.

15.2.2.5 Quality management interface

Regarding the quality management interface, levels 2 and 3 of the HOOD capability model for requirements management differ from level 1 only in that the analysis and review of the existing requirements must be carried out repeatedly and continuously, rather than only once.

There are however a few implications to this. First, with regular analyses and reviews it is no longer possible to carry out this activity just when it seems comfortable to do so. Rather, there must be a plan or at least an idea of how to regularly carry out the analysis and review cycles during the course of the project.

Second, as this is no longer a single activity, resources must be explicitly assigned and planned for. This usually means that there is a special group of people that will carry out the analyses and reviews, and this group normally does not change during a project.

Third, as it is typically impossible to go through all existing requirements in every analysis and review cycle, the relevant people have to devise efficient ways of dealing with rework, re-reviews, changes and so on.

Last but not least, an official commitment to repeated analyses and reviews may lessen the natural resistance of the relevant requirements developers or authors against their work being quality checked and reviewed. The reason for this is that multiple analyses or reviews indicate that the quality management is an ongoing process, rather than something special where all work is being put to the test at once. With this concept in mind, analysis and review results will be seen as constant suggestions for improvement, not as a single assessment.

15.2.2.6 Project management interface

On level 2, the HOOD capability model for requirements management demands the definition of work packages and their control. There are quite a few implications associated with this, and thus with respect to the project management interface, the step from HCM-RM level 1 to level 2 is anything else but simple.

In order to be able to define work packages, a number of different tasks have to be carried out beforehand. First, an overview must be created of all necessary activities, and this must be done on each level of detail of the project management plan. The planning will usually reach a certain level of detail before the estimates can be assumed to be precise enough to be relied on. One of the effects of this is that such a detailed planning will minimise the risk of forgetting major or key activities, and will provide a good basis for any other estimates such as resources consumption.

Second, all the identified tasks or pieces of work on one level of detail have to be classified applying sensible and meaningful categories. Examples of such a classification could be sales activities, project management activities, requirements management activities and so on. There is no ready recipe for carrying out this classification, and it will heavily rely on the experience of senior staff and project managers. Project management plans from similar predecessor projects may provide an excellent starting point for the people faced with this task.

After the classification of all known necessary activities on one level of detail is finished, each class must be split up into pieces that form logical units and that may not exceed a certain size. Again, experience is mandatory for splitting the classes properly up into suitable chunks.

The logical units created this way may be called work packages on the different levels of detail. For example, on a very high level of the project plan the work packages could be "Define requirements", "Develop system", "Test system" and "Deliver system". On a very low level, typical work packages could be "Draw schematic", "Paint housing" and "Wire transformer".

After the work packages are defined, they have to be controlled. This means that project management has to check repeatedly whether the individual pieces of work are actually carried out. The normal way to do this is by using metrics and other information such as personal talks and the like. Thus although the tasks sounds quite basic and rather simple, project management has to decide how the project progress can be measured and the results visualised and what actions should be taken if one of the indicators approaches a critical value.

The following figure 15.12 shows an example of a project management plan with work packages on a comparably high level.

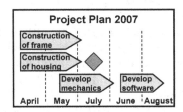

Figure 15.12: Example project management plan with work packages

15.2.3 Level 3: Expert

Similar to level 3 of the HOOD capability model for requirements definition, level 3 of the HOOD capability model for requirements management represents the top of what can be reached. Level 3 is a philosophy, rather than some level of maturity. Level 3 is what every organisation should aim for in order to reach what is possible. An organisation on HCM-RM level 3 will constantly produce an extremely high quality.

15.2.3.1 Risk management interface

With respect to the risk management interface, the highest level of the HCM-RM is reached when the risks are assessed and prioritised and when possible countermeasures are defined.

This goes hand in hand with the project management activities, because for a proper assessment and prioritisation of the risks, resources must be assigned, and there must also be resources in case of a danger when countermeasures have to be carried out.

The assessment and prioritisation of the risks makes it necessary that the impacts of each risk are roughly known or can be estimated. This in turn will only be possible if there are enough links between the various pieces of project information so that impact analyses can be carried out.

The risk management information will only be up to date if the risk analyses are carried out repeatedly, and this is necessary as the risk information feeds back into project management and planning. For example, there could be risks that are estimated to be very high with an immense possible impact on the project success but that are only relevant at the beginning of the project. Once the project has passed through the initial phase and reached a stable status, the risk no longer exists and it would be most desirable to free any resources that have been allocated in order to address the risk if this turns out to be necessary.

Project Risks					
ID	Text	Ref.	Author, Date	Priority	Countermeasure(s)
PR-71	Voltage could be too high.	UR - 12	John Wine, 12 Aug 2005	High	1) Add fuse 2) Add resistor
PR-14	Operator may get injured.	UR - 37	Roger Rabbit, 21 June 2005	High	1) Restrict robot work range 2) Add safety bars
PR-188	System may be delivered late.	UR - 66 UR - 67	Richard Nickson, 7 July 2005	Low	Renegotiate with customer
PR-3	Project may be cancelled.	UR - 105	John Wine, 23 June 2005	Mid	Show management the importance of th...
PR-	Speed exceeds legal limits.	UR - 3	Patricia Munch, 15 ...		

Figure 15.13: Example risk documentation on HCM-RM level 3

Figure 15.13 shows how the risk management information may look like on HCM-RM level 3.

15.2.3.2 Change management interface

On HCM-RM level 3 the change management information is complete in that all impacts of changes on all the other systems engineering disciplines are documented. This makes it necessary of course that the changes are assessed and all linked information is traced back for the impact analysis, see the following figure 15.14.

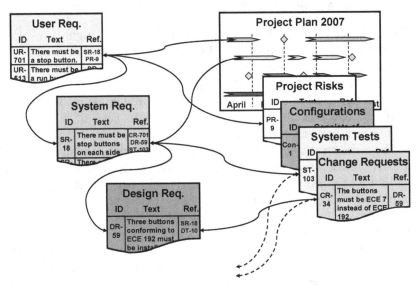

Figure 15.14: Change traceability using linked data on HCM-RM level 3

It is seen from the above figure that the quality of impact analyses for changes or change requests depends practically only on the density of the links between the various pieces of information. Thus in order to be able to reach level 3 of the HOOD capability model for requirements management, there must be a significant amount of project data connections.

It is clear that only project information organised in the proposed way allows for the impact of changes to be assessed on a reliable basis, but in our experience only a very limited number of organisations reach such a level of professionalism with regard to requirements management.

One reason for this is the effort it takes to create and maintain the project data. As has been mentioned before, the information links are not created only once, but must be checked and modified on a regular basis.

For many organisations, this appears to be too much time and money to invest in an activity with a seemingly unimportant outcome.

Another reason is often the lack of knowledge. Creating and maintaining project information as shown in figure 15.14 is far from being trivial, and a considerable number of otherwise well-reputed organisations fail in establishing the necessary processes.

A third reason is the psychological aspect that has also been mentioned before. Well organised project data will make activities and results more transparent, and this is inevitably connected with the people carrying out the activities becoming more transparent, too.

15.2.3.3 Configuration and version management interface

For HCM-RM levels 1 and 2 to reach it is sufficient to have versions and configurations as explained before. However, these versions and configurations may still be random in that they are created as appears necessary or logical.

This means for example that up to the point of time when some version or configuration is created, nobody knew that there would be such a version or configuration. This is unsatisfactory from a number of viewpoints.

First, the efforts and activities to reach a certain stage that may be freezed cannot be focussed because the goal is not known beforehand. Second, deviations of the actual project state from initial project plannings are harder to spot as it cannot be checked whether some stage should have already been reached or not. Third, the fact that the project has reached a milestone or an important stage may be missed because no one knows what to look for.

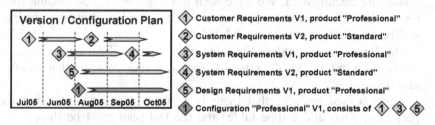

Figure 15.15: Example of an version and configuration plan

Thus on level 3 of the HCM-RM there must be an initial version and configuration plan and a policy for drawing baselines and making freezes. It can be seen that this is closely related to the project management activities, as the version and configuration planning will be connected to deliverables and project milestones. One example of an initial version and configuration plan is shown in figure 15.15.

It is clear that an initial version and configuration plan as shown in the above figure needs regular updates and checks, and quite often the initial dates will turn out to be impossible to meet. However, the value of such a planning must not be underestimated.

One of the main benefits of a version and configuration planning is the fact the project members must develop a rough idea of which milestones exist and how these will approximately be reached in terms of time and effort. Thus this planning goes hand in hand with the general project management planning and helps people not to forget some important activities or project results.

It is seen from figure 15.15 that planning will support project managers in prioritising activities and focussing efforts if necessary. By contrast, a collection of versions and configurations that came into existence more or less randomly, see figure 15.10, does not allow for any predictions of the future. With only figure 15.10, a project manager would be lost if he had to decide which activities to carry out next in order to complete the next necessary configuration.

15.2.3.4 Test management interface

Similar to the other systems engineering disciplines interfaces, there is a clear development of the test management interface from level 1 of the HOOD capability model for requirements management through level 2 to level 3.

On level 1 we suggested that a certain number of requirements are labelled as being key requirements, that these are tested and that the test results are documented. We have seen how the people responsible for the tests will begin to answer important questions when they start trying to satisfy the requirements to reach level 1.

On level 2 we added the idea that the verification method and verification criteria are documented for those requirements that should be tested.

Level 3 now requires that there is a proper test plan including work packages, costs and a time table, and the test plan must be linked to the requirements. figure 15.16 shows how this may look like.

The test planning is part of the overall project planning, and valuable information will be exchanged and reused between the various project plans. It is thus seen once more how the HCM-RM makes sure that step by step all relevant project data will mesh with each other so as to create maximum benefit.

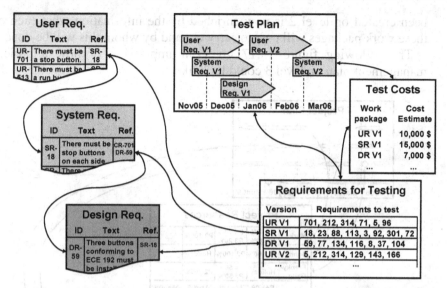

Figure 15.16: Example test plan information on HCM-RM level 3

This is the reason why we have deliberately excluded the planning of resources for testing. Resources may be assigned by a central project management, but the information provided by test management planning will make it easy for project managers to estimate the necessary resources consumption and to plan for this in due time.

It is of course clear that like all other project plans, the test plan must be maintained and updated regularly, otherwise the information represented by the plan will sooner or later be of very low quality. We point out again at the fact that working with old information that has not been updated on a regular basis can be much more dangerous than starting from scratch of making estimates as necessary, based on the current project status.

15.2.3.5 Quality management interface

It has been mentioned before that there is no difference in level 2 and level 3 of the HOOD capability model for requirements management with regard to the quality management interface, and the most important aspect here are requirements analyses and reviews on a regular basis.

15.2.3.6 Project management interface

On the last level of the HOOD capability model for requirements management, project management has to provide costs and resources information. This means that the information about work packages that has been created on level 2 is now enriched by the information what each of these work packages will cost to carry out and by whom this will be done.

The following figure 15.17 gives an impression of how a project management plan on level 3 could look like.

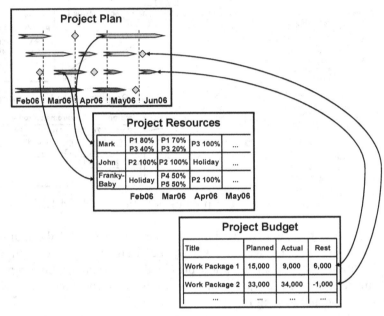

Figure 15.17: Example project management plan for HCM-RM level 3

It can be seen that this plan looks much more complete and the information represented by it much more valuable in comparison to the example project management plan shown in figure 15.12 to reach HCM-RM level 3.

The planning of costs will make sure that there is a basis for the prioritisation of work packages and activities, for example if the project runs short of budget and some tasks therefore have to be waived. It will also ensure that weaknesses of planning and obstacles that were not anticipated beforehand can be identified and focussed. It is quite common in some organisations for example that a project runs out of money before it is finished, but nobody knows exactly where all the money has gone or where more money than originally intended has been spent.

The planning of resources also allows for the prioritisation of activities if this turns out to be necessary. For example, key staff and specialists may not be available all the time. In such a situation a project manager may choose to start with the most important activities where the most experienced members of staff have to be present, and only then continue with the activities that could also be carried out by less senior project members.

Besides this, the planning of resources will also make sure that for each work package there is someone responsible, someone that can be asked if questions arise. This touches upon the psychological aspects of project management. In real life it can be observed every day that if some task is not explicitly assigned to someone, no one will feel responsible and no one will be able to tell anyone anything about the task.

Another aspect of both cost and resources planning is that it can provide input for risk management. For example, in a critical project it may be a significant risk that key staff could become ill or leave the company. Another example are very costly activities or work packages that may only be carried out if the customer is willing to continue with the project. This is clearly a risk from more than one point of view.

15.3 Summary

The present chapter gives an introduction to the HCM-RM, the HOOD capability model for requirements management. Using various examples, it is shown how the model may be best used.

The HCM-RM is the HOOD Group's standard model for the introduction and improvement of requirements management processes within an organisation. Similar to the HOOD capability model for requirements definition, HCM-RD, the HCM-RM is organised to consist of three levels (apart from level 0, no requirements management processes at all).

The HCM-RM is based on a step-by-step philosophy to introduce new concepts of working and thinking. The model provides a suggestion of how to start and in which order to proceed, but it can and should be tailored to the individual needs and situation of every organisation. The model covers the following interfaces to other systems engineering disciplines in order to make the requirements management information as complete as practically possible:

- Risk management
- Change management
- Version and configuration management
- Test management
- Quality management
- Project management

Using the criteria for reaching a certain level of maturity with respect to requirements management, the HCM-RM allows to assess which level has already been reached by an organisation. The criteria presented here represent good practice and are a result of our many years of experience with requirements management topics.

The two HOOD capability models, the HCM-RD and the HCM-RM, are engineered to go hand in hand with each other. It is strongly recommended to start with both models at the same time, rather than trying to reach a remarkable level of maturity in only one model and ignore the other in the meantime.

List of References

[Balz2000]   H. Balzert, *Lehrbuch der Softwaretechnik*, 2nd Edition, Spektrum Verlag, 2000.

[Bers1980]   E. Bersoff, V. Henderson, S. Siegel, *Software Configuration Management, An Investment in Product Integrity*, Prentice-Hall, 1980.

[Boeh1979]   B. W. Boehm, *Software Engineering; R & D trends and defense needs*, Research, Directions in Software Technology, MIT Press, Cambridge, MA, 1979.

[Boeh1981]   B. W. Boehm, *Software Engineering Economics*, Prentice-Hall, 1981.

[Boeh1988]   B. W. Boehm, *A Spiral Model of Software Development and Enhancement*, Computer Nr. 5, Mai 1988.

[Booc1994]   G. Booch: *Object-oriented Analysis and Design with Applications*, 2nd Edition, Benjamin/Cummings, Redwood City, 1994

[Broo2003]   F. P. Brooks jun., *Vom Mythos des Mann-Monats*, 1st Edition, mitp-Verlag Bonn, 2003.

[Cox1989]   B. Cox, *Study of effectiveness of process improvement in Software development projects*, Jourrnal of International Systems, May 1989.

[DeMa1979]   T. DeMarco, *Structured Analysis and System Specification*, 1st Edition, Yourdon Press, USA, 1979.

[DeMa1982]   T. De Marco, *Controlling Software Projects – Management Measurement and Estimation*, 1st Edition, Prentice Hall, USA, 1982.

[DIN199-1]   DIN 199-1, *Technische Produktdokumentation Technische Produktdokumentation - CAD-Modelle, Zeichnungen und Stücklisten - Teil 1: Begriffe - Teil 1: Begriffe*, 2002-03.

[Glin2005]   M. Glinz, *Einführung in die systematische Entwicklung und Pflege von Software*, 2005.

[Hall1998]   E. Hall, *Managing Risk: Methods for Software System Developments*, Addison-Wesley Longman, Reading, MA, 1998.

[Hass2003]   A. M. J. Hass, *Configuration Management Principles and Practices*, 2003.

[Hatl1988]   D. J. Hatley, I. A. Pirbhai, *Strategies for real-time system specification*, 1st Edition, Dorset House, USA, 1988.

[Hind2004]   B. Hindel, K. Hörmann, M. Müller, J. Schmied, *Basiswissen Software-Projektmanagement*, 1st Edition, d.punkt-Verlag, Heidelberg, 2004.

[Hoar1972]   T. Hoare, *Structured Programming*, Academic Press, 1972.

[Hood2004a]   HOOD Group, *RM&E – Methodik*, Course Notes, 2004.

[Hood2004b]   HOOD Group, *RM&E – Geschicktes Formulieren von Anforderungen*, Course Notes, 2004.

[Hood2005]   C. Hood, R. Wiebel, *Optimieren von Requirements Management & Engineering*, Springer Verlag, Heidelberg, 2005.

[Hull2004]   E. Hull, K. Jackson, J. Dick: *Requirements Engineering*, 2nd Edition, Springer-Verlag, Heidelberg, 2004.

[IEEE830]   IEEE Standard 830-1998, *Recommended Practice for Software Requirements Specification*, IEEE Computer Society, 1998.

[ISO15504]   ISO/IEC TR 15504:1998(E), *Information Technology – Software Process Assessment*, 1st Edition 1999.

[Jaco1994]   I. Jacobson, *The Object Advantage*, Addison-Wesley, USA, 1994.

[Kepp1981]   C. H. Keppner, B. B. Tregoe, *The new rational manager*, 1st Edition, Princeton Research Press, USA, 1981.

[Kres2004]   A. Kress, *Ein starkes Paar: Requirements Management & Engineering und Change Management*, http://www.HOOD-Group.com, 2004.

[Kreu2004]   A.s Kreutz, *Deutsche Informatik Akademie DIA*, 2004.

[Kruc1998]   P. Kruchten, *The Rational Unified Process (An Introduction)*, Addison-Wesley, 1998.

[Kruc1999]   P. Kruchten, *Der Rational Unified Process – eine Einführung*, deutsche Übersetzung, Addison.Wesley, 1999.

[Leff2000]   D. Leffingwell, D. Widrig, *Managing Software Requirements – A unified approach*, 1st Edition, Addison-Wesley, USA, 2000.

[Masl1954]   A. A. Maslow, *Motivation and Personality*, Harper and Row, New York, 1954.

[Mazz1994]   C. Mazza, J. Fairclough, B. Melton, D. de Pablo, A. Scheffer, R. Stevens, *Software Engineering Standards*, 1st Edition, Prentice Hall, UK, 1994.

[Meye1985]   B. Meyer, *On Formalism in Specifications*, IEEE Software, Jan 1985, 6-26.

[Oest2004]   B. Oestereich, *Objekt-orientierte Softwareentwicklung Analyse und Design mit der UML 2.0*, 6th Edition, Oldenbourg Wissenschaftsverlag, München, 2004.

[Ould1999]   M. Ould, *Managing Software Quality and Business Risk*, John Wiley and Sons, Chichester, 1999.

[Page1988]   M. Page-Jones, *The practical guide to structured systems design*, 2nd Edition, Prentice Hall, USA, 1988.

[Robe1999]   S. Robertson, J. Robertson: *Mastering the Requirements Process*, Addison Wesley, Harlow England, 1999.

[Rumb1991]   J. Rumbaugh, M. Blaha, W. Premerlani, F. Eddy, W. Lorenson, *Object-Oriented Modelling and Design*, Prentice Hall, Englewood Cliffs, 1991.

[Rumb1999]   J. Rumbaugh, I. Jacobson, G. Booch: *Unified Modeling Language,* Reference Manual, Addison Wesley, 1999.

[Rupp2001]   C. Rupp: *Requirements Engineering und –Management, professionelle Anforderungsanalyse für die Praxis.* Hanser Verlag, 2001.

[Schm2003]   K. Schmid, A. Birk, G. Heller, I. John, S. Joos, K. Müller, T. Maßen, *Report of the GI Work Group "Requirements Engineering for Product Lines"*, Fraunhofer IESE, 2003.

[SEI2002]   *Capability Maturity Model® Integration (CMMI)*, Version 1.1. SEI, Software Engineering Institute, Carnegie Mellon University, Pittsburgh 2002.

[Shel1992]   F. Sheldon, *Reliability Measurement from Theory to Practice*, U.S. Air Force Project Report, 1992.

[Shla1988]   S. Shlaer, S. J. Mellor, *Object-Oriented Systems Analysis - Modeling theWorld in Data*, 1st Edition, Prentice Hall, USA, 1988.

[Shla1992]   S. Shlaer, S. J. Mellor, *Object Lifecycles – Modeling the World in States*, 1st Edition, Prentice Hall, USA, 1992.

[Somm1997a] I. Sommerville, P. Sawyer, *Requirements Engineering: A Good Practice Guide*, John Wiley & Sons, Chichester, 1997.

[Somm1997b] I. Sommerville, G. Kotonya, *Requirements Engineering: Processes and Techiques*, John Wiley & Sons, Chichester, 1997.

[Somm1998]   I. Sommerville, P. Sawyer, *Requirements Engineering*, 1998.

[Somm2001]   I. Sommerville, *Software Engineering*, 6th Edition, Addison-Wesley, 2001.

[Spiv1988]   J. M. Spivey, *The Z Notation: a reference manual*, http://spivey.oriel.ox.ac.uk/~mike/zrm/, 1988.

[Stan2002]   Standish Group: *CHAOS Survey*.

[Stev2000]   R. Stevens: *Requirements Methodology Version 1.5*, Professional Services, QSS Inc., 2000.

[Stoe2003a] F. Stöckel, U. Sterr: *Anforderungen an Anforderungen*, http://www.hood-group.com, 2003 .

[Stoe2003b] F. Stöckel, U. Sterr, *Umsetzung von Qualitätskriterien an Anforderungen*, http://www.hood-group.com, 2003.

[Szym1985]   Szymanski, Neff, *Defining Software Process Improvement*, 1985.

[Vers1999]   G. Versteegen, *Das V-Modell in der Praxis*, dpunkt-Verlag, 1999.

[Vers2000]   G. Versteegen, *Projektmanagement mit dem Rational Unified Process*, Springer Verlag, 2000.

[Vers2004]   G. Versteegen, A. Heßler, C. Hood, C. Missling, R. Stücka, *Anforderungsmanagement*, 1st Edition, Springer-Verlag, Heidelberg, 2004

[Wall2001]   E. Wallmüller, *Software-Qualitätsmanagement in der Praxis – Software-Qualität durch Führung und Verbesserung von Software-Prozessen*, Hanser Verlag, 2001.

[Your1988]   E. Yourdan, *Managing the System Life Cycle*, 2nd Edition, Prentice Hall, 1988.

Index